"In an era of rampant misinformation regarding the origin, text, transmission, and translation of the Bible, James White has written a most timely and important book. We recommend it highly to anyone confused over the issue of the King James Version and modern translations."

Dr. John Ankerberg and
Dr. John Weldon

"This is by far the best and most balanced treatment of all the important issues involved in the controversy over KJV Onlyism. Kudos to James White and Bethany House!"

Dr. Kenneth Barker
Executive Director
NIV Translation Center

"One of the saddest signs of legalistic Christianity is the tenacious defense of the KJV as the only legitimate English-language translation. Almost as sad is that countless hours of scholars' and pastors' time must be diverted from the larger priorities of God's kingdom to point out the numerous historical, logical, and factual errors of KJV Onlyism—even though these errors have been repeatedly exposed in the past. Nevertheless, the job must be done, and James White does it masterfully in this book."

Dr. Craig Blomberg
Associate Professor of New Testament
Denver Seminary

"James White has thoroughly researched the background and sources of the Bible as we have it today, and he points out the serious weaknesses of the KJV Only position, a view seemingly based more on faulty, unprovable assumptions than on solid evidence. I have deep appreciation for White's scholarship and wholehearted concurrence with his handling of the data. His treatment is to be commended and granted close attention by evangelicals."

Dr. Gleason Archer
Professor of Old Testament and Semitics
Trinity Evangelical Divinity School

THE

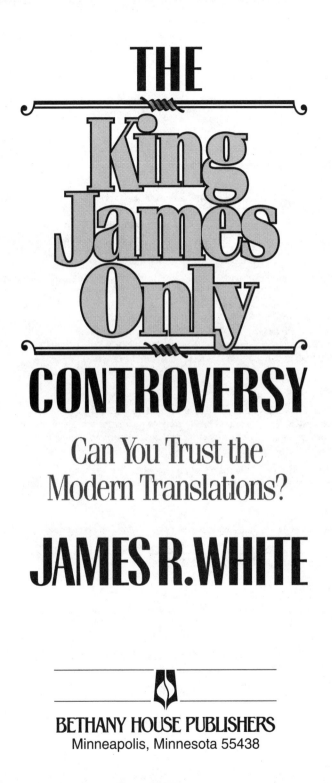

King James Only

CONTROVERSY

Can You Trust the Modern Translations?

JAMES R. WHITE

BETHANY HOUSE PUBLISHERS
Minneapolis, Minnesota 55438

The Greek font used in the body of this work was developed by Dr. William D. Mounce, and is used with his permission. A special thanks to Dr. Mounce for providing Bible students everywhere with such a fine biblical Greek font.

Scripture quotations marked KJV are from the King James Version of the Bible.

Scripture quotations marked NIV are taken from the HOLY BIBLE, NEW INTERNATIONAL VERSION®. Copyright © 1973, 1978, 1984 by International Bible Society. Used by permission of Zondervan Publishing House. All rights reserved. The "NIV" and "New International Version" trademarks are registered in the United States Patent and Trademark Office by International Bible Society. Use of either trademark requires the permission of International Bible Society.

Scripture quotations marked NKJV are from the New King James Version of the Bible, copyright © 1979, 1980, 1982, Thomas Nelson Inc., Publishers.

Scripture quotations marked NRSV are from the Revised Standard Version of the Bible, copyrighted 1989 by the Division of Christian Education of the National Council of Churches of Christ in the USA. Used by permission. All rights reserved.

Scripture quotations marked NASB are from the New American Standard Bible, © The Lockman Foundation 1960, 1962, 1963, 1968, 1971, 1972, 1973, 1975, 1977.

Published by Bethany House Publishers
A Ministry of Bethany Fellowship, Inc.
11300 Hampshire Avenue South
Minneapolis, Minnesota 55438

Printed in the United States of America.

Library of Congress Cataloging-in-Publication Data

White, James R. (James Robert)
    The King James only controversy : can you trust the modern translations? / James R. White.
        p.   cm.
    Includes bibliographical references and index.

    1. Bible. English—Versions—Authorized.   2. Bible. English—Versions.
3. Bible. N.T.—Textus receptus.   4. Bible—Criticism, Textual.   I. Title.
BS186.W45   1995
220.5'2—dc20   95–7770
ISBN 1–55661–575–2   CIP

*Every minister knows how blessed he is
when God places in his ministry a true friend,
brother, and compatriot—someone who is always
there, always willing, always supportive. God
has blessed my ministry with such a person, and
it is to him that I dedicate this book.*

*For Richard Pierce,
a brother at all times.*

Acknowledgments

Many people have contributed to making this book possible. I wish to give special thanks to Steve Laube, my editor, who shared with me the vision of what this book could be. I thank D.L. and Chris Culiver, Myles and Carol Grunewald, and all the folks who supported *Alpha and Omega Ministries,* so that I could concentrate upon the task at hand. Kathi Willeford deserves special recognition not only for handling a lot of extra work during the period this book was being written, but for having been used of the Lord to direct my attention toward this area in the first place. Words cannot express my heartfelt gratitude for Julius Amman and the people of Reformation Fellowship for their support in this project as well. I also thank those who have put up with my constant jabbering about this aspect or that of the entire KJV Only controversy, including the patient and supportive members of my home church, the Phoenix Reformed Baptist Church, and the poor souls in my beginning Greek and Hebrew classes. Thanks guys. And to Dr. Mike Baird, the patient professor who spent seven solid years instructing me in the Greek language, I am and always will be thankful. I am also grateful to those who have taken the time to read the manuscript and offer helpful suggestions and criticisms. Finally, to my loving and ever patient wife, Kelli, and my wonderful children, Joshua and Summer, a true word of thanks for putting up with the long nights and the preoccupation with the work at hand.

Contents

Recte Ambulamus ad Veritatem Evangelii

Foreword

In this age of uncertainty, the last thing we need is the suspicion that the Word of God is somehow faulty and misleading. Yet many, even within Christendom, have set about to undermine the authority of Scripture. This happens in places of radical higher criticism, but it also happens in places where we are least suspecting.

James White, in *The King James Only Controversy,* deals with this sense of uncertainty in God's Word promoted by those who defend the KJV as the only reliable Bible. With a clear outline and readable style, this book deals honestly with the issues raised by the KJV Only proponents. White's treatment is sensitive to the King James reader as well as the NIV reader. His larger vision is to help us as believers know the certainty of our faith in God and His Word.

This book, in eleven chapters plus a section dealing with more complex textual data, addresses the issue in a systematic way. White is constantly aware that you and I may not be as well informed as he is. The opening chapters give a brief, simple overview of the KJV Only position and history of the development of the King James Bible. In chapters 3 and 4, White introduces us to two important foundational concerns: the reliability of the modern Greek texts used to translate the NIV and other versions, and the development of the *Textus Receptus* and its translation by the men of King James. Incidently, if you don't know what the Textus Receptus is, read the book. White explains it very well. The next five chapters go into detail addressing the KJV Only position, helping us to understand the particulars of the criticisms leveled against the modern versions. White deals with differences in translation and textual basis between the KJV and the NIV and others. Particularly outstanding is the chapter dealing with the charge that modern versions downplay the divinity of Christ. White makes it clear that *neither* the KJV nor the modern versions have done this. The main part of the book concludes with an excellent summary of the issues using a clear and simple question-answer style.

I recommend this book to any faithful Christian who has wrestled with the issue of the certainty of God's Word. If you use the KJV and wonder about modern versions, you will find a sympathetic yet straightforward treatment of your views. If you have never encountered the KJV Only controversy, read the book! It will help you understand your modern version.

Dr. Mike Baird
Professor of New Testament
Grand Canyon University

Introduction

The salesclerk never saw it coming. He had just finished unpacking the new shipment of study Bibles and setting up the new display. He had been working at the Christian bookstore only a week. All seemed well. And then it happened. She seemed like any other lady looking for a Bible for her grandson. More than glad to help he pulled a nice NIV down from the shelf and opened the box. He noticed she immediately turned the Bible and looked at the spine. Her countenance changed. She put the Bible back in the box, withdrawing her hands quickly, as a person does when discovering an object is dirty or oily. "I would like a *real* Bible," she says. "A real Bible?" the salesclerk asks. "Yes," she replied, "a *real* Bible, the Bible God honors, the King James Bible, the A.V. 1611."

Scenes like this are repeated almost daily across the English-speaking world. Ask any person who has worked behind the Bible counter at a Christian bookstore. Many have been informed in no uncertain terms that the only Bible they *should* be carrying is the King James Version. The many others they offer are, in fact, nothing but perversions of God's Word.

The church today faces many difficult issues and questions. It would seem that a controversy revolving around a group of people who embrace one particular translation of the Bible is barely a bump in the rocky road upon which the church travels. One may well ask why we should take the time to examine an issue such as the King James Only controversy. Are there not more important things to do? Certainly it is true that far too much energy, in our opinion, has been expended upon this topic already, but that energy has come almost exclusively from one side of the debate. Most biblical scholars and theologians, even of the most conservative stripe, do not feel the issue worthy of any real investment of time. So why write an entire book on the topic? An illustration might help.

One of our faithful volunteers was on the phone. The pastor of her church had preached on Matthew 18 on Sunday, and had read verse 11, "For the Son of Man has come to save that which was lost" (NASB). She and her husband were both using the *New International Version*, the NIV, which does not have Matthew 18:11. Neither one saw the textual footnote at the bottom of the page that gave the translation of verse 11. Both were quite puzzled and wondered why the NIV would "delete" this verse.

These friends are not alone. Believers who were raised in good, solid Christian churches have to admit to a large measure of ignorance when it comes to the *text* of the Scriptures. Why are there different translations? Why are there controversies about words, phrases, sentences, even entire passages? Why does my pastor's Bible have a verse that mine does not? It is this kind of confusion that provides the perfect breeding ground for controversy. Our friends knew they could call upon us to explain the situation. Many do not know whom they can turn to.

The King James Only controversy, by its very nature, brings disruption and contention right into the pews of the local Christian church. KJV Only advocates, due to the nature of their beliefs, are often disruptive of the fellowship in churches, feeling that their message of "God's one true Bible" needs to be heard by all. Anyone who does not "know what they know" needs to be told quickly, and most often, forcefully. And since much of the KJV Only material alleges grand and complex conspiracies on the part of the modern translations, distrust of others who use (or would even defend) those translations often results in schisms within the fellowship and a debilitation of the local body.

Most important, men of God, pastors and elders entrusted with the care of the flock of God, are inevitably, and often unwillingly, drawn into this controversy. Time that should be spent in ministry to families, the sick, the hurting, has to be invested in explaining to zealous members of the congregation why their salvation is not dependent upon a seventeenth-century Anglican translation of the Bible. Energy that could be devoted to the study of the Word and the proclamation of God's truth from the pulpit has to be directed toward allaying fears inspired by KJV Only publications. These pastors often have to adopt a defensive posture, for KJV Only advocates are quick to spread suspicion of weakness, or even heresy, against those who do not agree with their position.

Those not familiar with KJV Only publications need only pick up *The Bible Believer's Bulletin* from Dr. Peter Ruckman (Pensacola Bible Institute) or books such as *Let's Weigh the Evidence* by Barry Burton (Chick Publications, 1983), *New Age Bible Versions* by Gail Riplinger (A.V. Publications, 1993), or *Final Authority* by Willam P. Grady (Grady Publications, 1993), to discover how vitriolic this argument can become. Charges of blasphemy, heresy, and even stupidity, fly thick from *some* elements of the KJV Only movement.[1] Thankfully, not all who hold to this position engage in such name-calling, but sadly the movement as a whole is marked by this kind of invective. The willingness of individuals such as Peter Ruckman to dehumanize those who disagree with him through personal attack breeds an "us versus them" mentality in those who buy into the KJV Only position. Anyone who would seek to reason with these individuals runs the risk of being identified as an "enemy of God's Word," i.e., the KJV.

Responsibility must be laid at the door of the KJV Only camp for the destruction of many Christian churches. Church splits have taken place as the direct result of the influence of KJV Only materials on elders, deacons, and other influential members. Many pastors have become quite wary of these materials, having experienced great troubles at the hands of those who become mesmerized by the KJV Only cry.

This book is written because of a desire for peace in the church of Jesus Christ. We are not speaking of a peace that is purchased at the price of compromise, but a peace that comes from single-minded devotion to the things of God. Our relationship with Jesus Christ is not based upon a particular Bible translation. Men and women had fine Christian lives for fifteen hundred years before the KJV came on the scene. Obviously one can live such a life without ever opening a KJV Bible. The church should not be distracted by even well-meaning people who seek to force others to read one particular translation of the Bible.

The KJV Only controversy feeds upon the ignorance among Christians regarding the origin, transmission, and translation of the Bible. Those who have taken the time to study this area are not likely candidates for induction into the KJV Only camp. Having a firm grasp of the issues that arise in transmitting an ancient text to the modern day and then translating that text from a rich foreign language into our less rich English tongue is not only vital in providing an answer to the KJV Only advocates, but it is also extremely important to the Christian mission in our day. As we proclaim the Gospel to an ever more skeptical world, we must be clear on why we believe the Bible to be God's Word. This calls us to be students of that book, and requires us to study its history and the reasons for our trust in its veracity and accuracy.

The Christian who wishes to "give a reason for the hope" that is within him will be quite alarmed at the logical conclusions that are to be derived from the KJV Only perspective. The body of this work will demonstrate that the KJV Only position is forced to make statements about the Bible that in reality undercut the very foundations of the faith itself. Furthermore, KJV Only supporters have to downplay the importance of properly translating various passages of Scripture that are central to the demonstration of the deity of Christ so as to maintain the alleged infallibility of the KJV (see chapter 8). Christian people who believe that the faith is true and able to withstand scrutiny cannot allow such assertions to pass unchallenged.

It is very important to understand the motivation behind this book. This book is not being written to push one particular translation of the Bible over another. There is no desire to get everyone to read the NASB, or the NIV, or the NKJV, or the RSV, or any other "modern" translation. On the other hand, I am not in any way seeking to stop those who use the KJV from reading that venerable translation. *This book is not against the King James Version.* I know many fine Christian people who use the KJV and for whom the translation works just fine. However, I do oppose those who would force others to use the KJV or risk God's wrath for allegedly questioning His Word. *I oppose KJV Onlyism, not the King James Version itself.*

It is not our intention to provide a history or even a full description of the KJV Only movement. This work is not designed to respond to specific individuals within that camp. Rather, the wish is to provide a broad response to the general claims, providing a reasoned response to the concept that there is any particular translation of the Bible in English that God *requires* the faithful Christian to use. There will also be an examination of the most commonly cited passages in the Holy Scriptures that are utilized by KJV Only advocates to "make their case."

The author of this work is a biblical conservative. In light of this, there are a number of Bible translations that I would not personally recommend. This work does not seek, by responding to the KJV Only position, to give carte blanche to any and all beliefs or theories that might be put forward under the guise of "academic freedom." I am no friend to those who would seek to undercut the very foundations of the Christian faith. Indeed, it is a concern for the integrity of the faith that drives this reply to the KJV Only position, for the cause of conservative values in the Christian faith is by no means aided by the existence of the KJV Only camp. The willingness of many to sacrifice all semblance of logic and rationality in the cause of defending a great, yet imperfect, translation of the Bible as if it were inspired is used by skeptics as evidence of how "backwards" conservatives *as a whole* truly are.

Whatever factors have motivated you to pick up this volume, let us ask for this one thing: a willingness to listen, to think, and to consider. Much time has been taken to hear the KJV Only position in its many and varied expressions. I have gone to great lengths to be accurate in representing a many-faceted movement. I ask only the same in return. Critical thought is encouraged, not in a humanistic sense whereby man is set up as some sort of demigod, capable of judging even the things of God by his own puny standards. Rather, I encourage the thinking that is marked by wisdom, a wisdom that examines the facts and holds to the highest standard of truth. Christians should not engage in circular reasoning and unfair argumentation. The KJV Only controversy should be examined in such a way that all of us, no matter what our perspective, seek to be consistent in our thinking, consistent in our argumentation, consistent in our beliefs.

Finally, for those who come to this discussion with deep and long-standing commitments to the Authorized Version (AV, as we shall call it at times), please consider well the necessity of examining your beliefs, no matter how cherished they may be, on the basis of God's truth. We all have our traditions. Yes, even those who claim to "go by the Bible alone" have their traditions, and the more aware we are of our traditions, the more fully we can test them by Scripture. Those who are blind to their own traditions are the least likely to be fully biblical in their beliefs. We all must constantly test our faith by Scripture, and we must pray for a willingness to abandon those beliefs that are found to be contrary to God's revealed truth.

Endnotes

[1] Grady identifies nearly all modern scholars who do not join the KJV Only ranks as "Nicolaitane priests" (pp. 312-314). This writer has been the object of this kind of attack by KJV Only advocates, but only after entering the arena and addressing the subject. For example, the following appeared in Peter Ruckman's *The Bible Believer's Bulletin* of August 1994, page 9:

> Out in Phoenix, Arizona, is James White, a member of the Alexandrian Cult who has been attacking the King James Bible most of his life while using it. He writes this in answer to a letter sent to him by a born again, saved, witnessing young man . . . . [Quotation of a letter follows] . . . . Blow it out your nose, kid. Out here in the traffic you're liable to get run over. Stick to fairy tales.

Another KJV Only advocate, Texe Marrs, wrote the following letter on July 28, 1994, in response to receiving twenty-eight pages of documentation demonstrating errors and misrepresentations in Gail Riplinger's book, *New Age Bible Versions:*

> Don't write me again unless in sincere repentance. You are a devil, plain & simple. And I understand well why Mrs. Riplinger does not respond to your ridiculous assertions. Why dignify the lying claims of a servant of Satan!

King James Only | 1 |

Movements, by their very nature, often defy exact definition. The "New Age Movement," for example, is actually made up of many different streams of belief and practice, many of which are, in reality, contradictory to one another. Yet they share a few common elements that make it possible to speak, however loosely, of the "New Age Movement."

The King James Only movement is similar in that it defies precise definition. One will find a range of beliefs within the broad category of "KJV Only." We run the risk of offending individuals within the movement when we make broad generalizations, but such cannot be avoided completely. Hopefully, by defining the various positions found within the movement, we can help to focus attention upon the important issues that are at stake.

GROUP #1: "I LIKE THE KJV BEST"

This group of individuals would believe that the King James Version is the best single English translation available today. This belief might be based upon the rhythmic beauty of the work as a whole, or upon its historical importance, or any number of other factors. This group, however, would not deny the possibility of a better translation being made. They would simply state that such a translation has not yet arrived.

These individuals are only marginally "KJV Only," as they would not be militant in their perspective, and would probably not insist that everyone else agree with them. We have no need to address this particular group, and have no reason to seek to discourage them in their use of the KJV as their translation of choice.

GROUP #2: "THE TEXTUAL ARGUMENT"

A large spectrum of people come together in this second group, joined by their common belief that the underlying Hebrew and Greek texts used by the King James translators are, for various reasons, superior to all other original language texts. These individuals would not necessarily believe that those texts are *inspired*, per se, but that they more accurately reflect the original writings of the prophets or the apostles.

There are a number of possible positions that fall within this one category. One group that would strongly reject the term "KJV Only," but who feel that the Greek texts used by the KJV translators were superior to those used by modern translations, would be the "Majority Text" advocates.[1] This viewpoint asserts that the best reading should be that which is supported by the consensus, or majority, of the existing manuscripts of the Greek New Testament. However, these individuals would also point out that the "Majority Text" differs in a number of places from the Greek text that was used by the KJV translators, a text that became known as the *Textus Receptus*, or TR.[2] Others would support the TR over against the Majority Text, often for reasons derived from theology and practice more than from the manuscripts themselves.

GROUP #3: "RECEIVED TEXT ONLY"

The next group of individuals would insist that the above mentioned *Textus Receptus*, or Received Text,[3] has either been supernaturally preserved over time or even inspired, and hence maintained in an inerrant condition. They would believe the same concerning the Hebrew text that was utilized by the KJV translators. This position would not *necessarily* insist that the KJV is an inerrant translation of these texts, leaving open the possibility of a better translation. Their focus is upon the differences between the Hebrew and Greek texts used between 1604 and 1611 in the production of the KJV and those texts that are used today in the translation of such modern versions as the *New American Standard Bible* and the *New International Version*. The reasons used to support this viewpoint are varied. Some see the providential hand of God in the work of those who created these original language texts, which would include men such as Desiderius Erasmus, Stephanus, and Theodore Beza. Others reason back from the fact that God has blessed the resultant translations, feeling this shows God's favor toward those texts.

GROUP #4: THE INSPIRED KJV GROUP

Most King James Only advocates would fall into this group. They believe that the KJV itself, as an English language translation, is inspired and therefore inerrant. Many of these folks believe the TR is inspired and inerrant as well (it would seem logical that the text from which the KJV was translated would have to be inerrant if the resulting translation is to be considered inerrant), but in practice the importance of the TR begins to fade when the direct claim of inspiration of the KJV is put forward.

The key affirmation of this group that gives form and substance to the entire KJV Only controversy is to be found in the following equation:

The King James Bible Alone = the Word of God Alone

It is extremely important to understand that this is the starting point in the thinking of most KJV Only believers. And it is this belief that gives rise to so much of the "heat" that marks this debate, for in the mind of a convinced KJV Only believer, any attack upon the KJV is an attack upon the Word of God.[4] A person who would dare to defend, or even use, another translation of the Bible is, for these people, rejecting the "true" and "real" Bible, and by doing so is rejecting the "true Word of God."

Furthermore, once the above equation is firmly instilled in a person's thinking, other items of the KJV Only position fall into place. For example, KJV Only books are filled to the brim with comparisons between the AV and other translations. Any difference between the KJV and these translations is considered a "change," an "omission," or "deletion." The standard that is used in these works is always the KJV. It seemingly never crosses the mind of the convinced KJV Only advocate that he or she needs to be just as concerned about the propriety of choosing the KJV as the "standard" as anyone else does when choosing his or her Bible translation. The KJV was not the first English translation, nor the last. Hence, it is perfectly logical to ask, "Why should I use it as the standard by which I am to test all others?" Yet the reason, almost always, is found in the equation, "The King James Bible Alone = the Word of God Alone." That's the starting point, the foundation of the entire system.

From this presupposition it is easy to understand why these believers view "other translations" (if they will even classify the KJV in the same realm of "translations" as the others) as "corrupt." Once you believe the KJV is the inspired, inerrant Word of God in English, you don't take kindly to change! And since all other translations will differ, in this point or that, from the KJV, all are therefore seen as "corrupt" and dangerous. The "changes" are seen to be attempts on the part of "someone" to "tamper with God's Word" and "deny Christian truth." And when one feels that he or she has discovered a massive conspiracy—one that is deceiving Christians right and left—it is easy to become very zealous for the cause.

GROUP #5: "THE KJV AS NEW REVELATION"

The final KJV Only group we need to introduce is that which occupies the most radical position in the spectrum.[5] This group, while mentioning at times the Greek and Hebrew texts, the academic credentials of the King James translators, and the doctrinal superiority of the KJV, in reality do not rely upon such things. This group truly believes that God supernaturally inspired the King James Version in such a way that the English text itself is inerrant revelation. Basically, God "re-inspired" the Bible in 1611, rendering it in the English language. As a result, these folks go so far as to say that the Greek and Hebrew texts should be changed to fit the readings found in the KJV! Though this position might strike most as rather extreme, we have found this group to predominate in many areas due to the influence of key proponents of this system of belief.[6] These individuals are often quite militant and vocal in their opposition to the "perverted Bibles" used by so many Christians today. They are quick to identify anyone who would oppose their position as a "Bible hater," and most will suspect some kind of demonic activity in the heart of any person who would take an opposing position. In my experience, it is next to impossible to reason with such a person, for facts are not the issue. Their belief in, and one might well say worship of, the King James Version of the Bible becomes the central aspect of their religious faith. One will, it is sad to say, often hear more about the KJV than about the Lord Jesus from these people.

THE ROLE OF CHRISTIAN FREEDOM

The use of a particular English translation of the Bible is surely a personal choice. Many factors can, and should, go into your decisions as you purchase Bible translations.[7] Whether you like a more literal, formal translation, or a more "dynamic," free-flowing translation will impact your choices. Study editions, companion volumes, concordances, even the print style and size, are all issues to take into consideration. What translation is predominant in your local church is important as well, especially if you will be teaching or leading Bible studies. But one thing that should never be a factor is intimidation. You should never have to wonder if you are going to be accepted by others if you use an NIV rather than a KJV (or vice versa!). Fellowship should never be based upon the English translation one carries and studies.

I firmly believe that if people wish to use the KJV, they should feel free to do so. If they find its poetic form, its rhythmic beauty, to be preferable to "modern language," let no one be critical. God made us all differently, for which we should be very grateful. But while quick to grant this freedom to others, it cannot be expected that this freedom would be given by those who have joined the KJV Only movement. For them this is not an issue of freedom, but of doctrine, belief, and faith. While never making their use of the KJV a barrier to our having fellowship with them, sadly, they very often make my use of anything *but* the KJV an impediment to our relationship. That sharing in the gospel of Christ can be disrupted by such an issue should cause anyone a moment's reflection, and more than passing concern.

Endnotes

[1] The prime example of this position is provided by Dr. Zane Hodges and Dr. Arthur Farstad, *The Greek New Testament According to the Majority Text*, 2nd ed. (Nashville: Thomas Nelson, 1985). This position at least attempts to present a meaningful defense of its beliefs, and, like the preceding group, does not require a militant, adamant insistence upon everyone else agreeing and toeing the line. Both Dr. Hodges and Dr. Farstad have been quite helpful in providing information in support of their own position, and have been Christian gentlemen in their demeanor and

scholarship in their contacts with this author, even though I am not in complete agreement with their particular position on textual issues. Another representative of the Majority Text viewpoint comes from W.G. Pierpont and M.A. Robinson, *The New Testament in the Original Greek According to the Byzantine/Majority Textform* (Original Word: 1991).

[2] See chapters 2 and 4 for specific discussion of the *Textus Receptus* and its relationship to the King James Version. It is very important that the reader recognize that the TR differs from the Majority Text, for arguments for the Majority Text are often intermixed with arguments for the TR by KJV Only advocates. One Majority Text advocate, Wilbur Pickering, has admitted that the TR would require correction in over a thousand places (" 'Queen Anne . . .' And All That: A Response," *Journal of the Evangelical Theological Society*, June 1978, p. 165). Dr. Daniel Wallace counted 1,838 differences between the TR and the Majority Text ("The Majority-Text Theory: History, Methods and Critique," *Journal of the Evangelical Theological Society*, June 1994, p. 194).

[3] Some people refer to the general Greek text used, as an example, in Greek Orthodox circles, as the "Received Text," while others reserve this title to the *Textus Receptus* itself. The TR differs in a number of places from the standard Greek text found in Greek Orthodox circles, which itself is more similar to the "Majority Text."

[4] Many KJV Only advocates prefer to speak of the "words of God" when they refer to the KJV, drawing from Psalm 12:6: "The words of the LORD are pure words: as silver tried in a furnace of earth, purified seven times."

[5] We have heard of small groups that go even further, claiming that the KJV was written in eternity, and that Abraham and Moses and the prophets all read the 1611 KJV, including the New Testament! These individuals believe that Hebrew is actually English, and when discussing religious topics, they will not so much as use a single word that is not found in the KJV! Such groups are, for rather obvious reasons, very small.

[6] Dr. Peter Ruckman of the Pensacola Bible Institute is the prime example of this perspective. See his chapter, "Correcting the Greek with the English" in *The Christian's Handbook of Manuscript Evidence* (Pensacola Bible Press: 1990), pp. 115-138. Note especially such statements as *"Mistakes in the A.V. 1611 are advanced revelation!"* p. 126 (emphasis in the original); "Moral: in exceptional cases, where the *majority of Greek manuscripts stand against the A.V. 1611, put them in file 13,*" p. 130; and "Where the perverse Greek reads one way and the A.V. reads the other, rest assured that God will judge you at the Judgment on what you know. Since you don't know the Greek (and those who knew it, altered it to suit themselves), you'd better go by the A.V. 1611 text," p. 138. Such statements personify the worst elements of "KJV Onlyism," a term we will utilize to describe the entire movement that centers its very religious faith upon a

particular translation of the Bible.

[7] We strongly encourage Christians to purchase and use multiple translations of the Bible so that comparison can be made between translations. It is best not to be limited to just one translation when studying Scripture. Cross-reference between such fine translations as the *New King James Version*, the *New American Standard Bible*, and the *New International Version* will allow the student of the Bible to get a firm grasp upon the meaning of any particular passage.

If It Ain't Broke... | 2

"New and Improved!" When we were children we were taken in by this advertising claim. We wanted the "New and Improved" version of that toy we were given only last month. The "New" game was a must; we had to have the "Improved" baseball bat or we would *never* make it in the Little League. But as we got older we learned that "New and Improved" was rarely new, and hardly ever improved. We surely took a great step toward adulthood when we realized that advertisers were not the most honest people in the world.

Mankind seems to have a strong desire for change. We are a restless lot, always seeking to experience "different" things. Most of us believe we can improve our life, our surroundings, and the key is always the same: change.

Change, for the simple sake of change, is not a Christian virtue. Such an attitude comes from Madison Avenue, not the Scriptures. There is nothing good about being quick to grab at the newest thing that comes down the road. Contentment with God's gifts and provisions is indeed a rare possession of Christians today.

In religious matters the two extremes are always present. There are always those who seek novelties in religious experience. At the same time, there are always those who resist any change—all change—at *all* costs. "Traditionalists" view any suggestion of variety or novelty with suspicion. "We don't need to change anything," we are told. "Everything is just fine. Follow the old ways. Don't be open to any new ideas."

Believers have to walk the narrow path between these two extremes. We are never to look for "new truths" that take us beyond the rich revelation God has already given us in Christ Jesus. Such an attitude demonstrates a deep misunderstanding of the riches that are already ours in Christ. At the same time, we are not to be so attached to our traditions, to our "way of doing things," that we are unwilling to improve ourselves or our service to Christ. Balance is the key.

When it comes to the KJV Only controversy, we encounter both extremes yet once again. It is very true that the modern church in America has seemingly gone bonkers when it comes to Bible translations. How many Bible translations do we need? Do we need to have a Bible translation for every group, sub-group, and splinter group? Do we need a translation in every American dialect? Some people have two dozen different Bibles sitting on their shelves, and to what end?

On the other hand, the position taken by KJV Only advocates has a long history within the church as well. Terms such as "traditional biblical texts" abound in KJV Only literature. Many such believers see themselves standing for the "ancient truth" of the Scriptures, valiantly attempting to stem the tide of "modernism" by holding to a seventeenth-century translation of the Bible. It is an old joke that has been told far too many times: "If it was good enough for the apostle Paul, it's good enough for me!"

KJV Only individuals are not generally interested in church history as a subject. Surely there are some who take an interest in it, but by and large such people suffer from the same apathy about our Christian heritage as most other Protestants in America.[1] If those who hold to the KJV Only position were to take the time to look back through the centuries, they might be surprised to encounter their own arguments, but in foreign settings. For you see, this is not the first time in history that people have argued that a particular text, a particular translation, should be used exclusively by those who would be faithful to God. And just as those who argued in this way were in error long ago, so the modern advocates of the KJV Only position err today.

JEROME AND AUGUSTINE

Traditions take time to develop. One of the first traditions to develop with reference to the Bible had to do with the common Greek translation of the Old Testament known as the Septuagint, often abbreviated "LXX." Many Christians believed the Septuagint to be an inspired translation of the Hebrew Old Testament. The story was that 70 (or 72) Jewish translators were given the task of translating the first five books of the Bible, the writings of Moses called the Pentateuch.[2] Earlier versions of the tale indicated close cooperation on the part of the translators, resulting in a particularly pure product. Later stories, however, spoke of the scholars retiring to their workplaces, completing their work, and, upon comparing the end result, discovering that they had produced identical translations, word-for-word—a sure sign of divine providence and inspiration. While such anecdotes are somewhat amusing today, they carried great weight, especially when the only translation of the Scriptures the early Christians had ever known was, in fact, the Septuagint. Indeed, it is hard to resist drawing the parallel between how the LXX was viewed then and how some AV Only individuals view the KJV today. Both see some kind of miraculous event taking place in the translation of both documents, despite the fact that there are many plain facts that contradict such a conclusion. Furthermore, the real source of this kind of dedication to a particular translation is rather easy to identify. An incident in the lives of Augustine and Jerome will be helpful in identifying the source of such devotion.

In the early fifth century Jerome provided a fresh translation of the Old Testament in Latin. What made his work unique was that it was based not upon the Greek Septuagint version, but upon the actual Hebrew of the original Old Testament. Jerome was one of *very few* early Christians who was able to read both Greek and Hebrew. As he translated from the Hebrew, his version varied both in content (the LXX having some additions and some deletions when compared with the Hebrew text) and in style (Jerome did not feel he had to accept every interpretive translation that was to be found in the Septuagint). When his translation reached North Africa, it caused a stir in the churches overseen by Augustine, the great bishop of Hippo. One aspect of his work that caused consternation among the people was that he did not use the traditional translation in the book of Jonah regarding the "gourd." The Hebrew is difficult here,[3] and Jerome decided not to follow the LXX's identification of the plant as the "gourd," but instead followed the Palestinian Jewish understanding and identified it as the caster-oil plant. In any case, there was a near riot when this passage was read in Carthage. Augustine objected to the reading of Jerome's translation, and explained why in a letter to Jerome, written in A.D. 405:

> [M]y only reason for objecting to the public reading of your translation from the Hebrew in our churches was, lest, bringing

> forward anything which was, as it were, new and opposed to the authority of the Septuagint version, we should trouble by serious cause of offense the flocks of Christ, whose ears and hearts have become accustomed to listen to that version to which the seal of approbation was given by the apostles themselves.[4]

While we can appreciate Augustine's concern over offending the "flocks of Christ," it is important to note that he does not object to Jerome's work on the basis of it being *inaccurate* but rather simply *unfamiliar*. He is basing his objections upon tradition and use, not upon the actual words of Jerome's translation. The Christians in Carthage were taking the Septuagint as the "standard" and comparing Jerome's translation to that standard. Of course, the standard to which both the Septuagint and Jerome's translation *should have been* held was the original writings of the prophets themselves, but since almost no one could read those books or that language, a "new standard" developed over time, that being the Septuagint. It became, *by traditional usage, the Bible* for these Christians. Jerome's new translation was seen by many as a threat to what was familiar, customary, and "friendly."

I would like to suggest that we find here one of the main forces that has given rise to KJV Onlyism in our day: traditional use. Many of us were raised using the KJV. We are familiar with its tone, its cadence, its poetic beauty. Phrases like "Give, and it shall be given unto you" (Luke 6:38) and "And as ye would that men should do to you, do ye also to them likewise" (Luke 6:31) are familiar and even comforting to us. We have heard it preached from the pulpit; many of our highest spiritual experiences have been associated with the KJV and its wording. It is natural, then, for there to be resistance to any perceived "change" in the norm, in our "standard." We are likely to distrust the "new," and cling tenaciously to the "old."

It is important to point out, however, that what we have accepted as the "standard" itself must be examined. When we "grow up" with a particular tradition, should we not be concerned to *test* that tradition to determine its validity, its truthfulness? For example, at the time of the Reformation the Reformers had to constantly challenge people to examine their traditional beliefs on the basis of Scripture. Is there truly a biblical basis, they urged, for holding to such beliefs as the papacy, purgatory, and prayers to the saints? Or are these traditions that you have been taught since infancy? Just because you have been taught something from childhood does not, in and of itself, make it true. Our most beloved traditions must be held up to examination if we are to be men and women of truth and honesty.

The same is true of Bible translations. The crowds in Carthage should have asked, "Is Jerome's translation more faithful to what is found in the prophet Jonah?" before they decided to riot. In the same way, if the KJV has been your "standard," have you ever really looked into *why* you accept it as such? Where did the KJV come from? Who translated it? What texts were used in its translation? Who produced those texts? Are these not important questions for any honest person who wishes to "prove all things" as the apostle Paul expressed it (1 Thessalonians 5:21)?

The dispute between Augustine and Jerome was not the last time the matter of a "traditional text" came to light. Ironically, over a thousand years later it was Jerome's text that again entered the picture, but this time as the text that had become "traditional" over against a new translation.

ERASMUS AND THE VULGATE

Over the 1,100 years following Jerome's publication of his Latin translation of the Bible, which became known as the *Vulgate*, his work became the most popular translation in Europe. By the early sixteenth century the *Vulgate* was "everyone's Bible." It held the position in the minds of Christians that the Septuagint had held a millennium before. And, just as Jerome himself had ruffled feathers with his "new" translation, so along came a great scholar who again upset the apple cart. The man's name was Desiderius Erasmus.

Erasmus is known today as the "Prince of the humanists." But we need to be careful that we do not understand the term "humanist" in its modern sense when we apply it to Erasmus. He was no modern secularist trying to pry God out of every aspect of life. Instead, the term "humanist" at that time referred to those who felt that God had endowed man with certain abilities of mind and thought that they should, to God's glory, cultivate. The motto of the humanists of the fifteenth and sixteenth centuries was, *ad fontes!* This is a Latin phrase that means, "To the source!" These men did not want to hear about the opinions of men passed down through the centuries. They wanted to go directly to the sources, directly to the ancient documents, so that they could learn for themselves. A burst of interest in ancient writers like Aristotle or Cicero had taken place in the Renaissance, and this drive continued into the days of Erasmus. And one can hardly pass over the introduction of printing in the mid-fifteenth century, an innovation that revolutionized the entire European culture.

This new curiosity led to a renewed emphasis upon the original texts of the Bible as well. While the Latin *Vulgate* had sufficed for centuries, now men were seeking to examine the basis upon which the *Vulgate* had been translated. In the fifteenth century an Italian humanist, a man far ahead of his time in the scholarly realm, Lorenzo Valla, began to study the text of Jerome's work. He discovered that the text that was current in the editions of the Bible that were in circulation differed in a number of places from the text that he found in Jerome's commentaries on the Bible. He reasoned that since Jerome's commentaries were seldom read, and hence seldom copied, they would be less likely to have suffered the normal changes that take place when a document is copied by hand than the text of the Bible, which was constantly being copied. As a result, he produced a "corrected" version of Jerome's work, one which was, in point of fact, much closer to Jerome's original than the text in use in his day in the Roman Church.

It is hard for modern readers to understand the situation that existed in the days of Valla and Erasmus. Valla did not publish his findings with reference to Jerome's *Vulgate*, and it was probably just as well for him. Doing the kind of work he was doing was simply quite dangerous. Why? It was considered heretical. Valla was "tampering with God's Word," or at least that is how his work would have been viewed at the time. Those were dark days in which heretics suffered the ultimate penalty for their beliefs. In fact, the Roman Church looked upon the humanists with suspicion. Why did anyone need to learn Greek? Latin was the language of the church, and Latin was the language that God had used to preserve the Bible, that is, the *Vulgate*. The Greeks (as in the Orthodox churches of the East) were heretics, it was reasoned, and had been excommunicated from the Holy Church centuries before (A.D. 1054). Why learn the language of heretics? And if it was suspicious to learn Greek, it was downright heretical to learn Hebrew. Hebrew was the language of the Jews, and everyone well knew in those days that the Jews were dangerous heretics. While we may be shocked at such thoughts today, this was the general belief of the citizens of Europe only a few centuries ago. Since the only way to learn Hebrew at that time was to study with a Jewish rabbi, some brave souls, such as Johannes Reuchlin,[5] took the chance and learned the language, eventually producing a Hebrew grammar and lexicon so that others, too, could learn the Hebrew language.

Years after Valla's death, Erasmus came upon his notes on the *Vulgate* and was so impressed that he took the risk of having them published.[6] Erasmus was a naturally adventurous soul when it came to academic pursuits. He seemed to enjoy the battle and did not mind "going out on a limb." He was famous during his lifetime for writing works that intensely ridiculed the institutional church. He exposed the rampant debauchery of the clergy in his day (though he himself was a Roman Catholic priest), and stepped on so many toes in the process that he constantly kept busy dodging all the darts that were sent his direction.

Erasmus' interest in the text of the Bible, seen in his publishing of Valla's work, prompted him to begin work on publishing the first printed edition of the Greek New Testament. Up to that time (around 1511) no one had printed the entirety of the Greek New Testament. Everyone was still utilizing hand-copied manuscripts. Up to the summer of 1514 Erasmus worked in England on this project, and then moved back onto the Continent to Basel, Switzerland, where he hoped to find many excellent Greek manuscripts. He was disappointed when he found only five, but he set to work with these. He obtained the assistance of John Froben, a printer there at Basel. Froben encouraged Erasmus to hurry with his work, possibly because he had heard that Cardinal Ximenes had already printed his *Complutensian Polyglot,* which included the Greek New Testament, and was merely waiting for approval to arrive from Rome before publishing his work. Time was running out to be the first to actually *publish* the Greek New Testament. As a result, the first edition of Erasmus' *Novum Instrumentum* ("The New Instrument") was hardly a thing of beauty, and as soon as it was printed Erasmus had to get to work editing the second edition. It was so hastily printed that Erasmus himself said it was "precipitated rather than edited"[7] and that it was "hurried out headlong." Since he was unwilling to wait for papal approval, he took a big gamble and dedicated his work to Pope Leo X, the same pope who excommunicated Martin Luther, hoping that the dedication would deflect any reprisals for his rushing his work to press. The gamble worked, and Erasmus had the first published Greek text on the market.

We will have much more to say of Erasmus' work a little later, as his work became, with a few changes, the basis of the New Testament of the King James Version itself. But for now we wish to note that the *New Instrument* as he first called it (he used the more familiar *New Testament* for the second edition) was actually a bilingual work. In one column was found the Greek text, in the other a fresh, new Latin translation done by Erasmus himself. Why is this significant? Erasmus had again managed to step on the maximum number of toes with one giant stomp of his academic foot. Not only was he dabbling with the language of heretics, Greek, but he *dared* "change" the ecclesiastical text, the Latin *Vulgate*! Such a brash move was certain to cause him no end of problems. If Erasmus was spoiling for a fight, he was not to be disappointed.

Martin Dorp, a young scholar from the University of Louvain, wrote to Erasmus about his work. Dorp was kind in his communication, though disagreeing with Erasmus' conclusions. The great humanist answered in a mighty epistle, described by one of Erasmus' biographers as a "veritable torrent of eloquent and victorious reply, where metaphor, metonymy, synecdoche, irony, and hyperbole vied with each other in hurrying the daring objector to the ocean of utter annihilation."[8] We note one element of Erasmus' reply to Dorp, "You must distinguish between Scripture, the translation of Scripture, and the transmission of both. What will you do with the errors of the copyists?"[9] Here the man who was primarily responsible for the origination of the very Greek text that was used by the KJV translators speaks plainly of the existence of "copyist errors" in the manuscripts of the New Testament. Other men entered the fray, including Luther's foe Johann Eck, Edward Lee, later archbishop of York, and Diego López Zúñiga of Spain. All came down hard on Erasmus for "altering" the Word of God, or so they thought.

One cannot but note the irony that faced Erasmus. Just as Jerome's work had received criticism for being "new" or "radical" back in the fifth century, so Erasmus was berated in the same manner for daring to "change" Jerome! What was once new had become traditional. The radical had become the accepted norm by which all others would be judged. And those in love with tradition were just as angry with Erasmus as the crowds in Carthage so long ago.

And so we see a second time in the history of the church where a translation of the Bible became the "norm" after centuries of use. When a new translation appears, a violent reaction erupts. The very same emotions that drive the modern KJV Only controversy are seen to be nothing new at all. This is a phenomenon we've seen before.

AND THE BEAT GOES ON. . . .

It would be funny, if it were not so serious. Jerome takes the heat for translating the *Vulgate*, which eventually becomes the standard. Erasmus then takes the heat for challenging Jerome and for publishing the Greek New Testament. Then, four hundred years later, it is Erasmus' work itself, in the form of the *Textus Receptus*, which has become enshrined as "tradition" by advocates of the AV! He who once resisted tradition has become the tradition itself. The cycle continues. Will there someday be an "NIV Only" movement? We can only hope not.

There is nothing wrong with tradition, as long as we do not confuse tradition with truth. As soon as we become more attached to our traditions than we are to the truth, we are in very deep trouble. The best tradition is that which is recognized for exactly what it is: a tradition that may help us to worship God or serve Him better, but which is not in and of itself the embodiment of truth. Traditions must be tested, and that includes traditions that touch on the use of particular translations or texts. As soon as we make our tradition the test of someone else's standing with God (as people did to Jerome, Erasmus, and today to those who would use a translation other than the KJV), we have elevated that tradition to a status that is anti-biblical.

Before we can enter into the specifics of Erasmus' work, and hence the translation of the KJV itself, we need to lay a groundwork in the history of the biblical text itself, and to this topic we now turn.

Endnotes

[1] KJV Only publications will often make reference to ancient heresies of

the church in attempts to connect modern Bible translations with such heresies. Rarely, however, are such attempts truly "historical" in nature, but are far more often meant to evoke emotional, rather than rational, responses. Examples of this are to be found in Riplinger, *New Age Bible Versions*, p. 345; Ruckman, *The Christian's Handbook of Manuscript Evidence,* p. 119; Norman Ward, *Famine in the Land,* (Which Bible? Society, n.d.), p. 46; and Jasper James Ray, *God Wrote Only One Bible,* (Eugene, Oreg.: Eye Opener Publishers, 1983), pp. 21-23.

[2] Later embellishments went so far as to include the entire Old Testament!

[3] The Hebrew term קִיקָיוֹן most probably refers to the caster-oil plant. The NASB's "plant" is probably the safest rendering.

[4] Letter LXXXII in *The Nicene and Post-Nicene Fathers*, Series I, (Eerdmans: 1983), I:361.

[5] Johannes Reuchlin was a scholar of the highest rank, remembered not only for his great ability in Greek, but most notably for his *De Rudimentis Hebraicis*, a Hebrew grammar and lexicon. For his interest in Hebrew he was drawn into unwanted controversy. Reuchlin is interesting to the modern student of church history for two other reasons. First, it was Reuchlin who lent Erasmus his sole copy of the book of Revelation, which Erasmus used in the production of his Greek text, which became known over a century later as the *Textus Receptus*. It was Reuchlin's text that was missing the last section of Revelation, forcing Erasmus to translate from Latin into Greek for the last six verses! Secondly, Reuchlin had a grandnephew who was to figure prominently in the coming Reformation, a man named Philip Melanchthon.

[6] Erasmus found Valla's notes in 1504 in the Praemonstratensian Abbey of Parc near Louvain. He was so taken with Valla's work that he had it published that same year in Paris.

[7] *praecipitatum verius quam editum*

[8] John Joseph Mangan, *The Life, Character, and Influence of Desiderius Erasmus of Rotterdam* (The Macmillan Company: 1927), I:346.

[9] Roland Bainton, *Erasmus of Christendom* (Charles Scribner's Sons: 1969), p. 134.

Starting at the Beginning 3

The KJV Only controversy plays upon the fact that most Christians today are more than slightly "fuzzy" on the particulars of how we got the Bible, how the Bible was passed down through the years, and how it has been translated into the English language. I am sincerely convinced that if most Christians had a solid grasp on the history of the Bible, and were familiar with at least the broad outline of how translation is undertaken, the KJV Only issue would be more of a slight disagreement than a full-blown controversy.

The goal of this chapter is to lay the most basic groundwork for the discussion of such things as "manuscripts," "text-types," and "textual variants" that follows. We cannot avoid dealing with such things if we are going to be thorough in replying to those who present the AV as the only true English translation of the Bible. I am also convinced that (1) Christians should have a knowledge of these things whether they are interested in the KJV Only controversy or not, and (2) any Christian who can read and understand the Bible is able to follow the discussion of texts and translations as long as a few definitions are provided right at the start.

If you are already familiar with such issues as the languages in which the Bible was first written, the types of manuscripts that Christians used, basic errors that men make when hand-copying documents, and the like, you may wish to move on to chapter 4. If not, you are encouraged to dig in and gather up all the information you will need to get the most benefit out of the discussions in the later chapters. *Do not be intimidated by the material presented here.* Most of the time the reluctance to tackle allegedly "scholarly" subjects is due to an unfamiliarity with terms and nothing more. Every effort will be made to ensure that terms are defined plainly and used in such a way as to promote understanding.

THE BIBLICAL LANGUAGES

I remember the first time I heard my pastor referring to "Greek." He was talking about what a word meant in the Bible, and I just couldn't figure out why he'd care about what the word meant in Greek when it was hard enough to figure it out in English! It was not long before I found out why he was talking about Greek, but that one Sunday he really lost me.

The Bible was initially written in three languages: Hebrew, Aramaic, and Greek. There are only a handful of chapters that were written in Aramaic, so one could basically limit the scope of the discussion to Hebrew and Greek. The Old Testament was written in the language of Israel, Hebrew, while the New Testament was written in the common Greek language of the day, the *koine* or "common" Greek.[1]

I count it a great blessing from God to have been allowed to study the Greek and Hebrew languages. I love both languages (though I admit to loving Greek a whole lot more than Hebrew!), and have received a tremendous amount of satisfaction from seeing men and women that I have taught in these languages using them to the glory of God. But I also recognize that most Christians who are reading this book have not had the same opportunity to learn the languages in which God originally inspired the Scriptures. I am also well aware that those of us who know the languages are often guilty of using them in a way that is opposite to our professed reasons for having learned them. That is, rather than making things *clearer,* we may well *obscure* God's truth by going off into some unnecessary (and cryptic) discussion of some point of grammar that is really not germane to the issue at hand. Those who have been given the privilege (and hence the responsibility) of knowing these languages should always strive to make their knowledge useful in the edification of others in the body of Christ.

Greek and Hebrew are very different languages. They not only *look* different, but they differ dramatically in their form and function. Because English is related through other languages to Greek, most people can make out some of the Greek letters and can understand certain Greek terms. Many people know that "Philadelphia" comes from two Greek terms, *philos,* which means "friendly," in the sense of

— Mortuary — Oregon —

"loving," and *adelphos*, which means "brother," hence, the "city of brotherly love." And one might even be able to make out most of both terms if they were to see them in the actual Greek script: φίλος (*philos*) and ἀδελφός (*adelphos*). But Hebrew is another story. There are very, very few terms in Hebrew that even *sound* similar to English terms. And most people think of "chicken scratchings" when they see the Hebrew script. Here, for example, is how Psalm 119 begins, in Hebrew:

אַשְׁרֵי תְמִימֵי־דָרֶךְ הַהֹלְכִים בְּתוֹרַת יְהוָה:

As anyone can see, Hebrew is a language far removed from English in form.

The two languages also differ in their complexity and flexibility. Hebrew is an ancient tongue, and as such is rather "concrete" in tone. What it says, it says, and it does not contain nearly the same ability to express subtle nuances and shades of meaning as either English or Greek. Often one is left with a number of possible renderings of particular Hebrew phrases. The language simply does not narrow down the possibilities as well as modern tongues. Greek, on the other hand, far exceeds English in its ability to convey intricate meanings and delicate turns of thought. This same ability makes it possible to narrow the spectrum of possible English translations to a much greater degree than that seen in Hebrew. Greek is a more *technical* language, a more *precise* language than either Hebrew or English.

DISPUTES OVER TRANSLATION

Disagreements concerning Bible translations arise almost completely from two areas of study. Unfortunately, many people confuse the two areas and the issues they involve. It is important for our purpose in this book to clearly define these two areas.

1. TEXTUAL DISPUTES: *Disagreements over what was originally written by the prophets and apostles themselves.* What did Jeremiah actually write? What words did John use to describe the Lord Jesus in John chapter 1? Can we determine what Paul said when writing to the Philippians? These are *textual* issues, issues that go to the actual *text* of the Bible.

2. TRANSLATIONAL DISPUTES: *Disagreements over how to translate what was originally written by the prophets and apostles.* The vast majority of the biblical text is without question when it comes to the original text. That is, we *know* beyond all doubt what was in the original writings of the biblical authors in the vast majority of cases. But there are still disputes over how to translate that established text into English or other languages.

The verses encountered in KJV Only works fall into one of these two categories. For example, there are comparisons between the AV reading of John 6:47[2] and modern translations in a format like this:

John 6:47	
KJV	**Modern Translations**
Verily, verily, I say unto you, He that believeth **on me** hath everlasting life.	Truly, truly, I say to you, he who believes has eternal life.

This is an example of a *textual* dispute. The Greek text used by the King James translators contained the phrase "on me" at John 6:47. The Greek texts used by modern translators do not contain this phrase at this particular point. The reasons for this will be discussed in chapter 7. The main thing to note is that this kind of dispute is based upon what the Greek and Hebrew texts used as the basis of a particular translation actually say. The other kind of dispute, a *translational* dispute, can be illustrated by the citation of John 3:36[3]:

John 3:36	
KJV	**NASB**
He that believeth on the Son hath everlasting life: and he that **believeth not** the Son shall not see life; but the wrath of God abideth on him.	He who believes in the Son has eternal life; but he who **does not obey** the Son shall not see life, but the wrath of God abides on him.

In this case the Greek text that underlies the KJV reads the same as that which was used by the translators of the NASB. Hence this is not a *textual* dispute, but a *translational* dispute centered on the proper way to translate and understand the Greek term that is rendered "believeth" in the KJV and "obey" in the NASB. The distinction between these two issues is *often* lost in pro-KJV Only writings, but as we shall see, it is vital that we distinguish between them.

METHODS OF TRANSLATION

Translating from one language to another is not as simple as it might seem. One cannot simply look at a word in Greek or Hebrew and assign one English term as "the" translation of that word in every instance. It would be nice if it worked that way, but it doesn't. Translation is, in fact, a complex undertaking involving the study of the vocabulary, the grammar, and the syntax of both the language *from which* one is translating, and the language *into which* the translation is taking place.

Those who have had the privilege of studying a foreign language even for a short time know that there is not just "one" correct translation of a word, phrase, or sentence of a foreign language into English. Often there are two or more "right" ways of translating a sentence in Spanish, German, French, or Italian into the English tongue. The same is true of Greek and Hebrew as well. Often the difference between two "right" translations will focus upon how *literal* a person wishes to be in his or her translation. Since this introduces us to one of the major areas of discussion regarding translations, a few examples would be helpful.

The French have a saying that goes, *"j'ai le cafard."* The most literal translation would be, "I have the cockroach." Why the French would have such a saying is beyond human reason, *until* one discovers that a literal translation does not always convey the real *meaning* of the original saying. *J'ai le cafard* is an *idiomatic expression*, one which has a special meaning that is not necessarily evident by the words themselves. Specifically, this saying means "I am depressed" or "I have the blues." If someone wanted to provide a translation from French to English that accurately reflected the *meaning* of the French, one would not have "I have the cockroach" but "I am depressed" as the translation.

Another example can be drawn from the German saying *"Morgenstund' hat Gold im Mund'."* Literally this means, "Morning hours have gold in the mouth." Again we would be left wondering what this means in a literal translation. This is an idiomatic saying that is similar to our English saying, "The early bird catches the worm." The point of both of these examples is that to say "I have the cockroach" is the *only* proper translation of the French *j'ai le cafard* is simply not true. One must make room for the *meaning* in one's translation as well.

These examples introduce us to the debate between *formal* and *dynamic equivalency*. *Formal equivalency* is the method of translation that gives as *literal* a translation as possible. This perspective seeks a word-for-word translation from one language into another. *Dynamic equivalency* seeks to translate the *meaning* from one language into another, even if this involves sacrificing a word-for-word translation in the process. In our preceding examples, "I have the cockroach" and "Morning hours have gold in their mouths" are the *formal* translations, while "I am depressed" and "The early bird catches the worm" are the *dynamic* translations. No translation is completely formal—even translations that are considered "formal," such as the KJV, NKJV, and NASB, contain "dynamic" translations, for at times there is simply no way to make sense of a *completely* literal translation. And even the most dynamic translations contain some formal elements as well. Therefore, what we find in modern translations is a spectrum extending from the most formal, literal translations to the most dynamic ones.

Some examples from the Bible would be helpful at this point. One passage that displays the difference between dynamic and formal equivalency is Luke 9:44. Note how this passage is translated by three English translations:

Luke 9:44		
KJV	**NASB**	**NIV**
Let these sayings sink down into your ears: for the Son of man shall be delivered into the hands of men.	**Let these words sink into your ears;** for the Son of Man is going to be delivered into the hands of men.	**Listen carefully to what I am about to tell you:** The Son of Man is going to be betrayed into the hands of men.

The literal rendering of the Greek is given by the NASB, "Let these words[4] sink into your ears." Obviously we do not speak this way any longer. One does not look at one's child and say, "Son, let these words sink down into your ears!" The NIV gives the dynamic equivalent that gives the actual *meaning* of the Greek phrase, "Listen carefully to what I am about to tell you."

A rather unusual example arises in the Old Testament at Amos 4:4. We say "unusual" because here the KJV and the NIV join together in giving the dynamic translation, while translations such as the NKJV and the NASB give the more literal reading. Here are the renderings:

Amos 4:4			
KJV	**NIV**	**NKJV**	**NASB**
Come to Bethel, and transgress; at Gilgal multiply transgression; and bring your sacrifices every morning, *and* **your tithes after three years:**	Go to Bethel and sin; go to Gilgal and sin yet more. Bring your sacrifices every morning, **your tithes every three years.**	Come to Bethel and transgress, At Gilgal multiply transgression; Bring your sacrifices every morning, **Your tithes every three days.**	Enter Bethel and transgress; In Gilgal multiply transgression! Bring your sacrifices every morning, **Your tithes every three days.**

The literal rendering of the Hebrew text is found in the NKJV and NASB, "every three days." The NIV and KJV give an interpretive translation, understanding "days" to refer to periods of time, that is, "years." While one can give a defense of understanding "days" as "years" in this passage, the fact remains that the *literal* translation must use "days," not "years."

There is much to be said on both sides of the formal vs. dynamic equivalency debate.[5] A balance between the two systems would seem to be the best approach. There seems to be no reason to insist upon having words "sink into ears" at Luke 9:44 when "listen carefully" does a much better job. At the same time, there is good reason to object to attempts to make the New Testament "simpler" than it was originally written under the inspiration of the Spirit. When the original text contains a complex sentence, do we need to break it up into a more simple form? I don't believe so. A balance between translating *meaning* and trying to make the Bible "easier" is needed.

Those who attempt to provide dynamic translations open themselves up to all sorts of criticism. It is much "safer" to translate literally in the sense that you are not "going out on a limb" in delving into the area of meaning. For example, the NIV provides numerous examples of dynamic translations for which it has been severely criticized. Probably the most famous of these is the NIV's rendering of the term "flesh" in Paul's epistles as "sinful nature." This is a bit too interpretive for my tastes, even in those places where "sinful nature" would be the understanding I would give to the term "flesh." Of course, the NIV gives textual footnotes that inform the reader that the term under discussion can be translated "flesh." But in other cases one is left without such helps. And the NIV is not alone in giving dynamic renderings. Even rather formal translations such as the NASB and NKJV utilize less-than-literal renderings at times when they were not actually forced to do so by the text itself. It is important to realize that the translators in each of these situations felt justified in their work. They were not sitting around tossing coins in the air, flippantly handling the biblical text. If one is interested enough, one can discover why a particular translation renders a passage the way it does. Unfortunately, KJV Only advocates are not generally interested in discovering the *real* reasons why the modern translations do what they do. It is enough for most to know that "heretics" are behind the new versions.

TEXTUAL CRITICISM

The very phrase "textual criticism" sounds ominous to many. To be a "critic" is often understood in a negative way. It carries connotations that are not normally seen as being consistent with a faith in the Bible and in Christ. It is vital to point out that each of us, willingly or not, is a textual critic. Each of us makes a decision about the Bible we will use and the readings it contains. Most people make this decision through reference to someone else; that is, we trust someone else to make that decision for us, whether that be a pastor, a friend, or an author or scholar. Most of the time people are unaware that they have even made the decision, as they simply adopt the prevailing viewpoint of the church in which they fellowship. But despite how "uninvolved" one might be, the decision is still made. It can be an informed decision, a decision based upon tradition, or a decision handed over to someone else. But no one can avoid the issue. Everyone has to take a stand.

Many people choose the "easier" road of simply trusting someone else. "Pastor Jones is a real smart man. I'll take whatever he says about this at face value." Pastor Jones may well be a smart man, but many smart men are woefully inadequate when it comes to the discussion of the text of the Bible and how we received it over time. "Dr. Smith is a brilliant scholar. He must know what he's talking about." Dr. Smith may well be a great scholar, but scholars have been known to let their pet theories and traditions interfere with their sound judgment, resulting in conclusions that lack a very vital element: common sense. "My dad used this version, so it must be good enough for me." Traditions are great things, but they are not infallible things. Did dad look into the issues himself, or was he just following the lead of grand-dad? Somewhere along the line someone has to do some study, some work.

I believe God deals with individuals as well as groups. I see the beauty of the corporate body of Christ, and I see the vital importance of the individual as well. It is both/and, not either/or; both the corporate body, the church, and the individual person, responsible before God. I cannot thrust my responsibilities off onto someone else. I have to take that responsibility seriously. If that involves "work," so be it. Those who are suspect of having to do "work" to come to sound conclusions do not seem to have listened very closely to the many exhortations in the New Testament aimed at admonishing Christians to "gird your minds for action" (1 Peter 1:13, NASB). Christians are to be hard workers in *all* aspects of their lives, *including* in their walk with the Lord.

Being an informed person on the subject of the text of the Bible would seem a basic, fundamental aspect of being a Christian today. Yet the vast majority of Christians have little or no knowledge at all of where the Bible came from, how it was transmitted over time, or why their translation differs from any other. This lack of study not only provides the breeding ground of the KJV Only controversy, but it is also an "opening" through which cultic groups often enter into the thinking of the unsuspecting believer.

There are two kinds of "textual criticism" that need to be clearly differentiated. The first is the kind we will need to discuss with reference to KJV Onlyism, and that is "lower" textual criticism. This activity involves the study of the manuscripts of the Bible, those written in Hebrew, Aramaic, and Greek, as well as ancient translations into other languages like Latin or Sahidic or Coptic. Its goal is to reproduce the original text of the Bible from this vast wealth of information. When practiced consistently, this kind of textual criticism does not involve subjective theories regarding authorship, alleged editors of the text, etc. It deals with the text and the facts.

The other kind of textual criticism, "higher" criticism, is not concerned primarily with the manuscripts as it is with questions of the *form* of the text and what this allegedly can tell us about the process of the writing and transmission of the text. Unfortunately, this "higher" criticism is often highly subjective, as can be seen from the fact that if you gather ten higher critics in a room and present to them a text, they will produce a minimum of a dozen different theories about how the text originated and how it came to have its present form. Anyone who thinks this assessment too harsh need only peruse certain journals dedicated to such "higher" criticism for more than sufficient evidence of its truth. The extremes to which this "higher" criticism can be taken, lacking as it does the restraint of facts imposed upon "lower" criticism by the manuscripts themselves, can be seen in the extravagant conclusions from the "Jesus Seminar" regarding the text of the New Testament. The unrestrained scissors of such groups as the Jesus Seminar have little, if anything, to do with serious textual study of the "lower" type.[6]

The textual differences between the KJV and modern versions derive from the Hebrew and Greek texts from which they were translated. Before discussing these texts we need to look at how the Bible was written and how we obtained the texts we will be discussing. We begin with a review of the manuscripts themselves.

Paul Didn't Use Thumb-Indexing?

From my desk I can see a total of forty-one Bibles. Some are Greek New Testaments, others Hebrew Old Testaments. Some are in Latin, some in French, some in German. Most are in English, and most are leather-bound, replete with cross-references, maps, and concordances.

I doubt Paul ever sat at a desk that provided him a view of forty-one Bibles. I know he never saw a complete copy of the entire Bible, that is for certain, as he died before the final sections of the New Testament were written. And what's more, the modern convenience of having all of the Bible in one book under one nice leather cover is a relatively modern phenomenon. We are truly blessed.

It may be difficult for us to imagine it, but people who lived not so long ago worked under conditions that most of us would have considered unbearable. Most Christians who have lived down through the ages never had a complete copy of the Scriptures to call their own. They may have had sections, such as a copy of the Psalter, or a copy of John, but rarely did they have a complete Bible all their own. Sometimes this was because the government would not allow it. This was the case when Rome forced the government in England to clamp down on the "Lollards," those brave Christians who loved the Bible so much that they insisted upon translating it into English. When the authorities began burning their translations, they took to memorizing them. They would memorize an entire book of the Bible, such as 1 Peter, or Mark, and would then take that name as their own. When they would gather, "Mark" would get up and quote from the Gospel of Mark, and then 1 Peter would render a section from his book as well. In that way they shared their love for God's Word.

But most of the time the reason for not having the entire Bible was much less sinister. The copies of the Bible owned by Christians well into the sixteenth and seventeenth centuries were *handwritten copies*. If you wanted a copy of the Gospel of John, you either had to pay a professional scribe to copy one for you, or you had to do it yourself. If you tried to do it yourself, you had to find someone to lend you their copy long enough for you to undertake the *very* difficult and *very* tedious task of copying, by hand, that manuscript. Given that staying alive (avoiding famine, the plague, or invading armies) was a full-time job that took a good deal of time and energy, it is easy to understand why most Christians did not have a closet full of handwritten copies of the entire Bible.

The Jewish people had a great reverence for the Bible and put great effort into preserving its text. The Hebrew texts we have today can boast great antiquity, as the great discovery of the Dead Sea Scrolls demonstrated. The Jewish Scriptures were written in the form of a scroll. When, for example, the Lord Jesus read from the "book of Isaiah" (Luke 4:17-21), it is almost certain that He was reading from a scroll containing the writing of Isaiah and most probably the other prophets. Some of these scrolls were extremely expensive, being made of materials that were quite costly.

Christians charted a new course almost from the very beginning. They utilized the "book" or "codex" style of manuscript, on which the copyist would write on both sides of a sheet of papyrus and would bind these sheets together in a book form. Papyrus was a relatively inexpensive writing material. It was not nearly as sturdy as the more expensive material that was used in later centuries—vellum or parchment—which was normally made of animal skins. The early Christians were not generally wealthy, which might explain the prevalence of papyri in the earliest centuries. As the church became more established, vellum took over as the material of choice.

The form of writing that was used in both the Old and New Testaments changed over time as well. The Hebrew language grew and changed over the centuries, as did the characters utilized to write it. Our modern Hebrew texts, as in the example on page 21, are written in a form of script that is different than that which was used originally. Furthermore, the dots or "vowel pointing" that you see under the Hebrew letters in that same sample were not part of the original text but added much later. Similarly, the New Testament manuscripts were first written in all capital letters (and are therefore called "uncial" texts) without punctuation or spaces between words. This literary form of writing prevailed until about the ninth century, when a different style of writing, the "minuscule" form, became predominant.

Over the years we have discovered examples of these kinds of texts buried in the earth or stored away in libraries. For example, one of the earliest records of Paul's writings is found in Papyrus 46 (abbreviated $\mathfrak{P}^{46}$). This work, dated to around the year A.D. 200, originally contained Romans, Hebrews, 1 and 2 Corinthians, Ephesians, Galatians, Philippians, Colossians, and 1 and 2 Thessalonians on about 104 leaves, 86 of which still exist today. It is surely one of the most important witnesses to the letters of Paul.

Another early papyrus manuscript that is very important is Papyrus 66 ($\mathfrak{P}^{66}$). Also dating from around A.D. 200, this manuscript contains a large portion of the Gospel of John. When joined with another papyrus manuscript from the early third century, Papyrus 75 ($\mathfrak{P}^{75}$), which also contains sections of John and Luke, scholars gained a tremendous insight into the earliest period of the history of the text of the New Testament. One can hardly avoid thinking about those ancient believers who once treasured these texts as their own. Their love for the Scriptures is one of those vital links that connects us across the span of time.

Another vital early papyrus manuscript is Papyrus 72 ($\mathfrak{P}^{72}$), the earliest manuscript of the epistles of Peter. This manuscript illustrates the fact that writing materials were precious and scarce, because it contains other works beyond Peter and Jude that were popular among Christians, but not considered canonical Scripture. Some have even vilified $\mathfrak{P}^{72}$ because it has other books in its pages, but the most logical reason for the inclusion of these other works is that it was easier for the owner of $\mathfrak{P}^{72}$ to copy all the books at once into one easy-to-carry form.

An ancient papyrus manuscript of the Gospel of John, $\mathfrak{P}^{66}$, from approximately A.D. 200.

As noted earlier, the form in which Christians copied their Scriptures changed over time. By the fourth century vellum became the "material of choice." Vellum lasts a lot longer than papyri. Therefore, we have many more of these kinds of manuscripts today than we do the less durable papyri. The single greatest example of an uncial codex written on vellum is Codex Sinaiticus, which today is almost always abbreviated with the single symbol of the Hebrew letter "aleph," written like this: ‎א. This great codex contains the vast majority of the Bible, both Old and New Testaments, in Greek. The story of how it was found[7] is evidence of God's providence. Constantin von Tischendorf embarked on a journey to the Middle East in 1844 searching for biblical manuscripts. While visiting the monastery of St. Catherine on Mount Sinai, he noted some scraps of parchment in a basket that was due to be used to stoke the fires in the oven of the monastery. Upon looking at the scraps he discovered that they contained part of the Septuagint, the Greek translation of the Old Testament. This was exactly what he was looking for, and so he asked if he could take the scraps to his room for examination, warning the monks that they should not be burning such items. His obvious excitement worried the monks, who became less than cooperative in providing further information about manuscripts at the monastery. Years passed by. Tischendorf attempted to find more manuscripts at the monastery in 1853, but to no avail. Six years later he visited yet once again, and this time on the very evening before he was to leave

A papyrus copy of Peter's epistles, $\mathfrak{P}^{72}$, from about A.D. 200.

he presented a copy of the Septuagint (which he had published) to the steward. Upon looking at Tischendorf's gift, the steward remarked that he, too, had a copy of the Septuagint. From the closet in his cell he produced a manuscript, wrapped in a red cloth. The monk had no idea of the treasure he held in his hands, for this was none other than Codex Sinaiticus, which at that time was no less than 1,500 years old! Tischendorf, having learned his lesson years earlier, hid his amazement and asked to examine the work. He spent all night poring over it, and attempted to purchase it in the morning, but was refused. The story of how the codex was eventually obtained is long, involved, and controversial. It resides today in the British Museum.

Codex Sinaiticus (א) is vilified more than any other manuscript by KJV Only advocates,[8] and for obvious reasons. So impressed were the scholars of the day like Tischendorf, Westcott, and Hort that claims were made for א (and another great codex, Codex Vaticanus,[9] abbreviated simply as "B") that later study has shown to have been at best unbalanced. Westcott and Hort used א and B to produce their New Testament, a work that displaced the text used by the KJV, later known as the *Textus Receptus*, in scholarly studies. Because of this, even moderate KJV Only advocates will accuse modern textual critics and translators of "worshiping" א and B, though this is hardly a reasonable charge.[10]

Codex Sinaiticus is not nearly as bad as its enemies would say, nor as good as Tischendorf or others wished. It is not infallible, nor is it demonic. It is instead a great treasure, for a while the oldest manuscript known, and for all time a tremendously valuable asset to our knowledge of the New Testament text. Those who say it is "corrupt" normally mean it is different at places than the traditional text that underlies the KJV. Others accuse it of being so full of errors as to be almost useless. There are indeed many corrections in the text of א, but such is hardly surprising. A handwritten text that is used for 1,500 years is going to collect a few corrections along the way! Moreover, there is a note in the Old Testament portion that even indicates that at some point in the past there had been an effort to correct the manuscript to a different standard, which, of course, would produce a fair amount of alteration. Imagine taking an NASB and trying to make it read like an NKJV!

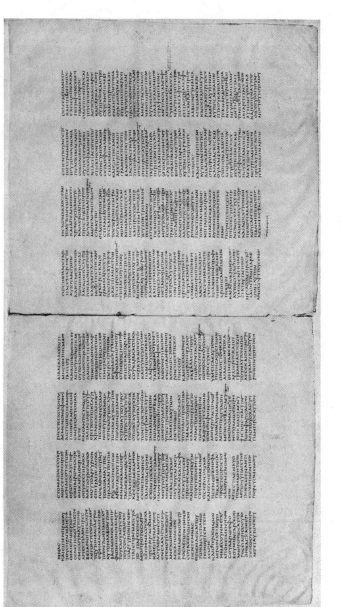

Codex Sinaiticus (ℵ), from the early fourth century.

As we mentioned before, around the ninth century a shift took place, and the "uncial" form gave way to the "minuscule." These texts look much more like our modern Greek texts. There are, quite literally, thousands of these texts, most of which date to the period after A.D. 1000. Some of these became quite ornate, replete with pictures, and even color!

Luke 1:1-6 in a minuscule text from A.D. 1292. Note the ornate styling.

TO ERR IS HUMAN

Men make mistakes, even when they are trying really hard. The greatest baseball player still strikes out. The greatest basketball player will miss the clutch free-throw and lose a game once in a while. The best archer will sometimes fire an arrow wide of the target. To err is human.

I am sitting at a computer writing this work. The computer checks my spelling (even while I am typing!), suggests other terms, and even analyzes my grammar. It prints out *exactly* what I tell it to print, and nothing else. And yet, I have made mistakes already in what I have written that others have pointed out to me as they have reviewed my work. Just today I was shown a rather obvious error in a later chapter. To err is human, even when that human is computer assisted.

There are dozens and dozens of citations in this work. As I sit here copying from a book, I make errors. My eyes skip to the next line; I misspell a word; I skip a phrase, or insert a phrase that is not in the original. Copying is difficult work, even with good lighting, a fresh set of eyes, and good conditions (a cool, air-conditioned room, no major distractions, etc.). Humans make mistakes when copying things. We were not born to be copy machines.

The scribes of old made errors, too. Even the best professional scribes had bad days. They made mistakes in what they were copying, even when they were copying the Scriptures. They worked under much more difficult situations. They often worked in the cold or the heat, and their lighting was almost always inferior to a good fluorescent lamp. Many of them had to work long hours at what they were doing. Fingers cramped, backs ached.[11] You may think of one of those long essay tests from college to get a slight idea of the rigor of the work. All of these things contributed to the simple fact that there is not a single handwritten manuscript of the Bible, in Greek or Hebrew, that does not contain, somewhere, an error, an oversight, a mistake. To err is human.

What kind of mistakes did scribes make? Most errors (the technical term that is used *incessantly* in scholarly works is "textual variants") were of little importance and are easily recognized today. A scribe might misspell a word. He might skip a phrase, or even a whole line, due to his eye catching a similar word, or a similar ending, somewhere else on the page as he looks back at the text he is copying (another technical term is used for this, the "exemplar"). There are all sorts of examples of this in the New Testament, as we will see when we examine textual variants in chapter 7.

Other errors had to do with hearing. In some instances a place called a *scriptorium* was set aside specifically for the production of manuscripts. One individual would read from the "master" document, and the other scribes would copy down what he was saying. It is easy to understand how certain kinds of mistakes could occur here. We all can imagine how the mind could wander after a few hours of listening to someone reading a text while you labor to write down what they are saying. Words that sound alike but differ in spelling could easily be substituted, and this is exactly the kind of thing that has been discovered.

Another kind of "scribal error" has to do with *harmonization*. Let's say you were used to the way a particular phrase sounds in a particular passage of Scripture because your pastor uses that verse all the time in church. But let's say that a similar phrase occurs elsewhere in Scripture—similar, but not exactly the same. As you are copying that other passage of Scripture it would be *very easy* to inadvertently make that passage sound like the one you are accustomed to. You might not even know you had changed anything! But this kind of harmonization is found in many, many places. We will see numerous examples of this later, but looking at at least one right now would be helpful.

When Paul wrote to the Ephesians, he said, "Grace to you and peace from God our Father and the Lord Jesus Christ" (Ephesians 1:2, NASB). This phrase early on had a part in the liturgy of the church. It was a Christian greeting, a blessing of sorts. Many people continue to use it in that way to this very day. But when writing to the Colossians, Paul was not as complete in his wording as when he wrote to the Ephesians. Instead he wrote, "Grace to you and peace from God our Father" (Colossians 1:2, NASB).

Now place yourself in the position of a scribe who has memorized Ephesians 1:2. Each Sunday you hear "Grace to you and peace from God our Father and the Lord Jesus Christ" as you leave the worship service. It is second nature to you. Now you start making a copy of Paul's letter to the Colossians. You start into verse 2 of chapter 1. "Grace to you and peace. . . ." "Ah, I know this one!" you think to yourself. And so you write out the whole phrase, *as you are accustomed to hearing it*, and move on with verse 3. In the process, you have added an extra phrase, "and the Lord Jesus Christ," without even knowing it. Or perhaps you look back at the original you are copying and notice that it does not say "and the Lord Jesus Christ." "That is strange," you might think. "It *should* say that! Well, the guy who copied this must have just missed it. I'll fix it. . . ." And so you put it in, again due to your familiarity with the same phrase but in a different context. This kind of *harmonization* is easy to understand, and it explains many of the most commonly cited examples of "corruption" on the part of KJV Only advocates. Indeed, this very example, Colossians 1:2 (the KJV *does* have the added phrase, "and the Lord Jesus Christ"), is found in nearly every KJV Only work in print as an example of an attempt to downgrade the lordship of Jesus Christ.[12] Instead, it is a perfectly understandable mistake involving harmonization between one passage and another. The fact that all modern translations have "and the Lord Jesus Christ" at Ephesians 1:2 should certainly cause us to question anyone who would ask us to believe that there is some evil conspiracy at work behind the non-inclusion of the same phrase at Colossians 1:2. If someone is tampering with the texts, why not take out the phrase at Ephesians 1:2? We will start to sound like a broken record as we point this out over and over again.

Thousands and Thousands of Variants

You may hear someone speaking of the thousands of variants in the manuscripts of the Bible, and in one sense, they are speaking the truth, as there are thousands of variants. One number that appears often in this context is 200,000 variants in the New Testament alone! But just as it is wise to listen closely to what a politician is saying, it is wise to look closely at this claim as well. If you put ten people in a room and asked them all to copy the first five chapters of the Gospel of John, you would end up with ten "different" copies of John. In other words, no two handwritten copies would be *absolutely identical* to each other. Someone would skip a word that everyone else has. One person would misspell that *one* word that they can *never* get right.

Someone would probably skip a line, or even a verse, especially if there were similar words at the beginning or end of the verse before and the verse after. So you would end up with a lot of *variants*. But would you not have ten copies of the same book? Yes, you would, and by comparing all ten copies you could rather easily reproduce the text of the original, because when one person makes a mistake, the other nine are not likely to do so at the very same spot.

When people speak of huge numbers of variants, they are referring to the fact that when one manuscript has a unique spelling of a word at one point, this creates a variant *over against all other manuscripts*. There are currently over 5,300 manuscripts catalogued of parts of the New Testament alone.[13] Obviously, with each one having small differences from each other, the number of "variants" becomes very high indeed. However, that does not mean that you have 5,000 *different* renderings of the New Testament. One can, by comparison of these many, many manuscripts, reproduce the original, just as we did above with the ten copies of the Gospel of John. Due to the fact that we are dealing with a more complex situation in the NT (the much longer period of time, the fact that we are working with copies of copies, etc.), things are not nearly as easy as our example would lead us to believe, but the principles are the same.

Taking the number mentioned above, 200,000, we first note that these variants occur in only about 10,000 places. How important are these variants? How do they impact the text? Textual scholars have answered in different ways, but with the same result.[14] Westcott and Hort, the two men most vilified by KJV Only advocates, indicated that only about one eighth of the variants had any weight, the rest being "trivialities."[15] This would leave the text, according to Westcott and Hort, 98.33 percent pure *no matter whether one used the Textus Receptus or their own Greek text!* Philip Schaff estimated that there were only 400 variants that affected the sense of the passage, and only 50 of these were actually important. He asserted that not one affected "an article of faith or a precept of duty which is not abundantly sustained by other and undoubted passages, or by the whole tenor of Scripture teaching."[16] The great American Greek scholar, Dr. A.T. Robertson, whose familiarity with the most intimate details of the Greek text is abundantly verified by his massive 1,454 page *A Grammar of the Greek New Testament in the Light of Historical*

Research, indicated that areas of real concern regarding textual variants amounted to but "a thousandth part of the entire text."[17] It is because of this that Dr. B.B. Warfield could state that "the great mass of the New Testament, in other words, has been transmitted to us with no, or next to no variations."[18] As Dr. Gordon Fee put it,

> It is noteworthy that for most scholars over 90 percent of all the variations to the NT text are resolved, because in most instances the variant that best explains the origin of the others is also supported by the earliest and best witnesses.[19]

The reality is that the amount of variation between the two most extremely *different* manuscripts of the New Testament *would not fundamentally alter the message of the Scriptures!* I make this statement (1) fully aware of the wide range of textual variants in the New Testament, and (2) painfully aware of the strong attacks upon those who have made similar statements in the past. KJV Only advocates are quick to attack such statements, but I stand by it and will document its truthfulness throughout the rest of this book. The simple fact of the matter is that no textual variants in either the Old or New Testaments in any way, shape, or form materially disrupt or destroy any essential doctrine of the Christian faith. That is a fact that any semi-impartial review will substantiate.

SCRIBES AND THEIR WORK

Back in kindergarten we used to play "telephone." We would sit in a circle and attempt to pass a message around the circle by whispering it to the person next to us. Normally, the message would not get to the other end without some kind of humorous alteration. The game illustrated how things can change when they are told and retold over and over again.

On another level we can see how the same thing can happen with written documents. We have already noted some of the kinds of errors that can take place when a person makes a handwritten copy of someone else's handwritten document. We might note some other problems that arise specifically in the course of repeated copying over time. For example, what if you have trouble reading the style of handwriting of the person who copied the book you are trying to reproduce? Some people write their *t*'s and their *f*'s alike; with others it is hard to distinguish between letters like *e* and *o* or *c*. The same kinds of problems exist in other languages. And if you are not in a position to ask the original author or copyist due to your geographic location, or due to the age of the document you are copying, you have to make your "best guess" at what is supposed to be on the page before you.

Another problem that crops up has to do with marginal notes. What if you are going along just fine, when all of a sudden you realize you skipped a line or a sentence up above. Remember, your writing materials are expensive. You can't just wad up a piece of papyrus and start all over again. If you are using vellum you might be able to erase what you wrote, but what if it was far enough back to make this too difficult? In either case, you might write the skipped portion in the margin in smaller letters, and give some indication that it is supposed to be included in the actual text. But this might lead to confusion further on down the line. Let's say you are copying someone else's work and you encounter something written in the margin. Did the original copyist intend this material to be included in the text, or is it just a note they have included there to explain a particular aspect of the passage? If you can't ask him, how are you to know? You don't want to put something in that isn't original, but at the same time you don't want to leave anything out, either. It seems that for most, it seemed safer to add the extra material than to leave it out.[20]

When we put the problems that arise with hand-copying manuscripts into the context of history, we begin to see the outlines of some of the major issues up for debate regarding the text of the New Testament. Since many fine works exist that go into great depth on this issue,[21] we will not repeat what others have done so well. Instead, we will summarize the important points.

First, the text of the Bible was transmitted in the context of history. That is, we cannot isolate the discussion of how the Bible came to us from the ebb and flow of history. The rise and fall of the Roman Empire, for example, is an important aspect of the transmission of the text of the Bible to our day. So, too, is the rise of Islam and the protracted conflict between Muslim and Christian forces around the ancient city of Constantinople. These things had great influence upon Christians and, necessarily, upon the manuscripts in their possession. This might seem rather elementary and not worthy of noting, but scholars have put forth entire theories about the text of the Bible that seemed to be utterly oblivious of the simple facts of history and how they impacted the entire process.

In some ways the text of the New Testament was more impacted by external forces than the text of the Old Testament. There are a number of reasons for this. There was a natural "isolation" of the text of the Old Testament due to the reverence given to it by the Jewish people, and by their distinct standing as a religious and ethnic group. Hebrew as a language was not well known outside of Jewish circles, which gave an added measure of "control" to the transmission of the text. In comparison, the Greek of the New Testament, at least in the first few centuries after it was written, was the "common language" of the people. Since the Gospel went to "all people," all sorts of different people had direct access to the New Testament and hence were able to make copies of those documents in a language they understood. Christians were very open about spreading their message far and wide, and as a result the text of the New Testament went far and wide as well. Rather than being limited to trained scribes, we discover that businessmen, soldiers, and even literate slaves often made personal copies of one of the Gospels so as to be able to read about their Lord Jesus. The less trained individuals might make more errors in their transcription than the experienced scribes, but this was unavoidable given the Christian belief that the message of Christ was to go to all men.

Text-types and Families

How is all of this important to us? Much in every way. One of the most critical elements of the entire KJV Only controversy, especially as it relates to the New Testament, revolves around the discussion of "text-types" or "text-families." We are now in a position to understand how "text-types" came into being. Basically, a text-type or text-family refers to a grouping of manuscripts that share common readings or characteristics that distinguish them from other text-types. Some manuscripts belong to more than one text-type, for they may have one kind of text in the Gospels, and a different kind of text in Paul's writings[22] or in the general Epistles. The lines between the various text-types that have been identified are often blurry. But in general, scholars have identified at least three, and probably four, "text-types" in the New Testament. They are:

(1) The Alexandrian text-type, found in most papyri, and in the great uncial codices א and B.

(2) The Western text-type, found both in Greek manuscripts and in translations into other languages, especially Latin.[23]

(3) The Byzantine text-type, found in the vast majority of later uncial and minuscule manuscripts.

(4) The Caesarean text-type, disputed by some, found in $\mathfrak{P}^{45}$ and "Family 1" (abbreviated f^1).

As one can see from the names, these text-types are tied to geographic locations. The Alexandrian is thought to originate in, or at least to have been predominant in, the area around Alexandria, Egypt, where early church fathers such as Origen, Clement, and later Athanasius flourished. The Byzantine text-type is found consistently in the area around Byzantium, or Constantinople, and the Western, of course, refers to the Western half of the Roman Empire (though this one is a little less specific in nature, examples of this type defying precise geographical location).

The two "ends" of the spectrum, so to speak, are the Alexandrian and the Byzantine. The Alexandrian is the more "concise," while the Byzantine is the "full" text. What does this mean? Most scholars today (in opposition to KJV Only advocates) would see the Alexandrian text-type as representing an earlier, and hence more accurate, form of text than the Byzantine text-type. Most believe the Byzantine represents a later period in which readings from other text-types were put together ("conflated") into the reading in the Byzantine text. This is not to say the Byzantine does not contain some distinctive readings that are quite ancient, but that the readings that are *unique* to that text-type are generally secondary or later readings. Since the Byzantine comes from a later period (the earliest texts are almost all Alexandrian in nature, not Byzantine), it is "fuller" in the sense that it not only contains conflations of the other text-types, but it gives evidence of what might be called the "expansion of piety." That is, additions have been made to the text that flow from a desire to protect and reverence divine truths. We will have more to say about this shortly.

The Byzantine text-type represents the vast majority of the Greek manuscripts we have available to us today. There is a fairly simple reason for this. Within a few centuries after the writing of the New Testament, Latin superseded Greek as the "language of the people" in the West. Obviously, when people are no longer speaking Greek the production of manuscripts in that language will be less than if everyone is still speaking that language.

Another historical event that greatly impacted the use of language was the rise of Islam and the Muslim invasion of Palestine, then North Africa, and finally all the way into Spain and southern France. Obviously, production of manuscripts in those areas was adversely affected by the rise of Islam as the predominant religion. If one thinks about a map, it becomes readily apparent that the only area that continued to speak and utilize Greek was the area under the control of Constantinople, also known as Byzantium. The brave people of this area withstood the attacks of the Muslim invaders for many years, finally succumbing in the middle of the fifteenth century. Given that these Christians continued to write and use Greek all through this period, while Greek had passed out of normal use throughout the rest of Europe and North Africa, the dominance of the text-type that was found in that area is easily understood.

KJV Only advocates disagree with this summary of the historical situation. The *Textus Receptus,* the Greek text from which the KJV New Testament was translated, is "Byzantine" in character, so AV Alone believers must find a way of defending the Byzantine text-type as the "best." They explain the lack of ancient examples of the Byzantine text-type by theorizing that those manuscripts "wore out" from excessive use over the years, while the "Alexandrian" texts were quickly seen as corrupt and hence just buried in the sand. Such a theory, of course, defies proof by its very nature, but it is the explanation used by many of those who would assert the superiority of the Byzantine text-type.

Another common claim made by those who defend the KJV is that the Alexandrian texts have been corrupted by "heretics." They point to men like Origen who did things and believed things that most modern fundamentalists would find more than slightly unusual,[24] and on this basis make the very long leap to the assertion that the manuscripts that come from the same area must be "corrupt." The problem is that you can also find excellent examples of orthodox

Christians in the same area just as you can find some rather heretical folks in the Byzantine area, too.[25]

As we noted before, it is important to emphasize that the differences between the Alexandrian and Byzantine text-types do not result in two different New Testaments. A person who would read Codex Sinaiticus and who would apply sound exegetical methods to its text would come to the very same conclusions as anyone reading a Byzantine manuscript written a thousand years later.

WHAT DO YOU MEAN BY "FULLER"?

Earlier we noted that the Byzantine text-type is "fuller" or "longer" than other text-types, and that this is taken as evidence of a later origin. An example would be helpful in demonstrating this. There are two main modern texts, the United Bible Societies 4th Edition, and the Nestle-Aland 27th edition, both of which have the same text but differ in other matters such as punctuation, textual apparatus, etc. These texts are more "Alexandrian" in character than the *Textus Receptus*, which was based upon Byzantine manuscripts, but *less* "Alexandrian" than the text produced by Westcott and Hort in 1881. Another text that is available is the "Majority Text," which is represented by the symbol "𝔐". This text is mainly Byzantine in character, too, for the obvious reason that the Byzantine manuscripts always form the majority. With these items in mind, let's note the following chart:

Reference	Nestle-Aland/UBS	𝔐 Text/Byzantine
Matthew 4:18	He	Jesus
Matthew 12:25	He	Jesus
Mark 2:15	He	Jesus
Mark 10:52	He	Jesus
Luke 24:36	He	Jesus
Acts 19:10	the Lord	the Lord Jesus
1 Corinthians 16:22	the Lord	the Lord Jesus Christ
Acts 19:4	Jesus	Christ Jesus
1 Corinthians 9:1	Jesus	Jesus Christ
2 Corinthians 4:10	Jesus	Lord Jesus
Hebrews 3:1	Jesus	Christ Jesus

Reference	Nestle-Aland/UBS	𝔐 Text/Byzantine
1 John 1:7	Jesus	Jesus Christ
Revelation 1:9	Jesus	Jesus Christ
Revelation 12:17	Jesus	Jesus Christ
1 Thessalonians 3:11	Jesus our Lord	our Lord Jesus Christ
2 Corinthians 5:18	Christ	Jesus Christ
Acts 15:11	Lord Jesus	Lord Jesus Christ
Acts 16:31	Lord Jesus	Lord Jesus Christ
1 Corinthians 5:4	Lord Jesus	Lord Jesus Christ
2 Corinthians 11:31	Lord Jesus	Lord Jesus Christ
2 Thessalonians 1:8	Lord Jesus	Lord Jesus Christ
2 Thessalonians 1:12	Lord Jesus	Lord Jesus Christ
2 John 1:3	Jesus Christ	the Lord Jesus Christ

There are two ways to interpret this chart. KJV Only advocates take it as evidence of an effort on the part of the Alexandrian text to denigrate the person of Christ. Yet, this is logically untenable. The full title of the "Lord Jesus Christ" occurs 86 times in the KJV; it is found 64 times in the New Testament of the NASB, and 61 times in the NIV. If the modern translations were trying to "hide" anything, why not exclude these other readings? There is another perfectly logical explanation, however, that requires no special theories and malevolent forces. Earlier we called it the "expansion of piety." We can see exactly how it functions in the chart above. It flows from a desire to safeguard the sanctity of the Lord Jesus. It led people to naturally expand the titles used of the Lord, possibly even without their conscious effort to change the text. The emotions that bring about this "expansion of piety" exist today as well. A number of years ago I was hosting a radio program on which we dealt with various religious groups. An elderly lady called in one week and took us to task for not being "reverent" enough. "Last week you talked about Jesus saying this and Jesus doing that. You need to say, 'the Lord Jesus said this' or 'the Lord Jesus Christ did that.' You need to show more reverence." One can certainly understand this woman's concern, and when that concern was shared by a scribe working on a manuscript of the New Testament, we can see how the later texts "grew" in their use of titles. This is what we mean when we say the Byzantine text is a "fuller" text.

A FINAL WORD ON THE TEXT OF THE NT

KJV Only advocates are quick to assert that those who do not join them in making the KJV the final authority in all things do not believe in the "preservation of the Scriptures." Almost all KJV Only books will contain a section on how God has promised to preserve His words, and they will, of course, assume that these "words" are found in the KJV. At this point they believe themselves to be holding the "high ground" in the debate, fighting for a belief that all Christians would naturally defend: the idea that God has revealed himself, and has done so in such a way that we can continue to know that revelation perfectly today.

The problem with the position taken by the defender of the AV is that he has not demonstrated that *his* way is the *only* way to understand the idea of "preservation." Does God have to preserve His Word in the way KJV Only advocates believe? Or might God have done this in another way?

Our brief look at the history of the text of the New Testament suggests that there might be a way other than "re-inspiring" the entire Bible (as some would have us believe God did in 1611), or even supernaturally guiding men to give us a particular translation. What if God preserved His Word in a much less flashy way?

When we look at how God led His people to recognize the canon of Scripture, the listing of the books that were inspired over against those books which were not, we note that God did not engage in any celestial fireworks in the process. No angels showed up with golden tablets marked "Divine Index." Instead, God worked with His people over time, leading them to recognize what He had already done through the act of inspiration. It took time, and some might wish for a more "spectacular" method, but God did it in His way, in His time.

The same thing is true regarding the protection and preservation of the text of the Bible. One might well see a tremendous amount of divine wisdom in the way in which God worked over the years. By having the text of the New Testament in particular "explode" across the known world, ending up in the far-flung corners of the Roman Empire in a relatively short period of time, God protected that text from the one thing that we could never detect: the wholesale change of doctrine or theology by one particular man or group who had full control over the text at any one point in its history. You see, because the New Testament books were written at various times, and were quickly copied and distributed as soon as they were written, there was never a time when any one man, or any group of men, could gather up all the manuscripts and make extensive changes in the text itself, such as cutting out the deity of Christ, or inserting some foreign doctrine or concept. No one could gather up the texts and try to make them all say the same thing by "harmonizing" them, either. If someone had indeed done such a thing, we could never know for certain what the apostles had written, and what the truth actually is. But such a thing did not, *and could not*, happen. Indeed, by the time anyone did obtain great ecclesiastical power in the name of Christianity, texts like $\mathfrak{P}^{66}$ or $\mathfrak{P}^{75}$ were already long buried in the sands of Egypt, out of the reach of anyone who would try to alter them. The fact that their text is nearly identical to even the most "Byzantine" manuscript of 1,000 years later is testimony to the overall purity of the New Testament text.

The side effect of this method of preserving the New Testament is the relatively small amount of textual variation that we will be discussing extensively below. But one point must be emphasized. Dr. Kurt Aland has pointed out what he calls the *tenacity* of the New Testament text.[26] This refers to the fact that once a variant reading appears in a manuscript, *it doesn't simply go away.* It gets copied and ends up in other manuscripts. Why is this important? It is important because readings don't just "disappear" in the New Testament. And that means that *we still have the original readings of the New Testament works.* You see, if readings could just "disappear" without a trace, we would have to face the fact that the *original* reading may have "fallen through the cracks" as well. But the *tenacity* of the New Testament text, while forcing us to deal with textual variants, also provides us with the assurance that our work is not in vain. One of those variant readings is indeed the original. We are called to invest our energies in discovering which one it is.

Endnotes

[1] Great controversy has raged over the past decades about the possibility of sections of the New Testament having been written in Hebrew or Aramaic. Though such is possible, we agree with Dr. Kurt Aland who wrote, "There is

no longer any doubt that Greek was the language in which all the parts of the New Testament were originally written" (*The Text of the New Testament,* Eerdmans: 1987), p. 52.

[2] See our discussion of this passage in chapter 7, pp. 170-173.

[3] See our discussion of this passage in chapter 6, pp. 132-133.

[4] Note that the KJV is just a little less than perfectly formal in translating the Greek phrase "words" as "sayings."

[5] For discussions on both sides see Kenneth Barker, *The NIV: The Making of a Contemporary Translation* (International Bible Society: 1991) for a defense of dynamic translation in the NIV, and Robert Martin, *Accuracy of Translation and the New International Version* (Banner of Truth: 1989) for a critique of the same.

[6] I am convinced that the conclusions of the Jesus Seminar have little, if anything, to do with *any* type of serious scholarly study, for that matter. The work produced by this group seems more designed to vent personal theories than to present serious material. See *The Five Gospels* by Robert Funk, Roy Hoover and The Jesus Seminar (Macmillan: 1993). For a critique of the Jesus Seminar, see Craig L. Blomberg, "The Seventy-Four 'Scholars': Who Does the Jesus Seminar Really Speak For?" in the *Christian Research Journal,* Fall, 1994, pp. 32-38.

[7] For a fuller rendition of the story, see, Metzger, *The Text of the New Testament: Its Transmission, Corruption, and Restoration* 2nd ed. (Oxford: 1968), pp. 42-45.

[8] Note the words of William Grady in *Final Authority* (Grady Publications: 1993), p. 100:

> Within two years of England's national acceptance of this depraved **Catholic** manuscript, the city of London was in smoldering ruins. *"The wicked shall be turned into hell, and all the **nations** that forget God."* (Psalm 9:17).

[9] Vaticanus is attacked on the basis of its being found in the Vatican library. Of course, the fact that the *vast majority* of "Byzantine" manuscripts were copied by Roman Catholic monks in the centuries prior to the Reformation seems to be overlooked. Note the conspiracy-laden words of Grady (ibid., p. 101):

> Strange as it sounds, the most heralded manuscript evidence for rejecting the King James Bible **has yet to be *handled* by serious Bible-believing scholars!** People like Beale, and Geisler and Nix have chosen a "slide presentation" put together by the most treacherous international gangsters in history over the blood-washed text of the Protestant Reformation!

[10] See for example D.A. Waite, *Defending the King James Bible* (The Bible For Today: 1993), p. 61, "They just about worship that manuscript." This was just after alleging, inaccurately, that ℵ was about to be burned (one

will note that the steward at St. Catherine's kept the manuscript in his cell, wrapped in a red cloth, hardly the way in which one treats trash). When Dr. Waite debated me in August of 1994, he dropped the "just about" and directly asserted that Westcott and Hort worshiped Sinaiticus.

[11] Dr. Metzger gives a fascinating discussion of these things in his work, *The Text of the New Testament*, pp. 16-21. For example, he cites a colophon (a note made by a scribe, normally at the end of the manuscript) from an Armenian manuscript of the Gospels which complains that "a heavy snowstorm was raging outside and that the scribe's ink froze, his hand became numb, and the pen fell from his fingers!"

[12] See Jasper James Ray, *God Wrote Only One Bible* (The Eye Opener Publishers: 1955), p. 49; D.A. Waite, *Defending the King James Bible,* p. 181; Gail Riplinger, *New Age Bible Versions* (A.V. Publications: 1993), p. 335, etc.

[13] Most of these 5,300 manuscripts are partial; that is, very few of them contain *all* of the New Testament. Some contain only a few verses, others only sections of the entire NT.

[14] The citations found here are taken from Geisler and Nix, *A General Introduction to the Bible* (Moody Press: 1986), pp. 473-475.

[15] Brooke Foss Westcott and Fenton John Anthony Hort, *Introduction to The New Testament in the Original Greek* (Harper and Brothers: 1882), p. 2.

[16] Philip Schaff, *Companion to the Greek Testament and the English Version,* (Harper: 1883), p. 177 as cited by Geisler and Nix, p. 474. We agree wholeheartedly with Schaff's appraisal.

[17] A.T. Robertson, *An Introduction to the Textual Criticism of the New Testament* (Broadman: 1925), p. 22, as cited by Geisler and Nix, p. 474.

[18] B.B. Warfield, *An Introduction to the Textual Criticism of the New Testament* (London: 1886) p. 14.

[19] Dr. Gordon Fee, "The Textual Criticism of the New Testament" in Gaebelein, *The Expositor's Bible Commentary* (Zondervan: 1979), I:430.

[20] This is probably how John 5:4 ended up in most Greek manuscripts, including the ones from which the KJV was translated. The simple mention of the sick lying next to the pool did not seem complete enough, so someone included a note in their manuscript explaining the tradition behind the sick and the pool. This manuscript was copied and the explanatory note inserted into the text itself.

[21] See especially the previously cited works, Metzger's *The Text of the New Testament: Its Transmission, Corruption, and Restoration,* as well as Geisler and Nix, *A General Introduction to the Bible.* See also Kurt and Barbara Aland, *The Text of the New Testament* (Eerdmans: 1987).

[22] Codex Alexandrinus (A) is an example of just such a text, having a "Byzantine" text in the Gospels, but an "Alexandrian" text elsewhere.

[23] See chart in J. Harold Greenlee, *Introduction to New Testament Textual Criticism* (Eerdmans: 1964), pp. 117-118.

[24] Indeed, it might be difficult for them to find *anyone* in the ancient

church, even around Antioch and Byzantium, who would *look* a whole lot like a modern fundamentalist Baptist. Even the most conservative of the ancient Fathers, like John Chrysostom, would provide KJV Only advocates with numerous reasons to object to his theology, beliefs, and practices.

[25] Alexandria gave us Athanasius, the great defender of the deity of Christ, while the area around Antioch and Byzantium was infested with Arians, those who denied it. Is this sufficient basis for rejecting the Byzantine text-type *a priori*? Of course not.

[26] Kurt and Barbara Aland, *The Text of the New Testament,* pp. 56, 286ff.

Putting It Together

We are now in a position to begin to discuss the specifics of the King James Only controversy. We have established the background. Now we need to apply this information to the conflict that prompts the writing of this book.

The New Testament of the King James Version of the Bible is based upon a printed edition of the Greek New Testament that finds its origins in the work of Desiderius Erasmus, the great scholar to whom we have already had occasion to refer.[1] Erasmus' text, which eventually became known as the *Textus Receptus,* was extremely popular in England, and was used by all of those who engaged in the translation of the Greek text. To fully understand all the arguments that are put forth regarding the KJV, we must take some time to delve into the process by which the texts used by the KJV translators came to be in their possession. This will necessitate our further discussion of Erasmus. This is not a hurdle, however, as much as it is a great help, for we shall also note that Erasmus was on "our side" in this raging controversy. How so? Many of the *exact same arguments* that are used today by KJV Only advocates were used *against Erasmus* nearly 500 years ago! The very man to whom AV defenders must defer for the vast majority of their New Testament text used the very same arguments and methodology to defend his work that modern textual scholars use to defend the readings of the NASB or NIV! Later in this chapter we will look closely at one of the most famous passages that is very important to the story of Erasmus' Greek text, that of 1 John 5:7-8, known by many as the *Comma Johanneum,* or as the "Three Witnesses."

Having traced the genesis of the *Textus Receptus,* and its transmission from the days of Erasmus to the days of the KJV translators, we will take the time to note the words of those translators, and the initial form of their work. Most people are not aware of the substantial use of textual notes and alternate readings in the original

1611 KJV, because most modern editions do not contain these items. Finally we will note that not all KJV's today have the same text; that is, printed editions of the KJV differ from one another, presenting more difficulties for the most radical proponents of the infallibility of a human translation.

ERASMUS UNDER ATTACK

In chapter 2 we noted briefly the work of Desiderius Erasmus, both in his production of a printed Greek text (1516), the first of its kind to be published, and a fresh Latin translation as well. His Greek text went through a number of revisions, with new editions coming out in 1519, 1522, 1527, and 1535, the year before his death. Attached to his texts were his *Annotations* that included, initially, notes on various passages and comments on scriptural themes. As the controversy over his work grew, the *Annotations* grew as well, for he provided an explanation and defense of his stands in its pages. The *Annotations* give us a great insight into the thinking and beliefs of Erasmus and, when coupled with the many apologies he wrote against his chief opponents, make it possible to understand the methods and goals of this great scholar in his work on the text of the New Testament.

One of the marvels of Erasmus' work is that he was able to produce such a fine text with so few resources. He drew from barely half a dozen Greek manuscripts in his initial work, not including those he would have examined in England. Over the years he took advantage of his travels to examine other texts, but even if one added them all together the final number would still be rather small. Despite the paucity of manuscripts available to him, Erasmus showed himself a true scholar, and his *Annotations* address many of the same textual variants that are discussed today by modern scholars, many of which are relevant to the KJV Only discussion as well.

Erasmus was aided by two scholars in his initial work, Nikolaus Gerber and Ioannes Oecolampadius, later an aid to Ulrich Zwingli and a leader in the Reformation movement. Oecolampadius looked up all the references to the Hebrew of the Old Testament as Erasmus did not know Hebrew. Refusing payment for his services, Oecolampadius accepted only one of Erasmus' manuscripts, the introduction to the Gospel of John, and is said to have treated it as a relic, kissing it and hanging it on a crucifix while he prayed, that is, until it was stolen.[2]

It is well known that Erasmus struggled with the text of Revelation. Not finding any manuscripts that contained the book, he borrowed one from his friend Reuchlin. Erasmus was quite pleased with the text, feeling that it was "of such great age that it might be thought to have been written in the time of the apostles."[3] He had an unknown copyist[4] make a fresh copy and returned the original to Reuchlin. The copyist had difficulty with the text (the manuscript contained a commentary on the book of Revelation, and the actual text of Scripture was imbedded in the commentary), and as a result made some mistakes that found their way into the printed editions of Erasmus' Greek text, and finally into the text of the King James Version.

The printer, John Froben, began work on the project October 2, 1515. The final product emerged March 1, 1516, weighing in at around 700 pages, a hefty volume to be sure. Over the span of the next four editions, Erasmus' text would be reprinted 69 times, and though we don't know exactly how many copies that represents, a conservative estimate would be right at 300,000, an *incredible* number for the sixteenth century.

I emphasize the work of Erasmus for two reasons. First, his text was the beginning of what eventually would become known as the *Textus Receptus.* Hence, the sources he used, the methods he employed, and the conclusions he came to are *vitally* important to any real discussion of the topic at hand. Second, Erasmus encountered the *very same kind* of resistance to his work that is put forward by KJV Only advocates today against modern translations. His answers then are just as valid today. The great irony is found in comparing the arguments of Erasmus' opponents to the arguments used by AV Alone people today. Let's look at some of these arguments and Erasmus' replies.

It is very common to find the KJV Only advocate dismissing any appeal to the Greek or Hebrew manuscripts. "So you have to know Greek to know what God says" is the comment that has been made to me many times. "You are limiting God's Word to scholars. What about those of us who do not know Greek or Hebrew? Can't we know what God has revealed?" Recently I mentioned to a KJV Only advocate that I was teaching both Greek and Hebrew classes. He asked me what percentage of Christian people today know Greek or Hebrew. I answered that it is a very small number, to which he replied, "Good. No need to waste time with such things anyway, since you have God's words in the AV 1611." Erasmus encountered the same thing. Within three years of the publication of the first edition of his New Testament text, Jacobus Latomus published a treatise titled, *The Three Languages and the Study of the System of Theology,* which had the subtitle, "Whether a knowledge of the three languages is necessary for a theologian." One can guess to what conclusions Latomus arrived. Erasmus responded with a written defense in which he stated, "no subject area depends more on languages than theology"[5] and,

> With the help of Greek . . . many passages in the Vulgate have been restored that before were corrupt; many passages have been clarified that before were misinterpreted by commentators of great renown; much light has been shed on passages that before were covered by a cloud of ambiguity.[6]

Erasmus criticized both Thomas Aquinas and Augustine over and over again in the *Annotations* for their ignorance of the biblical languages. For example, he said of Augustine at Mark 16:14, "He would have had no reason to raise the question, had he consulted the Greek codices."[7] And with reference to Augustine's comments on John 18 Erasmus wonders "why he did not consult the Greek codices."[8]

We are often told that God has blessed the KJV more than any other translation of the Bible, and that the fact that it was the "only" Bible for hundreds of years should be grounds enough for us today to hold to it as the standard. We have already noted how attached many conservative theologians were to the "traditional" text of the Latin *Vulgate* in the days of Erasmus. Dorp had written to Erasmus even before his work was published and had asserted that no one would ever believe the *Vulgate* contained errors, "For it is not reasonable that the whole church, which has always used this edition and still both approves and uses it, should for all these centuries have been wrong."[9] Dorp went so far as to say, "If however they contend that a sentence as rendered by the Latin translator varies in point of truth from the Greek manuscript, at that point I bid the Greeks goodbye and cleave to the Latins."[10] How does this differ in the least from the words of a modern KJV Only advocate, Dr. Samuel Gipp, "Question: What should I do where my Bible and my Greek Lexicon contradict? Answer: Throw out the Lexicon"?[11] Or this statement by the same writer, "Question: What about a contradiction that can't be successfully explained? Answer: You will have to accept the perfection of the Authorized Version by faith."[12] Erasmus dismissed such arguments out of hand. "What will you do with the errors of the copyists?" Erasmus asked Dorp.[13]

Dr. D.A. Waite, a defender of the *Textus Receptus,* attacks the *New King James Version* in these words,

> The diabolical nature of the NEW KING JAMES VERSION shows itself in their printing all the various readings of the Greek text in the footnotes. They print all sides and take their stand in favor of none of them. By so doing, they confuse the readers. The editors have made no decision as to what God's Words really are.[14]

Dr. Waite is expressing the same concern that Dorp included in his letter to Erasmus, "For a great many people will discuss the integrity of the Scriptures, and many will have doubts about it."[15] Again Erasmus rejected these arguments out of hand. In fact, Erasmus presented to his critics many of the same arguments and facts used by modern textual scholars. With reference to the existence of textual variants and our need to deal with them, he wrote,

> Granted that the Greek books are just as corrupt as the Latin ones, yet by collating manuscripts that are equally corrupt one can often discover the true reading, for it frequently happens that what has been corrupted by chance in one is found intact in another.[16]

> Now granted that the Greek and Hebrew manuscripts are as corrupt as ours, does it follow that we are deprived of any hope of ever emending what is found to be corrupted in our manuscripts? Does it not happen frequently that from several faulty manuscripts—though not faulty in the same way—the true and genuine reading is found?[17]

How is this different than modern methods of textual criticism? Erasmus' *Annotations* reveal to us something that every KJV Only advocate should seriously consider: Erasmus used the very same basic methods of textual-critical study that modern scholars use. I am not saying that he had the full spectrum of textual tools available today, but the basic forms and methods of trying to arrive at the original reading were used by Desiderius Erasmus *even as he collated what became known as the Textus Receptus.* The TR did not fall down out of heaven complete. Instead, Erasmus, a classical scholar, used his best judgment in coming up with his Greek text, drawing from various sources, accepting some readings, rejecting others, as he saw fit. Anyone who believes the TR to be infallible must believe that Erasmus, and the other men who later edited the same text in their own editions (Stephanus and Beza), were somehow "inspired," or at the very least "providentially guided"[18] in their work. Yet, none of these men ever claimed such inspiration.

Lest anyone think Erasmus did not speak in the same vein as modern textual scholars, I offer the following citations. When discussing the catalog of human sins in Romans chapter 1, specifically verse 29, he commented, "Whenever a catalog of nouns occurs, whether you consult the Greek or Latin exemplars, there are differences. This is due to the forgetfulness of the scribes, for it is difficult to remember these kinds of things."[19] A similar comment is found later in his discussion of Romans chapter 8.[20] How Erasmus dealt with variants should be extremely important to any defender of the KJV, for the reading of that translation is often determined by Erasmus' decisions. At Romans 4:1 the order of words in the TR (and hence in the KJV translation) was determined not by the majority of Greek texts, but by Erasmus' examination of the early Fathers and the Latin text. At Romans 10:17, "So then faith cometh by hearing, and hearing by the word of God" (KJV), Erasmus realized that the *Vulgate* had "word of Christ," as did a number of early Fathers (what he did not know, however, was that $\mathfrak{P}^{46}$, $\aleph$, and B *also* have "Christ"). Basically, Erasmus "guessed" and chose "God," explaining, "It does not greatly affect the meaning except in the sense that the phrase 'voice of God' lends more dignity to the words of the Apostle and has a wider application."[21]

In another instance Erasmus indicated[22] that he "liked" one reading better than the other, even though the one he chose was the minority reading. Specifically, he liked "serving the time" at Romans

12:11 rather than "serving the Lord." He defended his choice by noting that the Greek terms for Lord (*kurios*) and time (*kairos*) could easily be confused because they look the same.[23] This was true, "especially considering that copyists often abbreviate syllables in their writing." Two things should be noticed about Erasmus' position. First, here we find him using the *exact same argument* that has been used to explain the difference between the readings "God" and "He" at 1 Timothy 3:16, a passage we will examine closely in chapter 8. KJV Only advocates ridicule modern scholars when they point to the same facts that Erasmus did long ago. Secondly, the only reason the KJV says "serving the Lord" at Romans 12:11 rather than "serving the time" is because the KJV translators chose that reading, which appeared in the first edition of Erasmus and in Beza's text, over the other reading that appeared in the last four editions of Erasmus and in Stephanus' text. We will have more to say about the various "flavors" of the *Textus Receptus* later on in this chapter.

In chapter 3 we noted how scribes could change a passage due to familiarity with a parallel account in another place, or due to their familiarity with the passage's use in the church. Erasmus realized the exact same thing. With reference to the phrase "Jesus Christ" at Matthew 1:18, Erasmus, noting that the Latin only had "Christ," said, "However I suspect 'Jesus' was added by a scribe because the passage is customarily recited in this way by the church."[24] In the same way he elsewhere noted that the scribes often wrote "not what they find in the manuscripts but what is fixed in their memory."[25] He recognized, correctly, the appearance of "harmonization" between parallel passages in the Gospels, even anticipating the decisions of modern textual scholars. One clear example of this is found at Matthew 20:22 where the KJV has, "Are ye able to drink of the cup that I shall drink of, and to be baptized with the baptism that I am baptized with?" The NASB has simply, "Are you able to drink the cup that I am about to drink?" While Erasmus kept the phrase "and to be baptized with the baptism that I am baptized with" in his text, he noted that it appeared to have been "transferred" from the parallel passage in Mark 10:38. Modern texts put this phrase in the footnotes due to the discovery of earlier manuscripts that support Erasmus' hunch. KJV Only advocates would not be listing this passage as yet another "deletion" on the part of the modern texts had Erasmus acted upon this inclination, something he *did* do in other places.[26]

The words of Erasmus himself are seen to refute many of the arguments used by modern defenders of KJV Onlyism. If KJV Only advocates were to be consistent, they would have to reject Erasmus' work, which is the basis for the KJV, on the *very same grounds* as the modern translations. Anyone engaging in textual criticism is said to be "judging God's Word," yet Erasmus did the very same thing! Of course, they do not reject Erasmus' work, thereby demonstrating their system to be inconsistent and self-contradictory. I can say with confidence that if Desiderius Erasmus were alive today he would *not* be an advocate of the AV 1611. He would, instead, reject vociferously the very same arguments that he faced so long ago, and in so doing would have to reject the very foundation of the KJV Only position.

Erasmus and the Comma Johanneum

The single most famous incident that is related to Erasmus' work on the New Testament revolves around the words of 1 John 5:7 as found in the KJV: "For there are three that bear record in heaven, the Father, the Word, and the Holy Ghost: and these three are one." Most KJV Only preachers and believers make the acceptance of this passage *the* test of "orthodoxy." If your Bible does not have this passage, you are in deep trouble.

The story of how this passage ended up in the King James Version is very instructive. When the first edition of Erasmus' work came out in 1516 this phrase, dubbed today the "Johannine comma," or in Latin, the *Comma Johanneum*, was not in the text for a very simple reason: it was not found in any Greek manuscript of 1 John that Erasmus had examined. Instead, the phrase was found only in the Latin *Vulgate*. Erasmus rightly did not include it in the first or second editions. The note in the *Annotations* simply said, "In the Greek codex I find only this about the threefold testimony: 'because there are three witnesses, spirit, water, and blood.' " His reliance upon the Greek manuscripts rather than the Latin *Vulgate* caused quite a stir. Both Edward Lee and Diego López Zúñiga attacked Erasmus for not including this passage and hence encouraging "Arianism,"[27] the very same charge made by KJV Only advocates today. Erasmus protested that he was simply following the Greek texts. In responding to Lee, Erasmus challenged him to "produce a Greek manuscript that has what is missing in my edition."[28] Likewise Erasmus rebutted Zúñiga by pointing out that while he (Zúñiga) was constantly referring Erasmus to one particular Greek manuscript, in this case he had not brought this text forward, correctly assuming that even Zúñiga's manuscript agreed with Erasmus' reading. He also said, "Finally, the whole passage is so obscure that it cannot be very valuable in refuting the [Arian] heresies."[29]

Since Erasmus had promised, in his response to Lee, to include the passage should a Greek manuscript be found that contained it, he was constrained to insert the phrase in the third edition when presented with an Irish manuscript that contained the disputed phrase, Codex Montfortianus, now at Trinity College, Dublin.[30] The manuscript is highly suspect, in that it most probably was created in the house of the Grey Friars, whose provincial, Henry Standish, was an old enemy of Erasmus,[31] and whose intention was simply to refute Erasmus. The text note in the *Annotations* grew tremendously, for Erasmus inserted many of the arguments and citations he had used in replying to Lee and Zúñiga. He remarked, "I have restored the text . . . so as not to give anyone an occasion for slander."[32] He concluded the note with the statement, "But to return to the business of the reading: from our remarks it is clear that the Greek and Latin manuscripts vary, and in my opinion there is no danger in accepting either reading."[33]

The *Comma Johanneum* is extremely important. Here we have a phrase that everyone will admit is manifestly orthodox. What it says is obviously *true*. Yet, we are in no way dependent upon the phrase for our knowledge of the Trinity or the unity of the three Persons: Father, Son, and Spirit. The doctrine of the Trinity does not stand or fall upon the inclusion of the *Comma*. Beyond this, however, we have a phrase that is simply not a part of the ancient Greek manuscripts of John's first epistle. The few manuscripts that contain the phrase are very recent, and half of these have the reading written in the margin. The phrase appears only in certain of the Latin versions. There are, quite literally, *hundreds* of readings in the New Testament manuscript tradition that have *better* arguments in their favor that are *rejected* by both Erasmus and the KJV translators. And yet this passage is ferociously defended by KJV Only advocates to this day.[34] We can see that Erasmus could have just as easily maintained his position against the *Comma*, resulting in a KJV without this inserted phrase. But aside from these considerations, we need to note what is really being said by the defenders of the AV. If indeed the *Comma* was a part of the original writing of the apostle John, we are forced to conclude that entire passages, rich in theological meaning, can *disappear* from the Greek manuscript tradition *without leaving a single trace.* In reality, the KJV Only advocate is arguing for a radical viewpoint on the New Testament text, a viewpoint that utterly denies the very *tenacity* that we discussed in chapter 3. Even "liberal" scholars will admit the outstanding purity of the NT text and the validity of the belief in the tenacity of that text. Here we find otherwise very conservative people, the defenders of the KJV, joining arms with the most destructive liberal critics in presenting a theory regarding the NT text that, in reality, *destroys the very basis upon which we can have confidence that we still have the original words of Paul or John.* Surely this is not their intention, but in their rush to defend what is obviously a later addition to the text that entered into the KJV by unusual circumstances, they have had to adopt a position that does this very thing.

The Greek Texts of Stephanus and Beza

Three men were primarily responsible for the creation of the Greek text utilized by the KJV translators in their work on the New Testament: Desiderius Erasmus, Robert Estienne (better known as Stephanus), and Theodore Beza. One can trace the text from Erasmus, who died in 1536, through Stephanus (died 1559), through Beza (died 1605), to the KJV translators. While the text produced by each of these men is substantially the same, there *are* variations between their various editions.

In the years that followed Erasmus' death, his Greek text continued to enjoy great popularity. It was the basis of the editions published by Stephanus. The third of the four editions published by Stephanus, that of 1550, was very popular in England, and was for most the "received text" of that day. Significantly, the third edition had variant readings printed in the margins, taken from the *Complutensian* edition (which was finally released in 1522) as well as about a dozen other manuscripts, showing that, along with Erasmus, the originators of the TR were not averse to showing the textual variations within the Greek text.

Theodore Beza is the third individual greatly responsible for the final form of the *Textus Receptus*. He was the successor of the great Reformer of Geneva, John Calvin. Nine editions of the Greek New Testament were published under his name during his life, four of which were independent works, the others being smaller-size reprints. Beza drew from Stephanus' listings of variant readings, and added many more of his own, drawing from important manuscripts in his possession. He also placed the information on the variant readings immediately under the text in the same style used by modern critical editions. Often his critical notes anticipate modern scholarship. For example, while maintaining the reading of Erasmus at Luke 2:14 in his text, Beza disputes this in his comments. Modern Greek texts agree with Beza, resulting in the differences between the KJV's "good will toward men" and the NASB's "among men with whom He is pleased."

While following Stephanus' editions closely, Beza did introduce changes based upon his own textual expertise.[35] Some of these were "conjectural emendations," that is, changes made to the text without any evidence from the manuscripts. A few of these changes made it into the KJV, the most famous being Revelation 16:5, "O Lord, which art, and wast, and shalt be" rather than the actual reading, "who art and who wast, O Holy One."[36]

Two decades *after* the publication of the King James Version, the Elzevir brothers, Bonaventure and Matthew, and later their nephew Abraham, produced their second edition of the Greek New Testament. In the preface is the claim that this text is the "text . . . now received by all," which in Latin was, "*textum . . . ab omnibus receptum*," from which came the phrase, *textus receptus*, the "received text." This edition, published in 1633, mainly followed Beza but also drew from other sources. Even the standard "*Textus Receptus*" (printed by the Trinitarian Bible Society) that is used today by nearly all KJV Only advocates is not identical to Erasmus, Stephanus, or Beza, but is instead an "eclectic" text that draws from various sources.[37]

A CLOSER LOOK AT THE TEXTUS RECEPTUS

The textual differences that exist between the KJV and the modern translations of the Bible such as the NASB or NIV are due to the fact that the TR follows the "Byzantine" text-type, while modern texts draw from the Alexandrian, Western, Caesarean, and Byzantine text-types, creating an "eclectic" type text that seeks to give the original readings as they have been preserved in these various textual families. It should be noted that the TR follows one *stream* of the Byzantine text-type; that is, there are times when the Byzantine family will give variant readings, and the TR will follow one particular element of that family, an element that is not always even the majority reading of the Byzantine text-type.

Most of the time the differences between the TR and the modern texts are the same differences that exist between the Byzantine text-type and the other text-types such as the Alexandrian and the Western. But, at times, the TR goes off by itself, and we find it either giving a reading that is not supported by Greek manuscripts at all, or by only a very few over against the large majority. It is important that the reader understand that the TR is *not* identical with the "Majority Text," even though it is closely related. The TR is its own text, and it is often found in disagreement with the Majority Text as well as with the modern critical texts. The textual variations that fall into the "Byzantine text-type versus other text-types" group will make up the bulk of chapter 7. For now let's look closely at the TR and some of its more interesting readings.

We noted earlier that Erasmus had a fresh copy of his friend Reuchlin's manuscript of Revelation made to both safeguard the original and extract the actual text from the commentary that surrounded it. This led to some problems in Erasmus' text of the book of Revelation. The most famous of these textual errors are found in Revelation chapter 17. In verse 4 the scribe created a new Greek word, never before seen, *"akathartetos"* (the actual term is *"akatharta"*), which is still to be found in the pages of the Trinitarian Bible Society's *Textus Receptus*. And then there is Revelation 17:8, where the scribe mistakenly wrote *"ouk esti kaiper esti"* ("and is not, and yet is," KJV) for the actual reading, *"ouk estin kai parestai"* ("and is not and will come," NASB).

There are other important errors in Erasmus' text in Revelation. The final six verses were absent from his lone manuscript. Pressed for time, Erasmus, so as to avoid a "gaping lacuna" in the text,[38] translated the passage from the Latin *Vulgate* into Greek. We may chuckle at such a procedure today, and certainly Erasmus took criticism for doing so, but anyone familiar with the languages involved has to admire how well Erasmus did, all things considered. Of course in the process he made a number of mistakes,[39] as we would expect. The amazing thing is that these errors *continue* in the *Textus Receptus* to this very day. Why Erasmus did not change these errors at a later time, we cannot say. He unashamedly made use of better texts of Revelation in later editions of the work, but he left these errors intact. Even more mind-boggling is the fact that these errors then survived the editorial labors of Stephanus and Beza, to arrive unchanged in the hands of the KJV translators, and subsequently ended up in the King James Version.

Other places where Erasmus' work, and hence the TR, fall short would include Revelation 1:6, where the KJV has "made us kings and priests," whereas the vast majority of manuscripts have "made us to be a kingdom and priests" (NIV).[40] Another place in the first chapter that *should* be significant to KJV Only advocates is found in verse 8, where the KJV reads "saith the Lord," while nearly every Greek manuscript[41] reads as the NASB, "says the Lord God." Surely if the modern texts deleted "God" in a passage that can be identified with the Lord Jesus Christ, and is hence relevant to His deity, we would never hear the end of it. Yet here the KJV simply has an errant reading that has almost no Greek manuscript support at all. Another important accidental deletion in the text of Revelation is found at the beginning of chapter 14. Compare the KJV and NASB renderings of verse 1:

KJV	NASB
And I looked, and, lo, a Lamb stood on the mount Sion, and with him an hundred forty and four thousand, having his Father's name written in their foreheads.	And I looked, and behold, the Lamb was standing on Mount Zion, and with Him one hundred and forty-four thousand, having **His name and** the name of His Father written on their foreheads.

The name of the Lamb, identified by the phrase "His name and," is not found in the TR. According to Hoskier, a grand total of six Greek manuscripts,[42] comprising one uncial text from the ninth century, and five minuscules, all dating quite late (two of which are highly suspect[43]), do not contain this phrase. The reason for its non-inclusion is quite simple: this is a case of *homoeoteleuton*, "similar endings."

The repetition of the phrase "his name and" caused those few scribes to skip to the second occurrence, deleting the reference to the name of the Lamb.[44] We risk the charge of repetition in pointing out yet once again that if the situation were reversed, this passage would be used by KJV Only believers as evidence of anti-Christian bias on the part of "modern translations."[45]

Two more interesting problems in the TR in Revelation should be briefly noted. The first is the addition of the phrase "him that liveth for ever and ever" at Revelation 5:14. This addition is found in only three suspect Greek manuscripts,[46] but is absent from Reuchlin's manuscript. And in Revelation 15:3, "King of saints," which should be either "King of the ages" (NIV) or "King of the nations" (NASB), the TR's reading again fails to have Greek manuscript support.[47]

The TR often gives readings that place it in contrast with the united testimony of the Majority Text and the modern texts such as the United Bible Societies' 4th edition and the 27th edition of the Nestle-Aland text.[48] Often this is due to Erasmus' importing of entire passages from the Latin *Vulgate*.[49] This is how Erasmus came up with "the book of life" at Revelation 22:19 rather than the reading of the Greek manuscripts, "the tree of life." Seemingly the edition of the Latin *Vulgate* that Erasmus used to translate the last six verses of Revelation into Greek contained this reading, and it survived all the editorial work on the text over the next century to end up serving as the basis of the KJV.[50]

Acts chapters 8 and 9 are also rather expanded in the TR due to material brought over from the *Vulgate*. If one looks up Acts 8:37 ("And Philip said, If thou believest with all thine heart, thou mayest. And he answered and said, I believe that Jesus Christ is the Son of God," KJV), for example, in the NIV, one will not find such a verse (outside of the textual footnote, that is). The reason is the verse is found in only a very few Greek manuscripts, none earlier than the sixth century, and Erasmus inserted it due to its presence in the *Vulgate* and in the margin of one Greek manuscript in his possession. We again note that this passage is surely very orthodox, and, in fact, is often laden with emotional attachments as well, making it very easy to "preach" against its "deletion" by modern texts. But, of course, we must overcome our emotionalism to again ask the central question, "What did Luke write at this point?" While the insertion surely speaks the truth, so would inserting the Westminster Confession of Faith between Titus chapters 2 and 3. But no one is going to suggest doing that. We cannot "improve" upon what God has revealed.[51]

Erasmus indicated that the *Vulgate* and the parallel passage in Acts 26 caused him to insert the phrase "it is hard for thee to kick against the pricks" at Acts 9:5 as well, again placing the TR in direct conflict with the vast majority of Greek manuscripts. The *Vulgate* is also the source of a large section of Acts 9:6, "And he trembling and astonished said, Lord, what wilt thou have me to do? And the Lord said unto him . . ." as well as the reading "the word of God" at Acts 19:20 rather than the reading of the Greek texts,[52] "the word of the Lord."

The TR stands against all other texts in reading "the eyes of your understanding" over against "the eyes of your heart" at Ephesians 1:18, and it likewise is alone at Ephesians 3:9 in reading "the fellowship of the mystery" over against the witness of the Greek manuscripts that reads "the administration of the mystery."[53] So too the TR reading "Let every one that nameth the name of **Christ** depart from iniquity" at 2 Timothy 2:19 is found in all of one uncial text and one minuscule text over against all other Greek texts that read, "Let everyone who names the name of the **Lord** abstain from wickedness."

What is often not understood by KJV Only advocates is that the KJV translators did not utilize just one Greek text when working on the New Testament. Instead, they drew from a variety of sources, but mainly from Erasmus, Stephanus, and Beza.[54] When these sources diverged, the decision lay with the KJV translators themselves. Edward F. Hills, a staunch defender of the KJV, listed a number of instances where the KJV translators had to decide between competing readings in the texts available to them, adding yet another step to the process that resulted in the text of the King James Version. As this is a vital point in examining the claims of KJV Only advocates, we provide here a summary of the information given by Hills, with some additional information from modern sources.[55] This chart provides the major passages where the various editions of the *Textus Receptus* differ from one another, a brief listing of the manuscript support behind each reading, and, when necessary, the editions of Erasmus or Stephanus when one edition differed from another.

The Textus Receptus Versus the Textus Receptus

Luke 2:22	*their purification,*[56] Erasmus, Stephanus, 𝔐	*her purification,* Beza, KJV, Complutensian, 76 and a few Greek minuscules, *Vulgate*
Luke 17:36	Erasmus, Stephanus 1, 2, 3, and 𝔐 omit this verse.	*Two men shall be in the field; the one shall be taken, and the other left.* Stephanus 4, Beza, KJV along with D and the *Vulgate*
John 1:28	*Bethabara beyond Jordan,* Erasmus, Stephanus 3, 4, Beza, KJV	*Bethany beyond Jordan,* Stephanus 1, 2, 𝔐, 𝔓[66], 𝔓[75], ℵ, B, *Vulgate*
John 16:33	*shall have tribulation,* Beza, KJV, D, *f*[1.13] *Vulgate*	*have tribulation,* Erasmus, Stephanus, 𝔐, 𝔓[66]
Romans 8:11	*by his Spirit,* Beza, KJV, ℵ, A, C	*because of his Spirit,* Erasmus, Stephanus, 𝔐, B, D, *Vulgate*
Romans 12:11	*serving the Lord,* Erasmus 1, Beza, KJV, 𝔐, 𝔓[46], ℵ, A, B, *Vulgate*	*serving the time,* Erasmus 2, 3, 4, 5, Stephanus, D, G.
1 Tim. 1:4	*godly edifying,* Erasmus, Beza, KJV, D, *Vulgate*	*dispensation of God,* Stephanus, 𝔐, ℵ, A G.
Heb 9:1	*first tabernacle,* Stephanus, 𝔐; KJV omits "*tabernacle*" and regards *covenant* as implied.	Omit "*tabernacle*" Erasmus, Beza, Luther, Calvin, 𝔓[46], ℵ, B, D, *Vulgate*.
James 2:18	*without thy works,* Calvin, Beza (last 3 editions), KJV, ℵ, A, B, Vulgate	*by thy works,* Erasmus, Stephanus, Beza 1565, 𝔐

As can be seen from this chart, the Greek readings of the KJV New Testament, word for word, did not exist prior to 1611; that is, it is a peculiar *"Textus Receptus"* that differs from any edition that preceded it. While flowing mainly from Erasmus via Stephanus and Beza, as a complete unit it did not come into existence until the first copies of the KJV were printed in 1611. Hence, when we speak historically of the *Textus Receptus,* we are speaking of a *text-type* that is found in various editions with minor differences between each edition. Most often when the term is used by KJV Only advocates, it refers to the KJV version of the TR, that is, the Greek text that flows from the textual choices made by the translators themselves, not to any one particular edition of Erasmus, Stephanus, or Beza.

When taken as a whole, the TR, absent the above abnormalities, is a fine representative of the Byzantine text-type. And, as we have already asserted in the strongest possible terms, the teaching of the TR is the same as the teaching of the Majority Text *and* any of the modern texts, such as the UBS 4th or the Nestle-Aland 27th. We have taken the time to note these items simply because of the *misuse* of the TR by KJV Only advocates. Erasmus did not think that his text was inerrant; Stephanus placed variant readings in the margins; Beza made conjectural emendations; the KJV translators chose between the differing readings of the different editions made by these men. None, obviously, would agree with the claims made by KJV Only believers about their work.

THE TEXT OF THE REFORMATION?

Often it is claimed that the *Textus Receptus* is the "text of the Reformation" or the "text of the Reformers." The desired effect of this claim is to add to the weight of the TR the witness of such great men of God as Martin Luther and John Calvin. Yet, is this claim tenable? Everyone admits that the Greek text utilized by Luther in his preaching, and Calvin in his writing and teaching, was what would become known as the TR. But we must point out that they used this text by *default*, not by *choice*. In other words, it was not a matter of their *rejecting* other "text-types" such as the manuscripts of the Alexandrian family, so much as it was a matter of using what was available. One cannot assert with any level of confidence that Calvin, were he alive today, would hold to the TR as the "inspired text." In fact, there is good reason to think otherwise.

Edward F. Hills, a Presbyterian scholar, even in defending the KJV, had to admit that Calvin made comments that demonstrated a willingness on his part to engage in the same kind of textual-critical thought that Hills identifies as "humanistic." Hills notes that in five places Calvin noted variant readings suggested by Erasmus, and that in three of those five times, Calvin agreed with the non-TR reading.[57] He cites as an example John 8:59, where Calvin agrees with Erasmus' contention that the phrase "*going through the midst of them, and so passed by"* was borrowed from Luke 4:30 (modern texts and translations agree). He also notes that Calvin went beyond Erasmus, adding eighteen other places where Calvin rejected the TR readings in favor of others.[58] Calvin also made two conjectural emendations: (1) at James 4:2 in reading "envy" instead of "kill," and (2) the deletion of 1 John 2:14 because it seemed to him a repetitious interpolation.

This review of Calvin's position makes it plain that the assertion that the TR was the "text of the Reformers" is more than slightly misleading, especially if it is meant to indicate that the Reformers were particularly choosing the TR *over against non-Byzantine texts* such as those used in modern textual criticism. The simple fact of the matter is that the research and study into those texts had not yet sufficiently advanced to allow the Reformers to have any particularly weighty opinion in matters that were not, at that time, under discussion.

The Translation of the KJV

There is no need to go into depth on the actual translation process of the KJV itself, since many fine works provide the basic outlines of how the translational work was undertaken.[59] No one doubts the tremendous ability of the men involved, nor the care that was given to the work of translation. We shall briefly note only a few general items.

First, the work was done in a way similar to many modern translations, that is, by the work of committee. Six groups, meeting at Westminster, Oxford, and Cambridge, worked on the Old and New Testament translations. The advantage of having groups of scholars rather than a single man is self-evident: a single translator is much more likely to allow his own theological viewpoint to enter the translation, and he is less able to check his own work for accuracy. A committee approach provides a means of balancing out individual theological perspectives, and the double-checking of the work that is inherent in a committee approach helps to weed out errors as well. Of course one drawback to the committee method can be seen in the final product produced in 1611—the final editors do not always catch different and inconsistent translations of the same Greek or Hebrew words, which can lead to confusion.[60]

Secondly, the KJV translators were not infallible human beings. Some, in fact, may have harbored less than perfect motivations for their work. Some hoped to gain favor with the king and advancement in their positions through their work on the translation itself. Some were far too enamored with the idea of royalty, a problem not too uncommon in that day.[61] But by and large the group encompassed some of the finest scholars the world has ever seen. One of the greatest, John Rainolds, a Puritan, was the one who suggested the new translation to King James at the famous Hampton Court encounter of January 16, 1604.[62]

Thirdly, the translators were Anglicans, members of the Church of England. It is very common for KJV Only advocates to attack such men as Westcott and Hort for being "baby sprinklers," yet the KJV was born in the heart of such a system of theology. The inconsistency of attacking modern translations due to the alleged theological irregularities of those associated with them while overlooking the very same problems with the KJV is striking.

Fourthly, the translators were given certain guidelines under which they were to work. Some of these fifteen rules that are of most interest include,

> The ordinary Bible read in church, commonly called the Bishops' Bible, to be followed and as little altered as the truth of the original[63] will permit.

> The old ecclesiastical words to be kept, viz. The word "church" not to be translated "congregation."

> When a word hath divers significations, that to be kept which hath been most commonly used by most of the ancient fathers.

> No marginal notes at all to be affixed, but only for the explanation of the Hebrew or Greek words, which cannot without some circumlocution be so briefly and fitly expressed in the text.

> When any place of special obscurity be doubted of, letters to be directed by authority to send to any learned man in the land for his judgment of such a place.

> These translations to be used when they agree better with the text than the Bishops' Bible—Tyndale's, Matthew's, Coverdale's, Whitchurch's, Geneva.[64]

These guidelines are very informative. They reveal that (1) the KJV relied heavily upon previous translations (prompting us to ask the KJV advocate, "When the KJV gives a reading that is identical to the Bishop's Bible, was the Bishop's Bible inspired and inerrant in that place, even before 1611?"); (2) Anglican ecclesiology had an impact upon the KJV's translation, a charge that has been made ever since the translation appeared; (3) translations were to follow the use of the early Fathers of the Christian faith, again a practice that would be inconsistent with the viewpoint of most fundamentalist KJV Only advocates; (4) marginal notes were to be used to help explain Greek and Hebrew terms; (5) it was recognized that there were places of "special obscurity" and that the translators were to make appeal to specialists in those fields who could be of assistance in understanding the text.

Finally we need to note, quite unfortunately, the fact that a number of the original translators died during the translation process itself. Why do we mention this? It is a sad fact that some KJV Only advocates, consumed by theories of conspiracy, have noted that some modern textual critics or translators have been "struck dumb" or have even died, this allegedly providing evidence of the divine wrath against them for tampering with the KJV. The fact that a number of translators died between 1604 and 1611 means nothing more than people died very regularly in seventeenth-century England, including godly scholars. But the KJV Only argument, if it were consistent, would lead us to believe that God was in some way showing His displeasure at the translation of the KJV. Such is, obviously, not the case at all.

LET THE TRANSLATORS SPEAK

One of the most eloquent arguments against KJV Onlyism is provided, ironically enough, by the translators themselves. Below are segments from the preface to the 1611 KJV, entitled *The Translators to the Reader*.[65] I provide only a small amount of commentary by way of introduction and explanation.

On the matter of the need for translations into other languages, we read,

> Translation it is that openeth the window, to let in the light; that

breaketh the shell, that we may eat the kernel; that putteth aside the curtain, that we may look into the most Holy place; that removeth the cover of the well, that we may come by the water, even as Jacob rolled away the stone from the mouth of the well, by which means the flocks of Laban were watered [Gen 29:10]. Indeed without translation into the vulgar tongue, the unlearned are but like children at Jacob's well (which is deep) [John 4:11] without a bucket or something to draw with; or as that person mentioned by Isaiah, to whom when a sealed book was delivered, with this motion, "Read this, I pray thee," he was fain to make this answer, "I cannot, for it is sealed." [Isa 29:11]

Now what can be more available thereto, than to deliver God's book unto God's people in a tongue which they understand?

The KJV translators faced the same arguments that are hurled against the godly men who worked on the NASB or NIV: "Wasn't the KJV good enough for you? Hasn't God blessed it? Why prepare a new translation?" Note their reply:

Many men's mouths have been open a good while (and yet are not stopped) with speeches about the Translation so long in hand, or rather perusals of Translations made before: and ask what may be the reason, what the necessity of the employment: Hath the Church been deceived, say they, all this while? Hath her sweet bread been mingled with leaven, her silver with dross, her wine with water, her milk with lime?

That is, "Do we condemn the ancient? In no case: but after the endeavors of them that were before us, we take the best pains we can in the house of God." As if he said, Being provoked by the example of the learned men that lived before my time, I have thought it my duty, to assay whether my talent in the knowledge of the tongues, may be profitable in any measure to God's Church, lest I should seem to laboured in them in vain, and lest I should be thought to glory in men, (although ancient,) above that which was in them. Thus S. Jerome may be thought to speak.

Regarding their reliance upon and use of the many English translations that preceded their work, the translators said,

> Yet for all that, as nothing is begun and perfected at the same
> time, and the later thoughts are thought to be the wiser: so, if
> we building upon their foundation that went before us, and
> being holpen by their labours, do endeavor to make that better
> which they left so good; no man, we are sure, hath cause to
> mislike us; they, we persuade ourselves, if they were alive,
> would thank us.

> Truly (good Christian Reader) we never thought from the
> beginning, that we should need to make a new Translation, nor
> yet to make of a bad one a good one . . . but to make a good
> one better, or out of many good ones, one principal good one,
> not justly to be excepted against; that hath been our endeavor,
> that our mark.

Some KJV Only advocates actually go so far as to deny the existence
of the Septuagint, the Greek translation of the Hebrew Old Testament,
prior to the time of Christ.[66] The KJV translators didn't see it that way:

> This is the translation of the Seventy Interpreters, commonly so
> called, which prepared the way for our Saviour among the
> Gentiles by written preaching, as Saint John Baptist did among
> the Jews by vocal. . . .The translation of the Seventy dissenteth
> from the Original in many places, neither doth it come near it,
> for perspicuity, gravity, majesty; yet which of the Apostles did
> condemn it? Condemn it? Nay, they used it, (as it is apparent,
> and as Saint Jerome and most learned men do confess) which
> they would not have done, nor by their example of using it, so
> grace and commend it to the Church, if it had been unworthy
> of the appellation and name of the word of God.

Likewise the KJV translators had a very different view of the use of
the Greek and Hebrew texts of the Bible:

> If you ask what they had before them, truly it was the Hebrew
> text of the Old Testament, the Greek of the New. These are the
> two golden pipes, or rather conduits, where-through the olive
> branches empty themselves into the gold. Saint Augustine

calleth them precedent, or original tongues; [S. August. 3. de doctr. c. 3. etc.] Saint Jerome, fountains. [S. Jerome. ad Suniam · et Fretel.] The same Saint Jerome affirmeth, [S. Jerome. ad Lucinium, Dist. 9 ut veterum.] and Gratian hath not spared to put it into his Decree, That "as the credit of the old Books" (he meaneth of the Old Testament) "is to be tried by the Hebrew Volumes, so of the New by the Greek tongue," he meaneth by the original Greek. If truth be tried by these tongues, then whence should a Translation be made, but out of them? These tongues therefore, the Scriptures we say in those tongues, we set before us to translate, being the tongues wherein God was pleased to speak to his Church by the Prophets and Apostles.

Their view that the Word of God is translatable from language to language is plainly spelled out:

Now to the latter we answer; that we do not deny, nay we affirm and avow, that the very meanest translation of the Bible in English, set forth by men of our profession, (for we have seen none of theirs of the whole Bible as yet) containeth the word of God, nay, is the word of God. As the King's speech, which he uttereth in Parliament, being translated into French, Dutch, Italian, and Latin, is still the King's speech, though it be not interpreted by every Translator with the like grace, nor peradventure so fitly for phrase, nor so expressly for sense, everywhere.

Did the KJV translators use the same sources and methods as modern translators, looking into the translations in other languages, consulting commentaries and the like? Most certainly.

Neither did we think much to consult the Translators or Commentators, Chaldee, Hebrew, Syrian, Greek or Latin, no nor the Spanish, French, Italian, or Dutch; neither did we disdain to revise that which we had done, and to bring back to the anvil that which we had hammered: but having and using as great helps as were needful, and fearing no reproach for slowness, nor coveting praise for expedition, we have at length, through the good hand of the Lord upon us, brought the work to that pass that you see.

One of the issues that arises in the Preface that is very relevant to the KJV Only controversy is the inclusion of alternative translations or marginal readings in the KJV. The translators defended their inclusion of these items, and in so doing demonstrated that those who would make their translation an inerrant and inspired work do so against their own statements:

> Some peradventure would have no variety of senses to be set in the margin, lest the authority of the Scriptures for deciding of controversies by that show of uncertainty, should somewhat be shaken. But we hold their judgment not to be sound in this point.

Note the emphasized portion of the following quotation closely:

> There be many words in the Scriptures, which be never found there but once, (having neither brother or neighbor, as the Hebrews speak) so that we cannot be holpen by conference of places. Again, there be many rare names of certain birds, beasts and precious stones, etc. concerning the Hebrews themselves are so divided among themselves for judgment, that they may seem to have defined this or that, rather because they would say something, than because they were sure of that which they said, as S. Jerome somewhere saith of the Septuagint. Now in such a case, doth not a margin do well to admonish the Reader to seek further, and not to conclude or dogmatize upon this or that peremptorily? *For as it is a fault of incredulity, to doubt of those things that are evident: so to determine of such things as the Spirit of God hath left (even in the judgment of the judicious) questionable, can be no less than presumption. Therefore as S. Augustine saith, that variety of Translations is profitable for the finding out of the sense of the Scriptures:* [S. Aug. 2. De doctr. Christian. cap. 14.] so diversity of signification and sense in the margin, where the text is not so clear, must needs do good, yea, is necessary, as we are persuaded (italics added).

When the very preface to the KJV says "variety of Translations is profitable for the finding out of the sense of the Scriptures," it is obvious that the KJV Only position is proven utterly ahistorical thereby. The position requires the translation to be something its own authors never intended it to be.

THE FORM OF THE 1611 KJV

The King James Version was printed by Robert Barker, the royal printer. Barker and his heirs maintained the right to print the KJV for a hundred years. The 1611 edition was handsomely printed in a typeface both beautiful and yet difficult to read for modern readers.[67] It was laid out in such a way as to provide for notes in the outer margins on both sides of the two columns of text. Even though the guidelines had called for a limited number of notes, F.H.A. Scrivener indicated that the original 1611 edition contained 6,637 such notes in the Old Testament (4,111 expressing the more literal rendering of the Hebrew or Chaldee, 2,156 giving alternative readings "which in the opinion of the Translators are not very less probable than those in the text"[68]) and 767 in the New Testament[69] (37 of which relate to variant readings, 112 providing a more literal translation of the Greek, 582 giving alternative translations, and 35 giving explanatory notes or brief expositions), making a total of 8,422 such marginal notes.

The importance of the marginal notes to the KJV Only controversy should not be overlooked. We have already seen the defense of these notes on the part of the KJV translators. A brief glance at just a couple of them will indicate how important they are to the arguments put forward by KJV Only advocates today.

At Luke 17:36 a marginal note is attached that reads, "This 36. verse is wanting in most of the Greek copies." Modern Greek texts remove the verse and place it in footnotes, the NASB puts it in brackets, and the NIV removes it completely, relegating it to a textual footnote. At Acts 25:6 the marginal note reads, "Or, as some copies read, no more than eight or ten days." KJV Only works are filled with attacks upon the modern translations for noting that certain verses are not found in ancient manuscripts, or that some manuscripts read differently, yet you will search in vain for the same kind of denunciation of the KJV's textual notes.

Of course, the process of printing such a large and cumbersome work created printer's errors as well. Even today we find such things in our computer type-set Bibles, so it is easy to understand how mistakes could creep into the text of the Bible, printed as it was in a much more laborious and difficult manner.

Some of the printer's errors that have found their way into the KJV are more than slightly amusing. One of the first errors entered the text as early as 1611, where, at Matthew 26:36, some AV Bibles had "Then cometh Judas," when it should read "Then cometh Jesus." Other intriguing errors included the deletion of the word "not" from the Seventh Commandment (earning that printing the title "The Wicked Bible"), the deletion of "no" from "no more sea" at Revelation 21:1, the unrighteous inheriting the kingdom at 1 Corinthians 6:9, "printers have persecuted" rather than "princes have persecuted" at Psalm 119:161, the use of "sin on more" rather than "sin no more" at John 5:14, the "parable of the Vinegar" rather than "Vineyard" at Luke 20, Philip denying Jesus rather than Peter at Luke 22:34, the use of "lions" instead of "loins" at 1 Kings 8:19, the use of "the fishes shall stand" rather than "fishers" at Ezekiel 47:10, the switching of "wife" for "life" at Luke 14:26, and the switching of "camels" for "damsels" with reference to Rebekah at Genesis 24:61.

The Revisions of the KJV

The KJV that is carried by the average KJV Only advocate today looks very different than the edition that came off the press of Robert Barker in 1611. Not only do many printings of the KJV today lack the marginal notes and references, but the form of the text, *and the wording of the text*, has undergone change over time. Editions with changes in the text came out as soon as 1612, another in 1613, followed by editions in 1616, 1629, and 1638. By 1659 William Kilburne, in a tract titled *Dangerous Errors in Several Late Printed Bibles to the Great Scandal and Corruption of Sound and True Religion* could claim that 20,000 errors had crept into six different editions printed in the 1650s.[70]

Most modern KJVs follow the revision made by Benjamin Blayney in 1769. Jack Lewis notes that Blayney "did extensive revision, added 76 notes—including many on weights, measures, and coins—and added 30,495 new marginal references."[71]

Does the modern edition of the KJV differ *significantly* from the 1611? That depends upon how one defines the term "significantly." For the general audience who are seeking merely to understand the textual tradition of the KJV, no, most of the revisions have dealt with small matters of spelling, punctuation, etc. But for those who assert the absolute inerrancy of the KJV the question looms large: which KJV? Note some of the changes that have taken place over the years as indicated by F.H.A Scrivener: the change of "the LORD" to "the LORD thy God" at Deuteronomy 26:1; "Manasseh" to "the children of Manasseh" at Joshua 13:29; "seek good" to "seek God" at Psalm 69:32; "inherit God" to "inherit Gad" at Jeremiah 49:1; "Thou art Christ" to "Thou art the Christ" at Matthew 16:16; "there is no man good, but one" to "*there is* none good but one" at Mark 10:18; "approved unto death" to "appointed unto death" at 1 Corinthians 4:9; and "hath not the Son" to "hath not the Son of God" at 1 John 5:12.[72]

Are these changes significant? Surely they present a sticky problem for the radical proponent of KJV Onlyism. How are textual changes like this to be handled? How can one determine the "right" reading, when the KJV is made the absolute standard? Of course, the non-KJV Only believer has recourse to Greek and Hebrew manuscripts. But once a person has invested the English translation with inspiration itself, that route is no longer a consistent option.

DIFFERENCES IN MODERN EDITIONS OF THE KJV

It may surprise some readers to discover that there are differences between various printed editions of the KJV, even today in our age of computer-typesetting and proofing. Yet this is most definitely the case. For most people the changes are both minor and essentially trivial, for no one would seriously consider the idea that a printer's error, or even a difference in the final printed editions that ends up being copied by other publishing companies, is truly relevant to the Word of God. But for the zealous defender of the word-for-word inspiration and inerrancy of the KJV, differing readings can cause quite a problem indeed!

Lewis notes that the American Bible Society examined six editions of the KJV in the nineteenth century and discovered 24,000 variants in the text and punctuation as a result of this survey.[73] Even today differences remain, sometimes in editions printed by the very same publisher. For example, at Matthew 4:2 some modern KJV's have "he was afterward an hungred," while others have "he was afterward an hungered," and another has "he was afterward ahungered."

Note the comparison of the 1611 KJV with the 1769 Cambridge edition at the final clause of Ruth 3:15:

1611 Edition	1769 Cambridge Edition
and he went into the citie.	and she went into the city.

We note that there is a dispute about how this passage should read that continues to this day, for the NASB has "she" while the NIV has "he." The KJV, however, has had *both* readings at some point in time in its history. Why do we present this point? Because differences in currently printed versions of the KJV cannot be determined by mere reference to the 1611 edition, for changes have been made since the time of the original publication, as we have seen. This particular fact becomes quite important in trying to figure out the proper rendering of Jeremiah 34:16:

Cambridge Edition	Oxford Edition
But ye turned and polluted my name, and caused every man his servant, and every man his handmaid, whom **ye** had set at liberty at their pleasure, to return, and brought them into subjection, to be unto you for servants and for handmaids.	But ye turned and polluted my name, and caused every man his servant, and every man his handmaid, whom **he** had set at liberty at their pleasure, to return, and brought them into subjection, to be unto you for servants and for handmaids.

I have emphasized the differing term. You will find modern KJVs pretty well split as to whether they read "he" or "ye" at this passage. I spoke to a friend at Thomas Nelson Publishers who found one of their currently available KJVs had "he" while another had "ye." My own computer can't figure it out, either; one Bible program has "ye" and the other has "he."

As anyone can see, both readings make sense. "Ye" would refer to all the people who are being charged with wrongdoing in this passage; "he" would simply refer back to "every man his handmaid." The point is not to say that we don't know, or that this is a vital verse upon which a great doctrinal truth hangs. The question for the KJV Only advocate is, "How do you determine which one is right?" As we noted, you can't go back to the 1611 and use that, since we have seen that the 1611 has undergone changes of a similar nature over the years. So how can we determine the correct reading? The person who does not make the KJV the absolute authority in all things has an easy answer: look at the Hebrew text and find out. But the KJV Only believer cannot do this without betraying his position. If we have to refer to the original languages here, then we would need to do the same thing in other places where the KJV is shown to be wanting, such as Acts 5:30 or Titus 2:13. Plainly, if we make the KJV the starting point (and this is exactly what radical KJV Onlyism does), there is simply no way of determining the correct text of Jeremiah 34:16.

Thankfully we are not limited to the KJV as our only source of information. The Hebrew is plural here. There are no variants in the text—even the Septuagint gives the plural. The correct translation is the plural "you," i.e., "ye," which is, in fact, the reading found in the AV 1611. The NASB, NIV, NRSV, etc., all have "you." But there is one more important thing that can be learned from Jeremiah 34:16 and the ye/he question.

While discussing this passage with my friend at Thomas Nelson he exclaimed, "Say, the New King James Version says 'he' too!" I was quite surprised to discover that this was the case. Was there some reason for the use of "he" at this passage that I was missing? I checked many more sources and made some phone calls. I could find no reason for "he" at all on the basis of the text itself, but I did find a couple of other works that used "he" in the text. Finally I contacted the former executive editor of the NKJV Old Testament, Dr. James Price. He was very gracious and took the time to examine the Hebrew text with me, making sure there were no differences between the modern Hebrew text I was using and the version used by the NKJV translators.[74] He confirmed that the passage is in the plural, not the singular. He took the time to look into the situation and discovered that while the original translation committee had translated the passage using "you," a later English stylist, probably relying upon the Oxford edition of the KJV, had changed it back to "he," thinking "he" fit better in context than "you." This change somehow got past the final editing process and into print.[75]

We learn from this example that even in the age of computers and printing presses the translation of the Bible is still subject to simple human error and mistake. Here one error made long ago, the change of "ye" to "he," has not only been promulgated through many other editions of the KJV, but has even made its way into another translation, the NKJV! Without reference to the original languages, we might well wonder about the intended reading. But, of course, such/is not a problem to those who are willing to realize that we are dealing here with *translations* of the Scriptures into English, and God has never once promised that *translations* will be infallible or inerrant.

A Grand Work

Hopefully we can better analyze the claims of the KJV Only movement in light of the facts of how the KJV came into existence. The King James Version is a monument to those who labored to bring it into existence. Of this there can be no question. But as we have seen, it was a *human* process, and as in all of human life and endeavor, it did not partake of infallibility.

Endnotes

[1] See chapter 2, pp. 13-17.

[2] George Faludy, *Erasmus* (Stein & Day: 1970), p. 180.

[3] See Erasmus' *Annotations* note 2 on Revelation chapter 3. Cited from Erika Rummel, *Erasmus' Annotations on the New Testament* (University of Toronto: 1986), p. 38. In reality, Reuchlin's manuscript was only about four hundred years old at the time, dating to the twelfth century.

[4] Some have identified Gerber as the copyist; others have suggested it was poet laureate Henricus Glareanus who was in Basel at that time. See Rummel, note 16, p. 193.

[5] LB IX 85E, Rummel, p. 127.

[6] Ibid.

[7] Note 5 on Mark chapter 16.

[8] Note 5 on John chapter 18.

[9] Ep. 304:109-111, Rummel, p. 123.

[10] Ibid., lines 139-42, Rummel, p. 123.

[11] Samuel Gipp, *The Answer Book* (Bible & Literature Missionary Foundation: 1989), p. 148.

[12] Ibid., p. 156.

[13] Roland Bainton, *Erasmus of Christendom* (Charles Scribner's Sons:

1969), p. 134.

[14] D.A. Waite, *Defending the King James Bible* (The Bible for Today: 1992), p. 125. Dr. Waite seems to be ignoring the fact that the KJV translators also put variant readings in the margins of their translation. William Grady in his book *Final Authority* (Grady Publications: 1993) is just as vociferous in his attack on the NKJV for daring to give the reader the information concerning the readings found in the 𝔐 text and the modern eclectic texts. He writes,

> Now, although the Nelson Company pitched their Bible on the strength of the Received Text, they were soon caught talking out of both sides of their mouths. When a study is made of the footnote section in the NKJV, one discovers a classic example of compromise. Understanding the self-centered nature of today's carnal believers, Nelson Publishers decided to let their customers have a literal choice between *three different Greek readings!* With the main English Scripture **supposedly** translated from the traditional *Textus Receptus*, 774 instances appear where two alternative Greek texts are presented for consideration. These are the old Westcott and Hort readings, perpetuated by the Nestle's/United Bible Societies text, designated as "NU" and the Hodges-Farstad-Nelson Majority Greek text, denoted by "M" in the footnotes.

We note that Mr. Grady is in error to say that the Hodges-Farstad Majority Text and the Nestle-Aland/UBS Greek texts simply perpetuate the Westcott-Hort readings. But we note his continued comments:

> Can you imagine the confusion being wrought among laypeople as they suddenly discover their new responsibilities to become *textual critics?*

Mr. Grady is a Baptist. Yet when it comes to a person's responsibility before God with reference to the issue of the text and translation of the Bible, he becomes very *un*-Baptistic, seeking to have believers give over their responsibilities to someone else, specifically in this case, Erasmus, Stephanus, Beza, and the Anglican KJV translators. See our discussion of this denial of our personal responsibility in this matter in chapter 5.

[15] Ep. 304:150-1, Rummel, p. 123.

[16] *Capita contra morosos* 69, Rummel, p. 131.

[17] LB IX 88C-D, Rummel, p. 131.

[18] This is the position taken by Edward F. Hills in his work, *The King James Version Defended,* 4th ed. (The Christian Research Press, 1984), pp. 222-223:

> The texts of the several editions of the Textus Receptus were God-guided. They were set up under the leading of God's special providence. Hence the differences between them were kept down to a minimum. But these disagreements were not eliminated altogether, for this would require not merely providential guidance but a miracle. In short, God chose to preserve the New Testament text providentially rather than miraculously, and this is why even the

several editions of the Textus Receptus vary from each other slightly.

[19] Note 66 on Romans chapter 1. Erasmus is referring specifically to the textual variants surrounding the term πλεονεξία.

[20] Note 49, "It almost always happens in this kind of catalog of single nouns that somewhere the codices will have variants, due to lapses of memory by the scribes."

[21] Note 15 on Romans chapter 10, Rummel, pp. 115-116.

[22] Note 21 on Romans chapter 21, Rummel, pp. 116-117.

[23] Compare κυριος with καιρος.

[24] Note 15 on Matthew chapter 1.

[25] LB IX 128B, Rummel, p. 113.

[26] Rummel notes other examples of Erasmus' recognition of harmonization, such as note 12 on Matthew 13, "We often find one place changed on account of another when the reader thinks that what he has read elsewhere is better or suspects that the passage at hand has been corrupted because it is different." Rummel, p. 113. I provide here another example of Erasmus' textual discussion, this from his sixteenth note on Romans chapter 5 (Rummel, p. 118, Greek inserted from original text):

> Οὐκ ἐλλογεῖται, that is, *imputatur* in the present tense, to give the phrase a more general meaning; for the [preceding] phrase μὴ ὄντος νόμου, 'there being no law,' fits either tense; as if one spoke generally: there being no law, no sin is imputed; ie, where there is no law there is no sin to be imputed. Origen read thus at any rate. And I found it written in this way in the Pauline manuscript, the oldest and most correct text. . . . . A certain scholar in a published book opines that the Greek reading was corrupt and that we ought to write ἐλλογεῖτο rather than ἐλλογεῖται — as if it were not impudent to dispute the reading in view of the great consensus among Greek manuscripts and as if the imperfect tense (if that was wanted) was not ἐνελογεῖτο rather than ἐλλογεῖτο. And this man claims to be a great scholar and never ceases to say haughtily that I know absolutely nothing. *Cum lex non est* (when there is no law) was written in the Donation manuscript; hence one may conjecture that *imputabatur* [the imperfect] is a corruption and should read *imputatur* [present tense]. ἐλογεῖτο would be acceptable if the verb was λογέω rather than λογίζομαι. The commentary of Chrysostom had ἐλογεῖτο. Theophylact's ἐλλογεῖτο, but both are errors, if I am not mistaken.

[27] Arianism takes its name from Arius, a fourth-century presbyter in Alexandria who taught that Jesus was a created being. Erasmus was attacked on almost all fronts due to notes such as this in his work. Indeed, he had to write apologies defending his belief in the proper words of "consecration" to be used at Mass, wherein he demonstrated his Roman Catholic system of belief in saying, "One can only accept the decrees of the church, for it will be difficult to prove by human reasoning which words the priest ought to use in consecration . . ." (Rummel, p. 158) and another defending his belief in

Transubstantiation as well (*Detectio praestigiarum*) in which he refuted allegations of Protestant thought by stating that in his notes, "There was not even a syllable to indicate that the Eucharist was not the true body of the Lord" (LB X 1564C, Rummel, p. 159).

[28] 277B, Rummel, p. 133.

[29] Rummel, p. 133. Controversy exists over the specifics of Erasmus' challenge and the insertion of the *Comma*. Metzger cites H.J. de Jonge's work in the 3rd edition of his *The Text of the New Testament* (p. 291), as saying that there is "no explicit evidence that supports this frequently made assertion," yet Rummel cites the same passage from de Jonge but maintains that Erasmus did issue the challenge and inserted the *Comma* as a result.

[30] Rummel, p. 40. Metzger notes that this manuscript opens of its own accord to the passage in 1 John, so often has it been consulted at that place. Bruce Metzger, *The Text of the New Testament*, 2nd ed. (Oxford: 1968), p. 101.

[31] See Rummel, note 30, p. 194, and Metzger, p. 101.

[32] LB VI 1080D, Rummel, pp. 133-134.

[33] Ibid., p. 134.

[34] Most of those who defend the passage do so by merely repeating the maxim that the KJV is the Word of God, and hence the passage should be there (i.e., they use completely circular reasoning). Others, like Edward F. Hills, refer to the *Comma* and say it is a reading "which, on believing principles, must be regarded as possibly genuine" (Hills, *The King James Version Defended*, p. 209). Hills is rather reserved in his defense of the passage, though he does conclude,

> In other words, it is not impossible that the *Johannine comma* was one of those few readings of the Latin *Vulgate* not occurring in the Traditional Greek Text but incorporated into the Textus Receptus under the guiding providence of God. In these rare instances God called upon the usage of the Latin-speaking Church to correct the usage of the Greek-speaking Church (p. 213).

Hills is one of the few who seem to have thought through the matter to its conclusion, though he is not quick to bring out the fact that this means the Greek manuscript tradition can be *so corrupted* as to lose, without a trace, an entire reading. One of the more interesting attempts at defending the inclusion of the *Comma* is provided by Kevin James, *The Corruption of the Word: The Failure of Modern New Testament Scholarship* (1990), pp. 230-238. James uses many of the standard arguments, responding to (though not directly noting this) the presentation of Bruce Metzger in his work, *A Textual Commentary on the Greek New Testament* (United Bible Societies: 1975), pp. 715-717. He includes the "grammatical" argument that posits a problem in the masculine form of "three" and the genders of Spirit, blood and water. This is not a very major problem, as "three" almost always appears in the NT as a masculine when used as a substantive, the one exception being 1 Corinthians

13:13 where it appears as a neuter, though here referring to a list of feminines. This is more stylistic than anything else. James blasts modern scholars, identifying their reasoning as "incomprehensible" (p. 231), asserting that modern texts adopt readings with just as slim external support as that found at 1 John 5:7-8. He cites two passages, James 4:14 and 2 Corinthians 5:3, as evidence of this. Yet, neither passage is even remotely similar to the *Comma*. The variant he cites at James 4:14 involves at least six different (though very similar) readings, which, of course, results in the support for each reading being rather small. The UBS 4th gives a "C" rating to the chosen text, indicating the committee's recognition of the difficulty of the passage. The other passage, 2 Corinthians 5:3, is also extremely dissimilar to the *Comma*, as it involves only the difference between the words ἐκδυσάμενοι and ἐνδυσάμενοι. What is more, since James obviously had Metzger's textual commentary at hand, he should have noted Metzger's own words, appended to the entry on the passage, "In view of its superior external support the reading ἐνδυσάμενοι should be adopted, the reading ἐκδυσάμενοι being an early alteration to avoid apparent tautology" (p. 580).

[35] Eduardus Reuss, *Bibliotheca Novi Testamenti Graeci* (1872) lists 38 differences between Stephanus' 4th edition and Beza's final work (pp. 143-144).

[36] Beza replaced the reading in the manuscripts, ὅσιος, with the future verbal form, ἐσόμενος. We pause only long enough to note that the KJV Only advocate who asserts the verbal plenary inspiration of the King James Version has to believe that Theodore Beza, the successor of John Calvin, as strong a proponent of "Calvinism" as has ever lived (certain KJV Only advocates such as Peter Ruckman are strongly anti-Reformed), was divinely inspired to make this change without any manuscript support at all.

[37] It is ironic to note that this text, often referred to as being "inspired," did not exist in 1611; that is, the *Textus Receptus* in its modern form was not used by the KJV translators. Instead, the modern TR is a "made up" text that follows the English KJV in determining which renderings to include. Note the discussion of the variants found between Erasmus, Stephanus, and Beza and the KJV translators' choices between them.

[38] *ne hiaret lacuna*. See Rummel, note 15, p. 193. A "lacuna" is a hole, a gap in the text.

[39] Included are: Verse 16: ὀρθρινός in place of πρωϊνός; the insertion of the definite article τοῦ. Verse 17: the replacement of Ἔρχου with Ἐλθέ twice; the replacement of ἐρχέσθω with ἐλθέτω and λαβέτω with λαμβανέτω; the insertion of the definite article τό. Verse 18: Replacement of Μαρτυρῶ with Συμμαρτυροῦμαι; replacement of ἐπιθῇ ἐπ αὐτά with ἐπιτιθῇ πρὸς ταῦτα; deletion of the definite article τῷ. Verse 19: Replacement of ἀφέλῃ with ἀφαιρῇ and ἀφελεῖ with ἀφαιρήσει; the replacement of ξύλου with βίβλου; the insertion of καὶ and the deletion of τῷ. Verse 21: The insertion of the pronoun ἡμῶν. Interestingly, H.C. Hoskier theorized that Erasmus did not, in fact,

translate from the Latin into Greek, despite Erasmus' statements to that effect. See his work, *Concerning the Text of the Apocalypse* (London: 1929), I:477.

[40] Hoskier lists eight minuscules that have this reading, including Hoskier 1, the Reuchlin manuscript from which Erasmus was working.

[41] Only two minuscules do not have "God" at this point, Hoskier 141 and 187. As we will note, Hoskier 141 is almost certainly a copy of Erasmus' printed text, and is hence nearly worthless as a textual source (the same is true of Hoskier 57). Hoskier 187 is a fifteenth- or sixteenth-century minuscule that was poorly written. Even Hoskier 1, the Reuchlin manuscript, reads "God."

[42] Hoskier lists the uncial P, and minuscules 1, 57, 141, 146, and 159.

[43] These being 57 and 141, mentioned in previous note.

[44] Note the Greek: τὸ ὄνομα αὐτοῦ καὶ τὸ ὄνομα τοῦ πατρὸς.

[45] See discussion of this passage in chapter 5, p. 108.

[46] Hoskier 57 and 141, as well as 137*. Some Latin manuscripts have the phrase.

[47] Again we find 57 and 141 being the only ones to support the TR reading.

[48] One of the greatest advantages of the textual footnotes of the *New King James Version* is that the English reader can note these variations quite easily without having to access critical Greek texts. We could only wish that other modern translations would follow the example of the NKJV at this point.

[49] KJV Only advocates are quick to accuse modern Greek texts of being somehow "polluted" by Roman Catholicism, and yet it is the TR itself that often imports entire passages on the basis of the authority of the Latin *Vulgate*. William Grady spends a great deal of time in his book, *Final Authority*, forging a link between the Vatican and modern texts, yet he overlooks passages such as these with remarks like that found on page 72, "Have a problem with the *Textus Receptus*? **Tell it to the judge!**"

[50] We note the rather outrageous claims of Dr. Peter Ruckman with reference to this very passage. In his booklet, *Satan's Masterpiece! The New ASV* (Bible Baptist Bookstore: 1972), he writes concerning this reading,

> But God's *words* are written in *a book*. The Authorized Reading of the Holy Bible (1611) is entirely correct, and the NASV as the old ASV (1901) is in error. Furthermore, the reader may be interested to know (in the cause of scientific exegesis and documented evidence) that the Authorized Reading is found in the Greek Textus Receptus, *yet neither Kurt Aland (Metzger's text) nor Nestle's gives the reading or even mentions it as having a source.* **"Cunning craftiness"** (Eph. 4:14) again, eh, Doctor?

What Dr. Ruckman forgets to mention is *how* the reading got into the TR. The reason Aland does not give a reference note is simple: there are no Greek manuscripts to support the reading.

[51] Some have suggested (Hills, p. 201) that this passage was original, but

was deleted due to later ecclesiastical practices regarding baptism. The fact, however, that it is found in the Latin *Vulgate*, which certainly shows as much, if not more, evidence of ecclesiastical "concern" makes this argument somewhat tenuous.

[52] Codex E contains the reading "word of God." Codex E is a bilingual, Latin/Greek manuscript from the early seventh century.

[53] The other textual variant in this verse will be addressed in chapter 7. It is interesting to note the words of Hills upon finding these readings in the TR: "We solve this problem, however, according to the logic of faith. Because the Textus Receptus was God-guided as a whole, it was probably God-guided in these few passages also" (p. 208).

[54] Some interesting places where sources as divergent as the *Vulgate* and the Jewish commentaries in the Mishnah were used will be noted in Chapter 7.

[55] See Hills, pp. 221-222.

[56] It is interesting to note that Dr. D.A. Waite in a debate with me alleged that this reading of Luke 2:22 (found in Erasmus, Stephanus, and the $\mathfrak{M}$ text-type) makes Christ a sinner. Note his words from his book, p. 163:

> The word, "**her**," is changed to "**their**," thus making the Lord Jesus Christ One Who needed "purification," and therefore was a sinner! This is unthinkable! One of these perversions was used in 1991, in my home church in the Christmas program they were using, making Christ a sinner thereby! . . . **I hope you will check in advance your own church's** CHRISTMAS **and** EASTER **programs. Unless they use the KING JAMES BIBLE, they will be in serious doctrinal trouble!**

[57] Hills, p. 204.

[58] Ibid.

[59] See especially Gustavus Paine, *The Men Behind the King James Version* (Baker: 1977).

[60] See the discussion of how this problem appears in the text of the KJV in chapter 9.

[61] William Barlow, one of the NT translators who worked on the Epistles at Westminster, made a number of interesting statements about the rights of kings, such as asserting that the body of the king is "sacred by holy unction." See Paine, p. 43.

[62] KJV Only advocates should note Rainolds' own words, wherein he urged the study of the Bible in Greek and Hebrew, "not out of the books of translation" (Paine, p. 84). We note the irony of the strongly anti-Calvinistic bent of such KJV Only writers as Gail Riplinger in light of the fact that Rainolds, as a Puritan, was very much a Calvinist. The inconsistency of the KJV Only position is again seen with clarity.

[63] We note in passing the fact that KJV Only advocates are quick to attack the use of the term "originals" by modern defenders of newer translations.

[64] Paine, pp. 70-71.

[65] These citations are placed in modern English style and spelling.

[66] "People who believe that there was a Septuagint before the time of Christ, are living in a dream world." Peter Ruckman, *The Christian's Handbook of Manuscript Evidence* (Pensacola Bible Press: 1976), p. 50.

[67] It was set in an "Old English" typeface, similar to this: 𝔍𝔫 𝔱𝔥𝔢 𝔟𝔢𝔤𝔦𝔫𝔫𝔦𝔫𝔤 𝔊𝔬𝔡 𝔠𝔯𝔢𝔞𝔱𝔢𝔡 𝔱𝔥𝔢 𝔥𝔢𝔞𝔳𝔢𝔫, 𝔞𝔫𝔡 𝔱𝔥𝔢 𝔢𝔞𝔯𝔱𝔥.

[68] F.H.A. Scrivener, *The Authorized Edition of the English Bible (1611)* (Cambridge: 1884), p. 41. Dr. Scrivener includes other categories I did not mention. Hence, there are other marginal notes listed in his study. Therefore, the numbers given do not add up to the final totals.

[69] Ibid., p. 56.

[70] Jack Lewis, *The English Bible: From KJV to NIV,* 2nd ed. (Baker: 1991), p. 39.

[71] Ibid.

[72] See Appendix A of Scrivener's work, pp. 147-202.

[73] Lewis, p. 39.

[74] I was using the modern text, *Biblia Hebraica Stuttgartensia.* Dr. Price noted in his response to Gail Riplinger that the differences between that Hebrew text and the text used by the KJV translators, known as the *Ben Chayyim* text, Bomberg edition of 1525, are "microscopic." He listed a grand total of eight places in the Old Testament where the textual differences between the two texts impacted the English translation, specifically Proverbs 8:16; Isaiah 10:16; Isaiah 27:2; Isaiah 38:14; Jeremiah 34:1; Ezekiel 30:18; Zephaniah 3:15; and Malachi 1:12.

[75] Future editions of the NKJV will change the pronoun back to "you."

The King James Only Camp   5

Before diving into a close examination of specific texts and passages relevant to the claims of the KJV Only camp, I would like to take some time to familiarize the reader with the kind of literature produced by this group. If you have already been exposed to the writings of Peter Ruckman, Samuel Gipp, D.A. Waite, or J.J. Ray, you are already aware of the tactics and strategies employed in presenting the KJV Only position. But most people have not been exposed to such writings, so a *brief* review is in order. It is not my intention to provide an "internal critique" of the movement in this chapter. Others have done this work and there is no reason for me to repeat their fine efforts.[1] Instead, I wish to draw examples from different KJV Only writers to illustrate points regarding the errors made by these individuals in their writing, teaching, and preaching.

In my opinion many of the great scholars of the past who have defended the Byzantine textual tradition cannot honestly be included in the "KJV Only" camp (though they are often cited as if they were). Men like Dean Burgon, F.H.A. Scrivener, H.C. Hoskier—all of whom were true scholars of the first rank—were **not** KJV Only advocates. All saw the need for revision in the KJV and in the TR as well. Just to give an example from Dean Burgon, who is so often cited by KJV Only advocates, we provide his words regarding the need for revision of the TR, wherein he notes a textual variant at Matthew 10:8:

> For, in not a few particulars, the "Textus Receptus" *does* call for Revision, certainly. . . . To mention a single instance:—When our Lord first sent forth His Twelve Apostles, it was certainly no part of His ministerial commission to them to '*raise the dead*' (νεκροὺς ἐγείρετε, S. Matthew x. 8). This is easily demonstrable. Yet is the spurious clause retained by our Revisionists; because it is found in those corrupt witnesses—‏א‎ B C D, and the Latin copies.[2]

None of these scholars insisted that the KJV was "it." They did not believe that the KJV was completely without error, or that even the TR was infallible and inspired. Surely they differed with much of modern scholarship on the relative merits of various texts and manuscripts, but that is hardly the same as taking a KJV Only position.

In this chapter the words of three writers who would be properly identified as "KJV Only" will be examined. We will start with the least radical of the three, Dr. Edward F. Hills, the Presbyterian author of *The King James Version Defended*. Then we will look at Gail Riplinger and her book, *New Age Bible Versions*. Finally we will look at the most radical and probably the most popular of the KJV Only advocates, Dr. Peter Ruckman of the Pensacola Bible Institute. For most, the words will speak for themselves. I need only point out a few facts and provide a context for the reader to recognize the style of argumentation that is being put forward.

A REFORMED ADVOCATE OF THE KJV

Dr. Edward F. Hills represents the best of the KJV Only position in the sense that he does not engage in the kind of insulting rhetoric that is characteristic of the presentations made by other individuals. Instead, Hills' arguments focus upon the "logic of faith." Every problem one can present in the KJV or its underlying texts is answered by appeal to the "common faith," "the providence of God," or the "logic of faith." Hills does not ignore such things as the insertion of passages from the Vulgate into the text of Erasmus and hence into the KJV; instead, he argues that since God preserved the rest of the TR, He must have preserved those readings, too. It is quite plain that Dr. Hills began with the conclusion of his argument ("the TR is the God-preserved text") and did not hesitate to utilize the conclusion in the course of his argument, charges of circularity notwithstanding. However, much to the chagrin of the more radical elements of the KJV Only movement, Hills did not join them in granting inspiration to the AV. Note his words:

> God's preservation of the New Testament text was not miraculous but providential. The scribes and printers who produced the copies of the New Testament Scriptures and the true believers who read and cherished them were not inspired

but God-guided. Hence there are some New Testament
passages in which the true reading cannot be determined with
absolute certainty. There are some readings, for example, on
which the manuscripts are almost equally divided, making it
difficult to determine which reading belongs to the Traditional
Text. Also in some of the cases in which the Textus Receptus
disagrees with the Traditional Text it is hard to decide which
text to follow. Also, as we have seen, sometimes the several
editions of the Textus Receptus differ from each other and from
the King James Version.[3]

Dr. Hills' honesty is a breath of fresh air. If he had not begun with the
assumption of the superiority of the TR, he would undoubtedly have
been led to a conclusion in favor, at the very least, of the "Majority
Text" rather than the modern critical texts. But another argument
precluded his coming to any conclusions other than the ones he
presented, and that was the "argument for certainty" as I call it. This
argument is the "glue" that holds the KJV Only position together. It is
the common thread that ties Dr. Hills to someone as completely
different in approach and mannerism as Dr. Ruckman. Since it is
central to the KJV Only position, we will take the opportunity to
review the argument as presented in its best form by Dr. Hills. We can
see how it functions in this quotation by Dr. Hills:

In short, unless we follow the logic of faith, we can be certain
of nothing concerning the Bible and its text. For example, if we
make the Bodmer and Chester Beatty Papyri our chief reliance,
how do we know that even older New Testament papyri of an
entirely different character have not been destroyed by the
recent damming of the Nile and the consequent flooding of the
Egyptian sands?[4]

The desire for *absolute certainty* in all matters plainly lies behind
statements such as this, and the much less polished (and much more
emotional) versions of the same argument that are encountered in less
scholarly KJV Only materials. It is argued that unless we embrace the
KJV as our "final authority," we have no final authority at all, and
hence all is subjectivity and uncertainty. People do not want
subjectivity, but desire certainty and clarity, and so we must hold to the
"traditional" text.

This argument is extremely powerful and should not be under-estimated. Many people fulfill their longing for "certainty" in religious matters by swearing allegiance to a particular leader or system. For example, many Roman Catholics find the idea of an infallible pope very "comforting," for when things get confusing they always have a source of certainty and absolute authority to turn to. In a similar way many Mormons look to the Prophet and the Apostles in Salt Lake City, and Jehovah's Witnesses look to the Governing Body in Watchtower headquarters in Brooklyn, New York. Others find a TV preacher or evangelist and, without stating it in so many words, invest him or her with some level of infallible religious authority. The fact that groups that offer this kind of "trust us and we will give you absolute certainty in all religious matters" mentality continue to attract followers should tell us that the lure of "absolute certainty" is a strong one indeed.

Protestants, however, should be *quick* to question any such notion of absolute religious certainty. The concept of the individual's responsibility before God is deeply ingrained in Protestant theology. We cannot hand off our responsibility in religious matters to someone else. We cannot say "the pope told me to do that" or "the prophet instructed me to believe that doctrine." God holds us individually responsible for our beliefs and our actions. This was one of the great scandals of the Reformation: the idea of the plowman and the merchant carrying *and reading* the Bible was unthinkable to the medieval Catholic theologian. How could the layman understand religious things without asking the priest? The Reformers preached a radical concept: a man is responsible to learn God's Word as best he can, and to follow what he learns. We are called to be students, responsible men and women who make learning, and studying, God's Word a high priority in our lives. We cannot blame anyone else for our ignorance, or our errors.

As imperfect human beings we will make mistakes. As Paul said, we see in a glass darkly in this life. There are things that are unclear, things that are simply not as plain as they someday will be. The KJV translators themselves said in their Preface, quoted earlier, "For as it is a fault of incredulity, to doubt of those things that are evident: so to determine of such things as the Spirit of God hath left (even in the judgment of the judicious) questionable, can be no less than presumption." Those who offer us certainty beyond all questions, the translators would rightly say, are being presumptuous with God's truth. Those who offer absolute certainty do so at a cost: individual responsibility.

If we say that we can have no certainty regarding the biblical text unless we embrace the KJV (or the TR), we are simply moving the question one step back and hoping no one notices. How can we be certain of the textual choices of Desiderius Erasmus, or Stephanus, or Theodore Beza? How can we be certain that the Anglican churchmen who chose amongst the variant readings of those three men were themselves inspired? Are we not, in reality, saying, "Well, I *must* have certainty, therefore, without any factual or logical or even *scriptural* reason for doing so, I will invest the KJV translators with ultimate authority." This is, truly, what KJV Only advocates are doing when they close their eyes to the historical realities regarding the biblical text.

A Case Study in Misrepresentation

Belief in grand conspiratorial schemes often leads one to sacrifice commitment to fairness when it comes to representing "THEM," whoever *they* might be. If you are fully convinced that the translators and editors of the modern translations, for instance, are all out to lead people *away* from the truth and *away* from Christ, why should you be overly concerned about being accurate in your representations of what they say or believe? In fact, why not "fudge" just a little and make them look *even worse,* if that will, in fact, help to "warn" people about them? Isn't a little white lie in the service of God acceptable, once in a while?

Sadly, modern Christianity provides us with all too many examples of less-than-exemplary reporting in the cause of "good." It seems we are often guilty of focusing upon the extreme, the exciting, the sensational, all at the cost of being honest, forthright, and accurate in our speech and writing. Books or films that just "stick to the facts" gather dust on the shelves, while other works that dabble in the spectacular at the cost of exactness sell like hotcakes.

Christians are to be lovers of truth, and as such, should hold to the highest standards thereof. Misrepresenting others—even those we *strongly* feel are in error—is not an option for one who follows Jesus.

It has been my experience that the most widely distributed KJV Only materials are those that are the most riddled with misrepresentation. One cannot study the materials put forward in defense of KJV Onlyism without being struck by the fact that the arguments contained in the materials show little apparent interest in being fair with the writings, beliefs, or perspectives of those labeled as "heretics" and "haters of God's Word." "Anything goes" seems to be the watchword when it comes to making the "enemy" look as bad as possible.

In late 1993 a book appeared on the market entitled *New Age Bible Versions*. The book, printed with a menacing black and red cover, has the subtitle, "An Exhaustive Documentation Exposing the Message, Men and Manuscripts Moving Mankind to the Antichrist's One World Religion." Also on the cover, "The New Case Against the NIV, NASB, NKJV, NRSV, NAB, REB, RSV, CEV, TEV, GNB, Living, Phillips, New Jerusalem, & New Century," which is immediately followed by "The Latest Research Supporting the Authorized King James Version." The book's author is identified only as "G.A. Riplinger." The perspective of the book is plainly laid out in the materials printed on the back cover:

> This book is the result of an exhaustive six year collation of *new* bible versions, their underlying Greek manuscripts, editions, and editors. It objectively and methodically documents the hidden alliance between *new* versions and the New Age Movement's One World Religion.
>
> Each page opens a door exposing new version editors — in agreement with Luciferians, occultists, and New Age philosophy — in mental institutions, seance parlors, prison cells, and court rooms for heresy trials — and most shocking of all — denying that salvation is through faith in Jesus Christ. Five have lost their ability to speak.
>
> The emerging 'new' Christianity — with its substitution of riches for righteousness, a crown for a cross, and an imitation for a new creation — is shown to be a *direct* result of the wording in new versions.
>
> Documented are the thousands of words, verses, and doctrines

> by which new versions will prepare the apostate churches of
> these last days to accept the religion of the Antichrist — even
> his mark, image, and Lucifer worship.

The text of the nearly seven-hundred-page book carries the same kind of temperament throughout. No chance is missed to insult and attack men both living and dead, as long as they had *something* to do with "modern versions."[5] At least one can say that there is no misunderstanding the viewpoint of *New Age Bible Versions*.

The book has gained a wide audience. A number of Christian leaders unwisely gave their support to the work, though later admitting that they had not, in fact, read the work very closely. The book obtained entrance into churches all through the land. Since it cited hard-to-find works, the vast majority of those reading it gave the author the "benefit of the doubt" and accepted the citations and quotations as being accurate. Some went so far as to begin burning modern versions after sermons prompted by the work.

I became aware of the book due to the appearance of the author on a local Christian radio station. I was so distressed by the inaccuracies of the information being presented that I contacted the host of the program. This led to two debates with the author, Mrs. Gail Riplinger, and, due to the tremendous response from people all across the nation, a booklet refuting her book as well.[6]

New Age Bible Versions contains a plethora of out-of-context citations and edited quotations, frequently misrepresenting the positions of the authors it attacks. I wish to focus primarily upon its treatment of Christian scholars, both past and present, but one example of the book's disregard for fair argumentation is found in the discussion of what initially prompted Mrs. Riplinger to begin studying this particular area. She not only includes this story in her book, but repeats it often in her public appearances. Mrs. Riplinger reports that she was trying to counsel a student of hers who needed spiritual guidance. As she says, "My first glimpse down into this dark chasm full of Christians suffering from 'mental chaos' came via a distraught young Christian woman attending a campus bible study." One of the passages that she wished to share with this student was Isaiah 26:3. We pick up with her own words,

A second attempt to arm her (Ephesians 6:17) in her joust with the devil, found the NASB's sword sheathed hiding *the key* words, "on Thee."[7]

These words are immediately followed by this chart that appears at the top of page 455:

NASB	KJV
The steadfast of mind Thou wilt keep in perfect peace.	Thou wilt keep him in perfect peace, whose mind is stayed on thee. Isaiah 26:3

It certainly *appears,* if one takes Riplinger at face value, that the NASB has indeed "deleted" something. And yet such would be a grand mistake. But notice the *actual* readings of both versions:

NASB	KJV
The steadfast of mind Thou wilt keep in perfect peace, Because he trusts in Thee.	Thou wilt keep *him* in perfect peace, *whose* mind *is* stayed *on thee:* because he trusteth in thee.

While *New Age Bible Versions* places a period after "peace" in its rendering of the NASB, we see that no such period exists. Instead, the rest of the verse actually contains the *"key words"* alleged to be missing![8] And note that *New Age Bible Versions* does not indicate that the KJV uses italics for the inserted clause "on thee," for quite simply, the Hebrew does not contain the phrase! This kind of actual mis-citation of the modern versions appears throughout the text of the book.[9]

The kinds of basic errors that fill the work are at times difficult to understand. For example, we are informed on pages 375-376, "The KJV is also the only bible[10] that distinguishes between the Hebrew *Adonai* and *JHVH*, using 'Lord' for the former and 'LORD' for the latter." Of course, this is simply untrue. The NASB, NIV, NKJV, RSV, NRSV, NAB, and others *all* use the "Lord/LORD" means of distinguishing between *Adonai* and *YHWH*. Even a brief glance at almost any page of the Old Testament in any of these other translations would have indicated the error of the statement. This kind of inaccurate statement is found all through *New Age Bible Versions*.

I do not wish to focus so much upon the errors regarding Bible verses, manuscripts, etc.,[11] as upon the obvious campaign to make Bible scholars, both of the past and the present, "fit the pattern" of the conspiracy that drives Riplinger's thinking. Lest someone think me harsh, it is important to recognize Gail Riplinger's own explanation of her motivations in writing *New Age Bible Versions:*

> Daily during the six years needed for this investigation, the Lord miraculously brought the needed materials and resources — much like the ravens fed Elijah. Each discovery was not the result of effort on my part, but of the directed hand of God — so much so that I hesitated to even put my name on the book. Consequently, I used G.A. Riplinger, which signifies to me, God and Riplinger — God as author and Riplinger as secretary.[12]

Those who are *that convinced* that they are right about the great conspiracy behind modern translations will go to immense lengths to *stay convinced of their position.*

New Age Bible Versions caricatures the views of several modern Christian scholars. We will focus on three biblically oriented examples of how a deep conviction about the evil nature of "modern translators" or "critics" can lead one to misrepresent their position.

KJV Only advocates love to hate B.F. Westcott and F.J.A. Hort. Westcott and Hort's work on the Greek New Testament is seen as a focal point of the attempt to "dethrone" the KJV and its underlying Greek text, the *Textus Receptus.* While modern Greek texts are not identical to that created by Westcott and Hort, one will still find defenders of the AV drawing in black and white, saying that all modern versions are based upon their work.[13] Entire books have been published that seek to do nothing but vilify these men.[14] The first example of misrepresentation is drawn from page 546:

> Westcott and Hort's *Introduction to the New Testament in the Original Greek* affirms:
>
>> [R]eadings of Aleph & B should be accepted as the true readings . . . [They] stand far above all documents . . . [are] very pure . . . excellent . . . and immune from corruption.

Riplinger provides a reference footnote for her citation that reads,

> B.F. Westcott and F.J.A. Hort, *Introduction to the New Testament in the Original Greek* (Peabody, Mass: Hendrickson Publishers, Orig. 1882), pp. xxii, 225, 212, 220, 239, 210.

Anyone reading this material would be led to believe that Westcott and Hort held a *very* radical view of the Greek manuscripts Aleph (א) and B. Since Riplinger then attempts to demonstrate that these manuscripts are, in fact, corrupt and unreliable, and later that they actually contain the "blueprint" for the "Antichrist's *final* bible,"[15] her purpose is clear: she is attempting to vilify Westcott and Hort and to destroy any last vestige of credibility these men might have in her readers' minds. What is more, how many individuals have access to Westcott and Hort's *Introduction to the New Testament in the Original Greek*, or even if they did, how many would look up these references?

As collecting Greek reference works has been a practice of mine for a number of years, I happened to have the work by Westcott and Hort close at hand when I first encountered this citation, and I was simply shocked by the blatant editing of the words of these two men by Gail Riplinger. The following charts will document my allegations.

First, there is nothing on page xxii that is in Riplinger's quote; the sentence "With these exceptions, readings of אB should be accepted when not contravened by strong internal evidence" appears on page xxiv. Next, the citation of page 225 shows how the ellipses can be used to give a false impression:

Riplinger's Version	What W&H Actually Said
[R]eadings of Aleph and B should be accepted as the true readings . . .	. . . readings of Aleph/B should be accepted as the true readings until strong internal evidence is found to the contrary, and (2) that no readings of Aleph/B can safely be rejected absolutely, though it is sometimes right to place them only on an alternative footing, especially where they receive no support from Versions or Fathers.

Contextually, at the top of this very page, W&H were talking about *errors* in Aleph/B. One would hardly get that idea from what Riplinger wrote. There is nothing on page 212 which is in any way relevant to the citation given by Riplinger, unless their use of "excellence" lies behind Riplinger's use of "excellent." On page 220 we find the context causing problems again:

Riplinger's Version	What W&H Actually Said
... [are] very pure ... excellent ...	These considerations shew that the common original of Aleph/B for by far the greater part of their identical readings, whatever may have been its own date, had a very ancient and very pure text, and that there is no sufficient reason for surmising that the rest of their identical readings came from any other source.

Note that W&H are not referring to Aleph/B here, as Riplinger indicates, but to the parent text of Aleph and B.

There is nothing even remotely relevant to the quotation on page 239. Finally, page 210 shows the same kind of error of citation that we saw on page 225:

Riplinger's Version	What W&H Actually Said
[They] stand far above all documents ...	We found Aleph and B to stand alone in their almost complete immunity from distinctive Syrian readings; Aleph to stand far above all documents except B in the proportion which the part of its text neither Western nor Alexandrian bears to the rest; and B to stand far above Aleph in its apparent freedom from either Western or Alexandrian readings with the partial exception in the Pauline epistles already mentioned more than once.

The fact that a number of pages cited by Riplinger in her note, in fact, contain nothing relevant to her excerpt, and the complete "cut and paste" nature of her citation, makes it difficult to identify the specific pages from which she is allegedly drawing her information. She might point to page 220 as the source of her "immune from corruption" quotation, for there we read,

> They prove that one of three alternatives must be true: either
> the respective ancestories of ℵ and B must have diverged from
> a common parent extremely near the apostolic autographs; or,
> if their concordant readings were really derived from a single
> not remote MS, that MS must itself have been of the very
> highest antiquity; or, lastly, such single not remote MS must
> have inherited its text from an ancestory which at each of its
> stages had enjoyed a singular immunity from corruption.

One also finds the term "immunity" used on page 225 as well, though
not in any context that would be remotely relevant to Riplinger's
citation. Remember, I am citing directly from the very same edition of
Westcott and Hort's work that she cites in her book. This kind of "take
a word from here, a word from there" quotation cannot be excused on
the basis of "differing editions."

Is it possible, to be fair, that Riplinger is simply not familiar
enough with the subject to follow such a complex work as this by
Westcott and Hort? And how would we know? If a pattern of this kind
of "cut and paste" citation is found, we can safely conclude that *New
Age Bible Versions* presents an unfair and unreliable view of modern
scholarship. Does such a pattern exist? An impartial review of the
work proves that such a pattern does indeed exist.

Dr. Edwin Palmer was the executive secretary of the NIV
translation committee. Consequently he is the subject of merciless
attacks in *New Age Bible Versions*.[16] But even worse is the
misrepresentation of his statements that, again, is for a very obvious
purpose. Edwin Palmer is the leading name in the origination and
translation of the single English translation that has most severely
challenged the preeminence of the KJV. If Riplinger can mislead her
readers with reference to the very executive secretary of the
translation committee of the NIV, she has gone a long way in
convincing people to abandon the use of the NIV. And how does she
go about her task? She first focuses upon one of the "hot" issues: the
great truth of the deity of Christ. She attempts to paint Dr. Palmer as a
closet Arian, a denier of the deity of the Lord Jesus Christ, through
the misuse of his own words. Compare her alleged "citations" with
his actual words:

Riplinger's Version	What Dr. Palmer Actually Said
Under the century old spell of the Westcott and Hort Greek Text, NIV Editor Edwin Palmer comes to his chilling theological conclusion!: [There are] few clear and decisive texts that declare Jesus is God.[17]	John 1:18, as inspired by the Holy Spirit, is one of those few and clear and decisive texts that declare that Jesus is God. But, without fault of its own, the KJV, following inferior manuscripts, altered what the Holy Spirit said through John, calling Jesus "Son."[18]

The fact that this kind of out-of-context quotation is inexcusable is made even more clear by the fact that Mrs. Riplinger misrepresented Dr. Palmer elsewhere, this time allegedly citing from Dr. Palmer's book, *The Holy Spirit*. I say inexcusable because *The Holy Spirit* affirms the deity of Christ over and over and over again. Surely if Gail Riplinger read Dr. Palmer's actual works,[19] she would know that she was misrepresenting him in the above citation. But instead, she compounds her error by misrepresenting him yet once again. Here is how she presented yet another attack upon Edwin Palmer in her book,[20]

NIV EDITORS	MORMAN [*sic*] DOCTRINE
"The Holy Spirit did not beget the Son." Edwin Palmer NIV Committee Executive Secretary	"He [the Son] was not begotten by the Holy Spirit . . ." Brigham Young

Riplinger claims that Edwin Palmer denies the role of the Holy Spirit in the Incarnation of Jesus Christ. Is this true? Certainly not. Her reference from *The Holy Spirit* is not from Palmer's discussion of the Incarnation at all, but from his discussion of the internal operations of the Trinity itself. Note what he said,

> There is among the three Persons of the Trinity a definite relationship and order. Because the three Persons are equally God, it must not be thought that they are all the same. Each one has distinctive properties and relationships to the others. Between the first and second Persons, for example, there is the relationship of Father and Son. From all eternity the Father begat the Son. The Holy Spirit did not beget the Son, only the Father did.[21]

This is, of course, historic Christian belief, based firmly on the revelation of Scripture itself, on the topic of the relationship between the Father and the Son in eternity past. Palmer is fully "orthodox" at this point. So what did he write about the Incarnation or the Lord Jesus Christ? Here are his words, which go completely unreported by Riplinger:

I. The Incarnation
The Holy Spirit was needed at the very start of Jesus' human life, at his incarnation. By the word incarnation we mean that act by which the Second Person of the Trinity, remaining God, "became flesh and lived for a while among us" (John 1:14). *This was an act effected by the Holy Spirit. . . . The Holy Spirit is the cause of the conception of Jesus.* He is the one, and not the Father nor the Son, let alone Joseph, who planted the seed of life in a mysterious way in Mary's womb.[22]

Sadly, people have burned NIVs as a result of this kind of distortion.

It is not only individuals from the past, such as Westcott and Hort or Edwin Palmer, who are liable to misrepresentation. No, living individuals are not immune from this kind of attack. I give only one example of how bold the defenders of KJV Onlyism can be. Here the object of attack is Calvin Linton, who wrote an article for *The NIV: The Making of a Contemporary Translation* titled "The Importance of Literary Style in Bible Translation Today." Again Riplinger is specifically attempting to create a dichotomy between the "New Version Editors" and her "Christianity," striving to make the new versions *anti-Christian* in their character and motivations in the hope of creating an emotional response on the part of the Christian who loves God's Word. To firmly implant this idea in the minds of her readers, Riplinger produces a chart that attempts to prove that modern versions de-emphasize the "Word." Here we reproduce a section of this chart, exactly as it appears in her work,[23] that provides us with yet another "cut and paste" quotation. Here Mrs. Riplinger is found to be taking bits and pieces from here and there, all the time ignoring context, all in the attempt to present a particular viewpoint on the part of Dr. Calvin Linton.

NEW VERSION EDITORS	CHRISTIANITY
Calvin Linton: NIV The bible is "God's message" and not his words, contends Linton. He believes the bible is "the wrong side of a beautiful embroidery. The picture is still there, but knotted, blurry— not beautiful, not perfect." He calls Christians "amusingly uninformed," who "presume the Holy Spirit dictated the actual **words** of the text of the original writers."	For verily I say unto you, Till heaven and earth pass, one jot or tittle shall in no wise pass from the law. Matthew 5:18 (A 'jot' is the smallest letter and a tittle is the smallest ornament placed on a letter.)

Here, however, is what Dr. Linton *actually* said:

> I recently received a lengthy letter from a devout reader of the Bible who asked why there needed to be any modern translations of the Bible at all. Why cannot we simply put down God's exact words in English form? Why dress them up in so many styles? . . . .
>
> Such questions, though amusingly uninformed, do actually touch on a profound consideration, one suggested by the great seventeenth-century poet and preacher John Donne, whose sermons as dean of Saint Paul's (in his later life) drew throngs. Speaking of the style of the Bible, he said, "The Holy Ghost is an eloquent author, a vehement and abundant author, but yet not luxuriant." This presumes that the Holy Spirit dictated the actual words of the text to the original writers, thereby (it is further presumed) investing the entire Bible with his own literary style. The style of the Bible, however, is not homogeneous. Rather, each writer has his own style, reflective of his personality, which a faithful translation must reflect in ways perceptible to the modern reader . . . .
>
> The Holy Spirit, while preserving the inspired writers from error, used the individuality of each writer as colors on his palette to paint a unified picture—or, to use another image, to weave a seamless garment. Such exploitation of the differing characteristics of the original writers—their learning, personality, environment, literary style, etc.—in no way impugns the inerrancy of the original autographs. It merely means that God did not expunge all individuality from the inspired writers, using them only as automata or as "word processors." The written Word comes to us through the "dust"

of our earthly nature, but it is uniquely breathed into (animated) by God. It foreshadows and testifies to the ultimate revelation of God in his Son, when "the Word became flesh and made his dwelling among us" (John 1:14). He, too, like the Bible, partook of our earthly condition (yet without sin, as the Bible in its original autographs is without error), possessing a human body, a certain physical appearance and manner of speech, and reaching us on our level, that God's message may be made wholly ours.

The translator must, among other things, strive to eradicate all characteristics of his own personal style, becoming a sounding chamber without strings. At best we probably must agree with the seventeenth-century writer James Howell when he says that a translator can do no more than reveal the "wrong side of a Persian rug." Fortunately the Bible is so gorgeously woven a tapestry that even the "wrong side" is wonderful![24]

One is left wondering where Riplinger came up with these alleged "citations." And yet, how many of those who read *New Age Bible Versions* ever bothered to check the sources cited before making a decision? People will continue to get away with this kind of activity as long as Christians remain unwilling to adopt a critical stance and allow anything to masquerade under the title "Christian."

Dr. James Price, the former executive editor of the NKJV Old Testament, responded to Gail Riplinger's book shortly after it was published by writing a letter that was later published.[25] He provided a number of examples where the "conspiratorial" kind of thinking that fills the pages of her book could be turned back upon the KJV Only advocate. I quote here only his comments that were based upon Old Testament references:

In Gen 36:24, all Hebrew manuscripts and other ancient authorities read "found water"; whereas the KJV reads "found mules" following a medieval Jewish commentator. Do you suppose this is a New Age attack on the Word of God for which water is a symbol, replacing it with mules?

In 1 Sam 2:25, all Hebrew manuscripts read "God"; whereas the KJV reads "judge," without capitalization. Do you suppose this is a New Age denial that God will judge sinners?

In Isa 19:10, all Hebrew manuscripts read "soul"; whereas the KJV reads "fish," following the Roman Catholic Latin Vulgate. Do you suppose this is a New Age attack on the spiritual nature of man, attempting to lower him to a mere animal?

In Hosea 13:9, all Hebrew manuscripts read "he destroyed you"; whereas the KJV reads "thou hast destroyed thyself," with no apparent support from any ancient authority. Do you suppose this is a New Age corrupting of the Word of God?

In Mal 2:12, all Hebrew manuscripts read "aware and awake"; whereas the KJV reads "the master and the scholar," following the Roman Catholic Latin Vulgate. Do you suppose this is a New Age attack on spiritual alertness, replacing it with godless scholarship?

Not only are these interesting passages, but the fact that these kinds of arguments can be turned back upon the conspiratorialists is plain evidence that they are using double standards.

But Gail Riplinger provides a fuller look into the thinking of the radical elements of KJV Onlyism as well. Recall that in describing her reasons for writing her book she had indicated that to her the initials of her name (G.A. Riplinger) spoke of "God and Riplinger," God as author, Riplinger as secretary. How this kind of thinking impacts what is reported can be seen by looking briefly at Riplinger's second book, *Which Bible Is God's Word?*[26] How has the refutation of many of her points in her initial work impacted this second book? Has she admitted her errors and changed her story? Not at all. Instead, we find a complete unwillingness to admit error. She responded to the correction of her misrepresentation of Dr. Edwin Palmer with the following paragraph:

Neither I nor my quote from Edwin Palmer mention the incarnation at all.[27] Palmer does not believe the word "*beget*" (John 1:14, et al.) refers to the incarnation. In spite of the fact that the verse is talking about his "flesh." [*sic*] Palmer's "*begotten God*" (John 1:18, *The NIV: The Making of a Contemporary Translation*, p. 143) is no more accurate theologically than the Mormon notion, "*The head of the gods appointed a God for us*" (*Teachings of the Prophet Joseph Smith,* pp. 370, 372).

There is no acknowledgment of error, only a complete misdirection of the line of thinking. Indeed, not only does the response make little sense, but amazingly enough, the quotation of Joseph Smith is not accurate, either![28] With reference to her statement that only a "tiny percentage of corrupt Greek manuscripts" contain the phrase "His name and" at Revelation 14:1,[29] I had responded in a review of her book that all Greek manuscripts contained the phrase. I assumed, incorrectly, that since the Nestle-Aland 27th edition cited no variant, and since even the Majority Text listed the TR as standing alone in the reading, the manuscript tradition was united in this reading. In fact, a small handful of very late manuscripts lack the phrase, as indicated in the discussion of the passage earlier in this work. When responding to my review, however, did Gail Riplinger admit that, in reality, it is a "tiny percentage of corrupt Greek manuscripts" that actually *lack* the phrase? Did she admit she had erred in her work? Not at all. Instead, she simply listed some Greek manuscripts that contained the phrase and passed over her own error in silence.[30]

But most interesting is her response given in reply to my pointing out the misspelling of the last names of men such as Richard Longenecker and D.A. Carson. I had raised this issue solely to open up the possibility that the many mis-citations and misrepresentations were due to the author's reliance solely upon secondary sources in her research, something Mrs. Riplinger has denied. Yet, she makes the following comment in regard to this, which I feel is *extremely* important for anyone wishing to understand the thinking of KJV Onlyism:

> The early printings of the 700-page *New Age Bible Versions* did accidentally drop the "e" from the name Longenecker and add an "l" to Carson. I only *reluctantly* fixed it, since these men advocate removing the name of deity from the bible about two hundred times.[31]

Gail Riplinger only *"reluctantly"* fixed her misspelling of these names (in a section wherein she accuses both men of being "cultists") because of her dislike of their textual choices. People who think in this way seem much more willing to allow the "ends to justify the means," which explains the incessant stream of misrepresentation that one finds in such works as *New Age Bible Versions.*

SPEARHEADING THE KJV ONLY MOVEMENT

To say Dr. Peter Ruckman is outspoken is to engage in an exercise in understatement. Caustic is too mild a term; bombastic is a little more accurate. His devoted followers see him in prophetic terms. He is the best-known advocate of KJV Onlyism in the United States. He is author of dozens of books and head of the Pensacola Bible Institute.

His critics are legion. Even those who support the King James Version find reason for criticizing Ruckman, because his writings are so acerbic, so offensive and mean-spirited that the entire movement has become identified with his kind of confrontational attitude. His followers exhibit such a close attachment to his words and his perspectives that the entire movement has been tagged with the term "Ruckmanism," and those who present his beliefs are often styled "Ruckmanites."

There is no doubt that Peter S. Ruckman is brilliant, in a strange sort of way. His mental powers are plainly demonstrated in his books, though most people do not bother to read far enough to recognize this due to the constant stream of invective that is to be found on nearly every page. And yet his cocky confidence attracts many people to his viewpoint.

His arguments represent the extreme of the KJV Only position. We have already noted his statements regarding the perfection of the KJV, even to the point of asserting that the Greek and Hebrew manuscripts should be changed to fit the AV 1611, since even mistakes in the AV 1611 are "advanced revelation."[32] His position, however, is so often clouded by insulting, demeaning language aimed at his opponents that few people get past the offensiveness to note that the arguments simply don't hold water. His followers, however, take his mannerisms as evidence of the truthfulness of his words, and accept his arguments without critical examination.

One could fill a book with examples of "Ruckmanite" language, but we will limit ourselves to a page or so before examining one sample of his argumentation. It is an axiom that we fight most against those who are closest to us, and this seems to be true for Dr. Ruckman as well. A graduate of Bob Jones University, Ruckman can find reason for denouncing BJU in the most amazing places. Dr. Stewart Custer of BJU finds a prominent place in Ruckman's list of targets, earning his own booklet in the process, *Custer's Last Stand*. A brief perusal of the book brings up the following quotations:

> In short, Stewart Custer's pitiful and disgraceful tract was written while turning tail and running from *all five issues* just as fast as his legs would carry him. But by far the most shameful and shocking thing about Stewart's work is not his *lying* (we would expect that) and his *stupidity* (we take that for granted, *but we will document it for the reader*); the most shocking thing was the performance of Robert Sumner *(Sword of the Lord)* and Bob Jones, Jr., (BJU) in actually seriously recommending the work as a "scholarly treatment of the Issues."[33]

> Is "the wording of the original Greek and Hebrew texts" the "last resort" in doctrinal matters (Custer, Introduction)? Are any of you deluded souls smart enough to know what a "RESORT" in that sense means? Did you look it up in a dictionary? No man on this earth, saved or lost, could go to ANY "original Greek and Hebrew texts" as a "court of last resort" because they are not there.[34] *Such a "court" doesn't even EXIST.* Custer knew it when he said it. He said it because the leaders of the Alexandrian Cult are going to USE that to prove that even though "we don't have the originals" we are "close to them"; therefore, we "Greek and Hebrew scholars" ARE THE FINAL AND LAST COURT OF RESORT IN DOCTRINE. Custer was just too yellow to carry you that far. We don't shrink from such issues; we face them head-on and deal with them *(in plain language!)*.[35]

Ruckman provides a citation of Custer, "The IMPORTANT THING to note is that each of these four types of texts is THEOLOGICALLY CONSERVATIVE." This happens to be a transparently true statement. Ruckman's response: "He expected you to accept that statement above without questioning it. We say he is a *deceived fool* and we will document *why* we say that."[36] He follows this on the next page with,

> On pages 7 and 8 of this pamphlet is the joke of the age. Here this poor, miserable little liar (see pages i, ii) tried to prove that the NASV was 'reliable' by comparing it with the AV and the NWT on SIX verses.

Later we read,

> Don't waste your time, kiddies. These half-baked upstarts just put out dogmatic fiats with the authority of a puffed-up toad full of buckshot, and they put them out without *one* source references, without *one verse* of scripture and with nothing to back them up but their own CONCEITED OPINIONS.[37]

In a fascinating chapter entitled "Treeing the Coon," we find,

> Who doesn't know *that* except Robert Sumner, Dayton Hobbs, A.T. Robertson, Cliff Robinson, John Broadus, J. Gresham Machen, Stewart Custer and the "vast majority of educated MEGALOMANIACS" who mistook earned *degrees* for *intelligence?*[38]

When Custer points out that Ruckman claims that the English readings are superior to the Greek readings, we find the following:

> Well, are they?
> If not, would you mind demonstrating why they are not?
> Surely Stewsie-woosie wouldn't accuse another Christian of *lying,* after the way he has been carrying on, without attempting to *prove* that the man was lying! If "Ruckman" said the above and it was *wrong,* then why didn't Stu baby list the chapter and verses in the Holy Bible that *prove* Ruckman was wrong?[39]

And to leave our quick review of this booklet we read,

> Well, not if you are so blind and perverted that you can't read a Bible in Braille, *you Bible-rejecting LIBERAL!!*[40]

Some might wonder if reviewing such material is worthwhile. Surely Ruckman's writing presents a side of KJV Onlyism that is less than appealing and uplifting, but it is important to recognize that it is also probably the most *pervasive* in the sense that his followers, picking up on his style, are *zealous* missionaries for the KJV Only cause. They will be found flooding computer bulletin boards with their arguments, writing letters to editors, and, sadly, causing problems for pastors and churches, all the while thinking they are "doing God's will" in defending the AV 1611. And, it is important to realize, the AV 1611 becomes the centerpiece of the entire Christian experience of these individuals. Ruckmanite churches will have "AV 1611" in their names, and the KJV will figure prominently in their preaching and teaching. Any disagreement with the KJV Only position is seen as an "attack" upon the "Word of God" by those who follow in Peter Ruckman's footsteps.

We will demonstrate that Ruckman's argumentation is circular at best, and often grossly flawed, by looking at his attack upon the NKJV. Again we find the same kind of emotionally laden invective used against those involved with the translation project that is the hallmark of Ruckmanism. As normal, Ruckman identifies the NKJV translators as being part of the infamous "Alexandrian Cult" (a term he uses to identify everyone who disagrees with him). We read,

> *The Alexandrian Creed* is the standard confession of every member of the Alexandrian Cult from Origen (250) to Farstad (1983). Not one member of the Cult can honestly deny a line of it, and no matter how subtly he tries to get around his adherence to it, the Creed is a true statement of what a real Cult member *believes.*
>
> *No honest man* could recommend the New "King James" Version (1982) to anyone.[41]

Ruckman later identifies the NKJV as an "ecumenical rat's nest" and goes on to say,

> It is true that the Holy Spirit can USE any version, and these apostate Fundamentalists will take anything they can use to make a fast buck; but they will have to promote sales to fake a "blessing." They are humanistic opportunists of the first order.

> Not one of them believes anything but the CREED. . . . They
> are HUMANISTIC RELATIVISTS for an apostate church
> (Laodicea), and their recommendations, criticisms, scholarship
> and advice may be rejected by any Bible believer without
> batting an eye (2 Cor. 2:17).[42]

How does Ruckman go about trying to prove such claims? We first
must remember the starting point of his thinking.

> Now the New "King James" Bible, *like every English
> translation since 1884,* had to compare itself with the original
> AV of 1611, for this is the STANDARD that God set up
> whereby to judge all translations. . . . No edition of the English
> Bible since 1880 . . . could sell unless it first compared itself
> with the absolute standard of truth set up by the Holy Spirit.[43]

As we said at the outset, the equation "the King James Alone = the
Word of God Alone" must be understood to grasp the kind of
argumentation presented in defense of this belief system. Of course,
the KJV has to be tested on the very same basis as any other
translation, just as its translators believed and stated in the Preface. It is
irrational to set it up as the standard by divine *fiat* and then judge
everything else by it, but this is *exactly* what Peter Ruckman does.

On pages 15-16 of his work, Dr. Ruckman provides five passages
of Scripture that he alleges prove his allegation that the NKJV "covers
up" sins in the Bible. He attempts to tie the NKJV to the "horrible"
RSV of the National Council of Churches (guilt by association) by
noting similarities in translation. All of this to arrive at his conclusion:

> Now, these verses were perverted because the New "King
> James" Version was aimed at a select type of clientele;
> certainly it was not aimed at anyone who READ the Bible and
> KNEW the Bible or BELIEVED the Bible. It was aimed
> pointedly and directly at a certain smooth, slick type of
> cultured intelligentsia who had *thick POCKETBOOKS.* To
> protect this bunch of apostate "Fundamentalists," the Falwell-
> Nelson-Hindson Dobson "Bible" altered 1 Timothy 6:10 . . . so
> that *the love of money* would NOT be the root of all evil.[44]

Does Dr. Ruckman provide solid, meaningful arguments to back up such strong language? Let's find out. Here is the first "sin" that is "covered up":

> 1. It is all right to *corrupt* the word of God as long as you don't "peddle" it. Observe how NO EDITION OF ANY KING JAMES BIBLE READS *with the Falwell-Nelson* in 2 Corinthians 2:17, "For we are not, as so many, peddling the word of God; but as of sincerity, but as from God, we speak in the sight of God in Christ" (NKJV).

When we look more closely, it appears that the NKJV simply translates the Greek text differently than the KJV, which has "corrupt the word of God." Is the NKJV (and NASB and NIV and RSV and NRSV) teaching that it is acceptable to corrupt the Word of God? The Greek term used here (there are no textual variants regarding the word) is *"kapeleuontes,"*[45] which literally refers to a peddler, a merchant, one who sells things, often with a negative connotation to the term. One source defines it, "to engage in retail business, with the implication of deceptiveness and greedy motives—to 'peddle for profit, to huckster.' "[46] Therefore we see that, in reality, the KJV rendering is inferior to all the modern translations, which more faithfully bring out what Paul is referring to. He is talking about those who seek to make a profit by preaching, and he contrasts this motivation with his own, that of "sincerity."

It is obvious, therefore, that the NKJV translators are not seeking to give anyone an excuse to "corrupt" the Word of God, but are instead doing just as the KJV translators before them: seeking to faithfully translate the Word of God into English. Surely if the KJV translators were alive today they would gladly admit that "peddle" is a better translation than "corrupt," and would adopt it themselves. The foolishness of the argument put forward can be seen simply by reversing it: is the KJV trying to say it is OK to peddle the Word of God, as long as you do not corrupt it? Of course not.

But it is just here that we have to realize that nothing we have said is slightly relevant to the KJV Only advocate who follows the thinking of Peter Ruckman. Remember, the KJV is the *standard.* What *"kapeleuontes"* meant to Paul or the original audience is *irrelevant.* Greek means nothing. Greek lexicons mean nothing. The verse says "corrupt" in the KJV, and hence it *must mean corrupt.* Period, end of discussion. God determined what it meant when He brought the AV 1611 into existence, and that's it. Facts are to be ignored; those who present the facts are to be insulted, belittled, and identified as "Alexandrians." The tight circularity of the position is almost painful to behold, but that is the situation when attempting to deal with the position held and espoused by Peter Ruckman. The same problem arises with the next allegation he provides:

> 2. It is proper to *hold* the word of God in unrighteousness as long as you aren't guilty of "suppressing" it. See the reading in Romans 1:18, "For the wrath of God is revealed from heaven against all ungodliness and unrighteousness of men, who suppress the truth in unrighteousness" (NKJV), where it matches the RSV of the NCCC.[47]

We again find nearly all modern versions using the term "suppress" here rather than the KJV's "hold." Why? The Greek term is *"katechonton,"* which means "to hold down, to suppress, to hold fast or firmly." Here the KJV rendering is better than it was in the previous example, though it is still found to be inferior to the modern versions. "To suppress" is a perfectly acceptable translation of the Greek term, and it vividly displays the action of sinful man in *suppressing* the truth of God (which every man has) in unrighteousness. The plain translation "hold" does not express this action very clearly at all.

So again we see the modern translations simply doing what translations are supposed to do: accurately render the Scriptures from Greek into English. The NKJV does read like the RSV at this point, and the reason is rather simple: both give the best translation of the Greek term that is possible! No conspiracies, no collusion, just good translation, just as the KJV translators would have wanted it. But again, this is all irrelevant to Dr. Ruckman. Romans 1:18 says "hold the truth" because the AV 1611 says so, Greek notwithstanding.

> 3. It is proper to *appear* to be doing evil as long as you don't actually DO evil. See the RSV reading of the NCCC in Falwell-Nelson's "Bible" in 1 Thessalonians 5:22, "Abstain from every form of evil" (NKJV), *which is not in line with any · line of Authorized Versions published by anyone in England or America in any century.*[48]

Here the difference is found between the NKJV's "Abstain from every form of evil" and the KJV's "Abstain from all appearance of evil." The word that is translated differently, *"eidos,"* can mean "form, outward appearance," but it also can mean "kind." The NKJV captures both possibilities with "form," while the KJV's rendering limits us to only one of the two possible meanings of the term.[49] Again the error of Dr. Ruckman's argument is plainly seen by simply reversing it: is the KJV trying to say it is OK to actually *do* evil as long as it does not *appear* that you are doing so? Of course not. The idea that there is some ulterior motive, some conspiracy involved in trying to twist and change the teaching of Scripture is a common element of KJV Only writing. Actually, of course, we are dealing with the various meanings and nuances of words in translation, seeking to do the best we can in communicating the same truths penned by (in this case) Paul so long ago.

> 4. It is all right to *change the truth of God* into a LIE as long as you don't "exchange" it for something. See in Romans 1:25, "Who exchanged the truth of god [*sic*] for the lie, and worshipped and served the creature rather than the Creator, who is blessed for ever. Amen" (NKJV), the RSV reading of the NCCC in Falwell's "Bible" which is no more an "edition" of the AV than Hansel and Gretel.[50]

Here we find another inferior rendering on the part of the KJV. The term translated "changed" in the KJV, "who changed the truth of God," is the word *"metallasso,"* which means to "exchange" one thing for something else.[51] Another source notes that in translating this term at Romans 1:25 "it is essential to avoid anything which might mean 'to change something into.' It is the substitution of one thing for another; hence, 'exchange' rather than 'change' is the correct gloss."[52] This makes perfect sense: men cannot "change" God's truth, as they do not *define* God's truth. God's truth remains inviolable no matter what man does. But man can *exchange* God's truth for "the lie," as Paul said, and engage in the perverted behavior that is the subject of this passage. Finally we examine the last cited passage,

> 5. It is all right to substitute financial gain for *godliness* or to accept financial income as a *proof* of godliness as long as you

don't think that godliness is a MEANS of gain. See in 1 Timothy 6:5, "Useless wranglings of men of corrupt minds and destitute of the truth, who suppose that godliness is a means of gain. From such withdraw yourself" (NKJV), the corrupt reading of the Falwell-Nelson which came from the Alexandrian text of 1910 (ASV).[53]

Anyone reading the KJV and NKJV at this point has a problem in following Dr. Ruckman's reasoning. The King James has "supposing that gain is godliness." The intention of the translation is clear: prideful men with corrupt minds who are destitute of the truth will cause problems in the church. These men think that godliness is a means of gain—they will *act the part* in order to *reap the benefits.* In this instance there is nothing wrong with the KJV rendering, but there is also nothing wrong with the NKJV rendering, either. The idea that bringing out the *instrumentality* of "godliness" to bring about "gain" in the NKJV is somehow meant to provide a cover for sin is simply unreasonable.

These kinds of arguments fill the pages of Peter Ruckman's books. He calls this "documentation" of errors in the modern versions, and since he has written a number of books, he and his followers truly believe that he has "documented" his position to the hilt. The problem is that Dr. Ruckman views his mere assertions as actual evidence, when such is surely not the case.

No review, no matter how brief, of Dr. Ruckman's position would be complete without a recounting of his "Creed of the Alexandrian Cult." His followers are quick to point to this "Creed" when accusing Christian leaders—ministers, scholars, or anyone else who opposes their position, of being members of the "Alexandrian Cult." I have often asked the followers of Peter Ruckman, "Where does this cult meet? What times are their meetings? I've never met an 'Alexandrian' before. What does one look like?" Of course from their perspective the entire Christian church in America and around the world is *filled* with Alexandrian cultists; nearly every seminary and Bible college has been taken over by these desperadoes. And what do "Alexandrians" believe? Let's look at the "Creed of the Alexandrian Cult" and see. Dr. Ruckman begins:

1. There is no final absolute authority but God.[54]

As it stands the statement is quite true, of course. God is the final authority in all things, and there is no authority above Him. The problem is that Ruckman will now begin to build a false edifice upon this statement, seemingly thinking that to believe that God is the final absolute authority means that God cannot *communicate* with final and absolute authority, which does not logically follow.

> 2. Since God is a Spirit, there is no final absolute authority that can be seen, heard, read, felt, or handled.

Untrue, of course. God is able to communicate His truth to man, both through creation (the law of God written upon the heart of man) and in special ways, that is, in Scripture and most fully in the person of the Lord Jesus Christ, God incarnate.

> 3. Since all books are material, there is no book on this earth that is the final and absolute authority on what is right and what is wrong; what constitutes truth and what constitutes error.

Another untrue statement. It is important to observe, however, that Ruckman is attempting to focus upon a *particular book* not in the sense of "the Scriptures," but in the sense of *one particular word-for-word book,* specifically, of course, a particular *rendering* of the Scriptures. Ruckman is driving toward asserting that unless one believes in inspired, inerrant *translations* of the Scriptures, one cannot have any kind of "absolute authority" at all. Note the logical error: any level of uncertainty regarding textual matters (i.e., textual variants) means that one has no final authority. Such does not logically follow. When launching a rocket, for example, the "final and absolute authority" is found in the laws of nature. If your rocket follows those laws, all will be well. If not, the rocket is in big trouble. You do not have to have an exhaustive, complete knowledge of *every aspect* of the laws of nature (no one has such an exhaustive knowledge) to launch a rocket. Surely the more you know the better your chances of getting your rocket into orbit, but you do not have to have 100% of all knowledge in the universe about gravity, electron flow, etc., to launch your rocket into orbit. In the same way, we can have an absolute and final authority in Scripture without having **THE** "one and only

English translation" delivered to us via angelic messenger. Despite all protests to the contrary, God's authority in Scripture is not in the least bit diminished by controversies about translating Scripture into English (or any other language).

> 4. There WAS a series of writings one time which, IF they had all been put into a BOOK as soon as they were written the first time, WOULD HAVE constituted an infallible and final authority by which to judge truth and error.

Here Ruckman refers to the autographs and asserts that "Alexandrians" could only have an "infallible and final authority" if they had the autographs themselves. Since, however, the autographs do not exist, and since there is a small amount of textual variation in the manuscript tradition, there can be no infallible and final authority. It can be seen, then, that if Ruckman is the least bit consistent it must follow that he views the AV 1611 (or at least the 1769 edition being used today) as being on the same authoritative level as the autographs themselves, and that is indeed the case. While other KJV advocates such as D.A. Waite deny the idea, it is obvious that the logical conclusion of Peter Ruckman's position is that there was a "re-inspiration" of the biblical text sometime between 1604 and 1611, giving the KJV the same status as "revelation" that was held by the autographs themselves.

> 5. However, this series of writings was lost and the God who inspired them was unable to preserve their content through Bible-believing Christians at Antioch (Syria) where the first Bible teachers were (Acts 13:1) and where the first missionary trip originated (Acts 16:1-6) and where the word CHRISTIAN originated (Acts 11:26).

Untrue yet once again. God was able to preserve their *content* (to use his own word) through Christians *everywhere* in the world, at Antioch as well as Alexandria, Jerusalem, Rome, etc. The *means* God used historically does not fit Dr. Ruckman's view of things and hence is dismissed in favor of the "inspired translation" theory.

> 6. So God chose to ALMOST [*sic*] preserve them through Gnostics and philosophers from Alexandria, Egypt, even

though God called His Son OUT of Egypt (Matt. 2), Jacob OUT of Egypt (Gen. 49), Israel OUT of Egypt (Exod. 15), and Joseph's bones OUT of Egypt (Exod. 13).

We note that Dr. Ruckman provides no evidence that "Gnostics" had anything to do with the production of manuscripts associated with Alexandria. This is a mere assertion without historical facts to back it up. It is also untrue that God "almost" preserved the Scriptures. He preserved them but in a way *different* than Dr. Ruckman would have liked.

> 7. So, there are two streams of Bibles: the most accurate— though, of course, there is no final, absolute authority for determining truth and error; it is a matter of "preference"—are the Egyptian translations from Alexandria, Egypt, that are "almost" the "originals" although not quite.

Having laid a false foundation, the rest of the house-of-mis-representation becomes easy to build. There are, in fact, *many* "streams" of Bibles, in the sense that we can even identify "streams" within the Byzantine text-type that Ruckman would trace to Antioch. The KJV's text is but one example of one "stream" within a larger river. And again it is untrue that there is no final, absolute authority for determining truth and error. Jesus said, "I am the way, the truth, and the life. No man comes to the Father but by me." It doesn't matter what translation you use, that truth remains true all the same. It is true for every man, woman, and child on the face of the earth, at all times in all places. It is an absolute, undeniable truth, and the idea that you *can't know* that it is absolutely true unless you buy into KJV Onlyism *should* cause any Christian person a *great deal* of concern.

> 8. The most inaccurate translations are those that brought about the German Reformation (Luther, Zwingli, Boehler, Zinzendorf, Spener, etc.) and the worldwide missionary movement of the English speaking people: the Bible that Sunday, Torrey, Moody, Finney, Spurgeon, Whitefield, Wesley, and Chapman used.

Here we have a thinly veiled attempt at what might be called the "argument from pragmatism." It goes like this: the KJV was used by God in great ways. Hence, it is the best translation (or, *only* translation). We have already seen that the claim that the TR was the "text of the Reformation" is less than honest when one examines Calvin's comments. It was the basic text used, but that by default, not particular choice. Luther used the *Vulgate* until he received Erasmus' text, and God used the Latin just as He used the Greek to lead the great Reformer away from the abuses of medieval Catholicism. Zwingli showed up for debates against Roman Catholic priests with three texts: the Greek, the Hebrew, and the Latin (not, we note with some sense of irony, the King James Version).[55] Most of the others cited were not particularly concerned about textual issues, and they used what was popularly available to the people. Spurgeon, in particular, is often misrepresented by KJV Only advocates,[56] though Dr. Ruckman admits he was willing to vary from the KJV at times.

> 9. But we can "tolerate" these if those who believe in them will tolerate US. After all, since there is NO ABSOLUTE AND FINAL AUTHORITY that anyone can read, teach, preach, or handle, the whole thing is a matter of "PREFERENCE." You may prefer what you prefer, and we will prefer what we prefer. Let us live in peace, and if we cannot agree on anything or everything, let us all agree on one thing: THERE IS NO FINAL, ABSOLUTE WRITTEN AUTHORITY OF GOD ANYWHERE ON THIS EARTH.
> This is the creed of the Alexandrian Cult.

The term "misrepresentation" seems, at times, simply too mild to describe this kind of writing. And when one remembers that this is directed toward servants of Christ who are working to proclaim His truth in churches and missionary works all over the land and even the world, one has trouble passing over Dr. Ruckman's invective in silence.

Endnotes

[1] We note especially the fine ongoing work of men such as Bob Ross, Doug Kutilek, and Gary Hudson.

[2] *The Revision Revised* by Dean John William Burgon (1883) pp. 107-

108. See also page 21 note 2, as well as page 392.

[3] Edward F. Hills, *The King James Version Defended* (The Christian Research Press, 1984) p. 224.

[4] Ibid., p. 225. We might note as well that Dr. Hills' argument is self-refuting. If we accept his constant use of the "providence of God," we cannot help but point out that if other NT manuscripts were destroyed by the flooding of the Nile, was this not as well under the guiding hand of the providence of God? Such arguments cut both directions.

[5] Modern scholars are associated with such individuals as Charles Manson (p. 91), the Mormon prophet Brigham Young (p. 344), Jehovah's Witnesses (p. 232), and New Agers (all through the book); they are called "cultists" (p. 345), Adoptionists (p. 345), and Arians (many places, including pp. 304-305). Their Christian commitment is not only denied but ridiculed. Even their *names* are used as jokes (p. 165).

[6] *New Age Bible Versions Refuted* (Alpha and Omega Ministries: 1994).

[7] Gail Riplinger, *New Age Bible Versions* (A.V. Publications: 1993), p. 454.

[8] As amazing as it might seem, some of Mrs. Riplinger's defenders have pointed to the difference between the italicized *"on thee"* and the actual rendering in both the KJV and NASB at the end of the verse, "in thee." It is obvious that there would be no difference between trusting *on* God and trusting *in* God.

[9] See *New Age Bible Versions Refuted* for further examples of this kind of misrepresentation.

[10] The reader will notice that Gail Riplinger refuses to capitalize the word "Bible." It consistently appears as "bible" throughout her book.

[11] Many of these errors are addressed in the chapters that follow, since they are common to the larger spectrum of KJV Only materials.

[12] As found in the January/February 1994 *The End Times and Victorious Living* newsletter.

[13] In the sense that Westcott and Hort correctly identified the need to examine the relationships of manuscripts, and demonstrated that it is simply not enough to *count* manuscripts, but instead we must *weigh* manuscripts (some manuscripts being more important than others as witnesses to the original text), one can say that modern texts are based upon their work. However, modern textual criticism has gone far beyond Westcott and Hort, and has in many instances corrected imbalances in their own conclusions.

[14] See for example D.A. Waite, *Heresies of Westcott & Hort* (The Bible for Today: 1979) and Grady's chapter, "Vessels of Dishonour" in his *Final Authority* (Grady Publications: 1993). As the KJV Only movement thrives most in conservative, independent Baptist circles, it is normally enough just to point out that Westcott and Hort were Anglicans, and hence "baby sprinklers" as one harsh KJV Only proponent puts it. Anglican piety, especially in the context of the times in which Westcott and Hort lived, provides all sorts of

ammunition for the demonstration that neither of these men was a fundamentalist Baptist, a point that Westcott and Hort would certainly have admitted. The fact that the KJV was translated by "baby-sprinkling" Anglicans does not seem to bother those who bring up Westcott and Hort, however.

[15] Gail Riplinger, *New Age Bible Versions* (A.V. Publications: 1993), p. 555.

[16] See especially pages 230 through 233, where Palmer's Reformed beliefs are not only misrepresented but mercilessly ridiculed. For example, note the use of such phrases as "His scandalous and sacrilegious statement will stun and shock the reader" (referring to the Reformed belief that regeneration precedes faith), "His 'Five Points' form a Satanic pentagram," "Sounding like one of the Jehovah Witness [*sic*] 144,000 . . . ," "Palmer and his cronies" and "Palmer's elite 'Elect.' "

[17] Ibid., p. 305.

[18] Kenneth Barker, editor, *The NIV: The Making of a Contemporary Translation* (International Bible Society: 1991), p. 143.

[19] I asked her specifically in our debate if, in fact, she had read Dr. Palmer's book, and she replied, "Of course."

[20] Ibid., p. 344.

[21] Edwin Palmer, *The Person and Ministry of the Holy Spirit* (Baker Book House: 1958, 1974), p. 15.

[22] Ibid., p. 65, emphasis added.

[23] *New Age Bible Versions*, p. 261.

[24] Calvin Linton, "The Importance of Literary Style" in *The NIV: The Making of a Contemporary Translation,* Kenneth Barker, Editor (Zondervan: 1986), pp.17-19.

[25] The letter was published by *Baptist Biblical Heritage*, P.O. Box 66, Pasadena, TX 77501-0066.

[26] Gail Riplinger, *Which Bible Is God's Word?* (Hearthstone Publishing: 1994).

[27] The tape of the radio debate between me and Mrs. Riplinger plainly shows that she *was* speaking of the Incarnation and asserting that Palmer denied the role of the Holy Spirit in it.

[28] The actual quotation is found on page 372 of *Teachings of the Prophet Joseph Smith,* and it reads, "The heads of the Gods appointed one God for us."

[29] Riplinger's specific claim in *New Age Bible Versions* was:

> All new versions, based on a tiny percentage of corrupt Greek manuscripts, make the fatefully frightening addition of three words in Revelation 14:1. [Citation of NIV version follows]. Will the unwary, reading Revelation 14:1 in a recent version, be persuaded that the bible sanctions and encourages the taking of "his name" on their forehead *before* they receive the Father's name?
> —*New Age Bible Versions* (A.V. Publications: 1993), pp. 99-100.

[30] Gail Riplinger, *Which Bible Is God's Word?* p. 62.

[31] Ibid., p. 63.

[32] Peter S. Ruckman, *The Christian's Handbook of Manuscript Evidence* (Pensacola Bible Press: 1990), p. 126.

[33] Peter S. Ruckman, *Custer's Last Stand* (Bible Baptist Bookstore: 1981), p. iii.

[34] This is the true mark of Ruckmanism: the denial, through the use of equivocation, of the existence of the original *readings* of the New Testament text. Ruckman continuously attacks the use of the word "original" (note the KJV translators' use of the term in their own Preface!), at times using it to mean "autographs," the original writings of the apostles themselves, and at other times using it to refer to the original *readings* that were found in those autographs. We do not have the autographs. In that sense there is no "original" any longer. The whole point of the tenacity of the New Testament text, however, is that the *original readings* still exist, faithfully preserved in the New Testament manuscript tradition. By denying the existence of the "originals," Ruckman reduces his reader to a need for a supernatural way to know what the "originals" read. This ignores, of course, the fact that God has preserved the *readings* of the autographs in the manuscript tradition down through the ages. This is why it can quite properly be said that Ruckmanism engages in a more radical and destructive form of textual criticism than even the "liberals" they decry, for they deny that the original *readings* have been faithfully preserved, requiring instead the supernatural inspiration of the AV 1611 so as to have *certainty* on those readings. Note the startling words of Peter Ruckman in his attack upon the NKJV:

> It is this maniacal obsession that makes men like Massey, at Rodney Bell's school, insist that he can find out the EXACT WORD that God gave Paul when Paul wrote his manuscripts; and it is this same egotism that makes patsies like Stewart Custer (Bob Jones University) tell us that he reads the "verbally inspired original" New Testament daily because he "holds it" in his hand (p. 14).

The meaning of these words should not be missed. Ruckman is ridiculing the idea that we can determine what words Paul wrote originally, and that solely on the basis that with a *small percentage* of those words we have textual variation, ignoring the entire fact of the purity of the New Testament text, and the fact that in the *vast majority* of the writings of Paul (or any other writer of Scripture) we *can* determine *exactly* what was originally written *because there are no textual variants to hinder us from doing so!* One example of this: at Colossians 2:9 Paul wrote that all the fulness of "deity" dwells in Jesus Christ in bodily form. The term "deity" is the Greek term θεότητος, the translation of which is discussed in chapter 8, pp. 203-204. There are no textual variants regarding this passage. We can be *certain* that when Paul wrote to the Colossians he used this very term. How Ruckman could deny this is beyond imagination.

[35] Ibid., p. 4. Since, of course, the AV 1611 was translated on the very same principles of textual critical study that Ruckman decries in modern translations, the argument is obviously circular.

[36] Ibid., p. 9.

[37] Ibid., p. 16.

[38] Ibid., p. 28.

[39] Ibid., p. 40. The position espoused by Ruckman is so utterly unfounded that it often leaves the Christian person befuddled as to how to respond to it (many would simply say you shouldn't bother responding to such thinking at all). Yet it is important to point out that asking someone to cite *Bible verses* about an issue of *translation* is tremendously silly. The issue is one of language and time. English did not exist when the Bible was written. The time difference between the first parts of the Old Testament and the KJV translation is a good 3,000 years; between the end of the New Testament and the KJV is about 1,500 years. It is simply irrational to believe that a translation into a language that did not even exist in the days of Moses or Isaiah or the Lord Jesus should *define* the original *readings* and *meanings* of documents written half a world away in a completely different language. It would be like someone translating the Declaration of Independence into a strange dialect found amongst tribes in the South Pacific and then asserting that the form and meaning of the Declaration should be determined on the basis of *that* language rather than English.

[40] Ibid., p. 52. In his attack upon the NKJV, Ruckman says of Custer that he "has about as much integrity and spiritual insight as you could put in the left eye of a blind mosquito." *About the "New" King James Bible* (Bible Baptist Bookstore, 1983), p. 2.

[41] Ibid., p. 4.

[42] Ibid., pp. 10-11.

[43] Ibid., p. 13.

[44] Ibid., p. 16. See our discussion of 1 Timothy 6:10 in chapter 6, pp. 139-140.

[45] καπηλεύοντες in the Greek in which Paul wrote; we are again without doubt that this term *is* what Paul wrote long ago.

[46] Johannes P. Louw and Eugene A. Nida, *Greek-English Lexicon of the New Testament Based on Semantic Domains* (United Bible Societies: 1988), 1:580.

[47] Ruckman, *About the "New" King James Bible*, p. 15.

[48] Ibid., p. 15.

[49] The KJV itself uses many different English words to translate the one Greek term εἶδος, including "sight" (2 Corinthians 5:7), "fashion" (Luke 9:29), and "shape" (John 5:37).

[50] Ibid., pp. 15-16.

[51] See Bauer, Arndt, Gingrich, and Danker, *A Greek-English Lexicon of the New Testament and Other Early Christian Literature*, 2nd ed. (The

University of Chicago Press: 1979), p. 511, and Fritz Rienecker and Cleon Rogers, *Linguistic Key to the Greek New Testament*, (Zondervan: 1982) p. 350. The *meaning* of the term is ignored by KJV Only writers who seek to attack the more accurate translation of the term. William Grady joins in Ruckman's attack on the NKJV's translation in his book, *Final Authority:*

> Suddenly, a profit-oriented corporation (the same crowd who manufactured the *enemies'* swords) would prevail upon the church to believe that the Holy Spirit had abruptly ordered a *weapon change—in the very heat of the battle!* Their corrupt rendering of Romans 1:25 says it best. Instead of the KJV's *"changed"* we read, "who **exchanged** the truth of God for a lie." A true Bible believer will never exchange his KJV for a NKJV. The reason for this resistance is the same today as it was in Bible days. . . . A person with an ounce of spiritual discernment can see that he who *"is not the author of confusion"* would *never* pick such timing to introduce yet another English revision! (p. 303).

[52] Louw and Nida, *Greek-English Lexicon of the New Testament Based on Semantic Domains*, p. 574.

[53] Ruckman, *About the "New" King James Bible,* p. 16.

[54] Each of the "Creed's" statements is taken from *About the "New" King James Bible*, pp. 38-39.

[55] Of course I am aware that Zwingli died before the KJV was translated; my point is two-fold. First, to point out that Zwingli utilized the original languages in a way that Ruckman would (if consistent) have to attack; secondly, to point out that Dr. Ruckman actually makes statements like the one I made above, statements involving pure anachronism. My favorite is found in his anti-Calvinistic booklet entitled *Hyper-Calvinism* (Bible Baptist Bookstore, 1984), p. 11, where we read with reference to John Calvin, "This led to a very embarrassing question asked of him by Jacob Arminius." John Calvin died May 27, 1564; Arminius was born in 1560. How a three- or four-year-old child could be asking Calvin "embarrassing questions" is difficult to figure out. Dr. Ruckman's materials are marked by this kind of "looseness" when presenting facts.

[56] See Doug Kutilek's *An Answer to David Otis Fuller: Fuller's Deceptive Treatment of Spurgeon Regarding the King James Version* (Pilgrim Publications).

Translational Differences | 6 |

"They've changed my Bible!" So we hear when someone encounters a difference in translation between their "old favorite" and a new translation. Like a pair of old slippers, we become accustomed to hearing our favorite verses in one manner, in one form, and we are generally uncomfortable with "change."

Over and over again KJV Only advocates accuse the new translations of "changing" this or "altering" that. They say that the NIV "deletes" this or "adds" that. It is vitally important to make sure that we see through this kind of argumentation before we begin the work of examining many specific differences between the KJV and modern translations. We wish to think clearly and honestly about this topic, and to do that, we must point out the most fundamental error of the KJV Only position.

A circular argument is one that starts with its conclusion; that is, you assume the point you are arguing for right from the start, and then "prove" it by using it as your basis. If I assume, right at the start of an argument with a nutritionist, that it is a true statement that "chocolate brownies are highly nutritious and good for you," it will be easy for me to prove that point, since I've started with that statement as the basis of my argument. As long as I start with that as a given fact, no amount of argumentation will persuade me otherwise, for I have assumed what I have yet to prove. My poor nutritionist friend can show me all the facts and data in the world, but as long as I've already accepted as an axiom "chocolate brownies are highly nutritious and good for you," I cannot step back and examine that statement and come to any other kind of conclusion. I am arguing in a circle, and circular arguments are, by nature, irrational.

KJV Only books, articles, and tracts share a common feature: *circular argumentation*. What is the bottom-line assumption of the writer? That the KJV is the only true English Bible (maybe the only true Bible in any language![1]), the standard by which all others are to be judged. This can be seen easily by looking at the terminology that is used. "See how the NIV *deletes* this passage. . . ." "Note how they have *changed* God's Word here to say. . . ." "Here they have *altered* the text to say. . . ." In each case the KJV Only advocate is using circular argumentation. How? The assumed standard is the KJV. Why is the KJV the standard? Why not the Geneva Bible, or the Bishop's Bible, or the Great Bible? Could we not choose any one of these earlier English translations and then make up page after page of comparisons showing how the KJV "altered" this or "changed" that? Certainly we could. As long as we allow the defender of the AV to determine the grounds of the argument by *assuming* the KJV to be the standard of all others, we will get absolutely nowhere.

The KJV must stand up to the exact same standards as any other translation. It cannot be made the standard by which all others are judged; it must take its place as one translation among many, so that it can be tested just as the NIV or NASB or RSV. In some places it may well excel; in others it may lag behind. But we must be careful to avoid making the basic error of setting up one translation as the standard over all others. Our standard must always be found in the question, "What did the original author of Scripture say at this point?" We must be concerned to know the words of Moses and David and Isaiah and Matthew and Paul first; the words of the translators in 1611 may be important, but they *cannot* take precedence over the words that were the direct result of divine inspiration.

With this in mind, we come to the examination of the differences that exist between the KJV and other English translations. The examination will be divided into three parts. The first part will examine differences that are *translational* in nature; that is, those differences that arise from the translation of the *same Greek or Hebrew text* by different English terms. The second section (chapter 7) will deal with *textual* differences, those that arise from differences in the underlying Greek or Hebrew texts that were used to translate the various versions of the English Bible. And finally, the third section (chapter 8) will examine those differences that relate to the crucial doctrine of the deity of Christ. It is not possible to examine every difference that exists between the KJV and every modern translation. It is my intention to examine the most commonly cited passages and to provide representative samples that should allow the reader to apply the general principles that will be discovered to any particular translational difference he or she might encounter.

A ROSE BY ANY OTHER NAME . . .

It has already been noted that there is often more than one correct way to translate certain Greek and Hebrew words and phrases into English. But when KJV Only believers set the KJV up as the *only* correct translation, they view any other translation, even if it is perfectly valid and proper given the Greek and Hebrew constructions, as a "change" (to use the nicer term), or a "perversion" (to use the more common term). In the vast majority of instances, the differences are not vital to an understanding of the passage. Often the KJV translation gives a more "literal" rendering, while the modern translation may throw much needed light upon what the author was attempting to convey. Most of the time the differences in translation can be a great *help* to the person who is seeking a fuller understanding of the original text. For example, note the translations of Acts 20:28:

KJV	NIV
Take heed therefore unto yourselves, and to all the flock, over the which the Holy Ghost hath made you overseers, **to feed** the church of God, which he hath purchased with his own blood.	Keep watch over yourselves and all the flock of which the Holy Spirit has made you overseers. **Be shepherds** of the church of God, which he bought with his own blood.

In this case the KJV translates the word that literally means "to shepherd" as "to feed," which, while acceptable, breaks up the connection between "flock" and "shepherd" in Paul's thought. At the same time, the KJV maintains the longer sentence structure of the passage, while the NIV simplifies it by breaking it into two sentences, which might cause a person to miss the fact that in Paul's speech to the Ephesian elders, shepherding God's flock was the purpose for which the elders had been appointed to their office. Neither translation is "wrong," they are simply *different* in certain aspects. By comparison of the two one has a better idea of what Paul said than would a person relying solely on one translation or the other.

Most of the time, differences in translation follow this pattern. There is certainly no malevolent intent on the part of the KJV translators in choosing the term "feed" over "shepherd," nor any evil intent on the part of the NIV translators in breaking the Greek sentence up into two parts. We simply have two different translations of the same passage, both of which provide us with a good idea of what Paul said to the Ephesian elders. Those who are intent upon *finding* problems with the modern translations may well come up with some reason for finding fault with everything that differs from the AV, but such an activity is based not upon the truth of the matter but upon an inordinate devotion to a particular translation.

The same can be seen in comparing the KJV and NASB at Ephesians 4:24:

KJV	NASB
And that ye put on the **new man**, which after God is created in righteousness and true holiness.	and put on the **new self**, which in *the likeness of* God has been created in righteousness and holiness of the truth.

One can see a number of differences in the two translations, yet the simple fact of the matter is that *both* are perfectly acceptable translations of the very same Greek text. The KJV is more literal in having "new man" rather than "new self," and in having "after God" rather than "in *the likeness of* God," but the NASB is closer with "has been created" rather than "is created." Both "in righteousness and true holiness" and "in righteousness and holiness of the truth" are perfectly proper possibilities as well.

These examples teach us to look closely at alleged "changes" as well as proposed reasons for these "changes." Most of the time there is a perfectly logical, rational reason drawn from the Greek or Hebrew text for any particular translation, whether in the KJV or modern translations. Very rarely is the reason to be found in conspiratorial theories or attempts to alter God's truth in Scripture.

A DIFFERENT GOSPEL?

One of the arguments used by KJV Only advocates is that the

new translations present a "different gospel" than the KJV. Allegations of conspiracies on the part of the "new translations" (as if there was one malevolent force behind *all* new translations) abound with reference to any passage that could possibly be construed as presenting a "false gospel." An excellent example of this desperate search for conspiracies on the part of the new translations is provided by Gail Riplinger in her book, *New Age Bible Versions*. Here is a chart that is found on page 256 of her work[2]:

NEW VERSIONS		KJV
persevere [work]	Rom. 5:4 2 Cor. 12:12, 6:4	patience [wait]
endurance endurance	Heb. 10:36 2 Cor. 6:4	patience patience
steadfast [don't mess up]	Col. 1:23	settled [resting]
if we endure [if we made it]	2 Tim. 2:12	suffer [if we suffer]
to remain true [don't mess up]	Acts 11:23	cleave unto [rely on him]
are protected by the power of God [Is God a body guard?]	1 Peter 1:5	are kept [God keeps you]
confidence of our hope [I 'hope' I make it!]	Heb. 10:23	profession of our faith

This chart is presented as part of an entire section that alleges that the new versions are presenting a "works-salvation" system. And yet I have written entire books defending salvation by grace through faith that utilized translations other than the KJV, as have many others. How can this be? Men who strongly believe in salvation by grace alone have been involved in the translation of many of the modern versions. How could they be convinced (and by whom?) to sacrifice their beliefs by allegedly mistranslating the text? Isn't there another way of understanding the differences in the translations given above? Most certainly.

In each and every case cited by Gail Riplinger, there is simply no reason at all to think that the modern translations are even hinting at her suggested comments, let alone trying to teach works-salvation. For example, the first citation given is Romans 5:4, where the KJV has "And patience, experience," while the NIV has "perseverance, character," comparing "patience" versus "perseverance." But, the word that is found in the Greek text means "patient endurance, steadfastness, perseverance." Are we to think that God does not engender perseverence and steadfastness in the Christian character? Surely not. The NIV translation is just as acceptable, if not more so, than the KJV's.

Some of the citations given above demonstrate inconsistencies in the KJV's translation of terms. Second Timothy 2:12 is cited where the KJV has "If we suffer, we shall also reign with *him,*" while the NIV has "if we endure, we will also reign with him." The term "endure" in the modern translations is contrasted with "suffer" in the KJV, and the assertion is that this somehow presents a "works-salvation" concept. Yet, the Greek term that is found here is not the term that is translated "suffer" in most places in the New Testament, but is instead a term that *even the KJV itself* translates as "endure" in other contexts! At 1 Corinthians 13:7 we are told that love "Beareth all things, believeth all things, hopeth all things, *endureth* all things." The KJV translates the very same term that is found at 2 Timothy 2:12 as "endureth" here in 1 Corinthians. If our writer is consistent, doesn't this then teach a "works-salvation" system as well? And when we examine another of the passages cited, Hebrews 10:23, we discover that the modern translations are *much* more accurate than the rather free, and misleading, translation of the KJV at this point.

The same is to be said of the other passages that are cited. In each instance the modern translations are seen to be at least as accurate and acceptable, if not more so, than the KJV. But these are not the only passages cited in the attempt to substantiate this charge. Note the following chart:

NASB	απειθω	KJV
not obey	John 3:36	believeth not
disobedience	Romans 11:32	unbelief
disbobedient	Romans 15:31	do not believe
disobedient	Hebrews 3:18	believed not
disobedience	Hebrews 4:6	unbelief
disobedience	Hebrews 4:11	unbelief

KJV Only advocates often allege that the use of terms related to obedience by the NASB in translating the particular Greek term that is translated "believe" many times in the KJV, John 3:36 being the prime example, is indicative of a tendency toward "works-salvation" on the part of the modern translations. Yet, again, a small amount of reflection demonstrates why this is untrue. First, the KJV itself translates the very same term using "obey" in other places! See 1 Peter 3:1; 4:17; and Romans 2:8. Secondly the translation "disobey" is the *primary* meaning of the term. The idea of "disbelief" is *secondary* and by *extension*. It is not the directly *literal* translation. This is not to say that the KJV is mistranslating the term, but that it is not giving the most literal translation at a number of places. And finally, there is no conflict between obedience to Christ and belief in Christ. True faith is obedient to Christ, and there is no such thing as a "disobedient faith." Just because there are those who might *misuse* the term "obey" so as to promote a works-salvation viewpoint does not in any way change the meaning of the term itself. Men will misuse God's truth no matter what words are used to express it. Men have used the KJV to promote the very same error for centuries. The KJV is the favorite version of a number of groups that promote works-salvation.[3] Should we blame the KJV translators for the misuse of their work? Hardly.

Another aspect of the Gospel that is brought into the debate is the issue of the ongoing nature of God's act of saving men. The Bible is plain in presenting the "now and the not yet" aspect of salvation. We *are* saved, and yet we are *being* saved, and we *will be* saved as well. Passages are to be found in any translation that will present these various aspects of God's work in the Christian's life. Defenders of the AV, however, find the literal translation of some of these passages offensive, because they feel the new versions are questioning the certainty of salvation itself. In fact, some use your position on these passages as a "test," so to speak, of your orthodoxy. Yet, this is a case in which the modern translations are more literal, and more correct, than the KJV. Note the following passages.

	NASB	Greek	KJV
Acts 2:47	those who were being saved.	Present Participle	such as should be saved.

	NASB	**Greek**	**KJV**
1 Cor. 1:18	those who are perishing . . . us who are being saved	Present Participles	them that perish foolishness . . .us which are saved
2 Cor. 2:15	those who are being saved . . . those who are perishing	Present Participles	them that are saved . . . them that perish
2 Cor. 4:3	those who are perishing	Present Participle	them that are lost
Eph. 4:22	which is being corrupted	Present Participle	which is corrupt

In each of these passages the NASB translates the present participle in such a way as to communicate the present character of the word to the reader. In all three passages from Paul's letters to the Corinthians we are given a plain indication of the fact that he intends us to see and understand this ongoing nature of the words, for it is obvious that those "who are perishing" are in the process of doing so and have not, as yet, completed that process. They have not yet "perished," but are on the road that will take them to that destination unless they are saved by God's mercy and grace. Paul obviously parallels "those who are being saved" with "those who are perishing" in both 1 Corinthians 1:18 and 2 Corinthians 2:15. If the process of perishing is ongoing, so is the process of being saved in the same contexts. The KJV rendering of these passages, while technically allowable, does not do a very good job in expressing the intention of the author at these places. And as far as the theological element of the KJV Only argument at this point, we must be continually reminded that our theology must be derived *from* the text of Scripture, not forced *onto* it. If Paul said we are "being saved" in 1 Corinthians 1:18, he also said that we "have been saved" at Ephesians 2:5, and that we "shall be saved" in Romans 5:9-10. If our theology can't handle each of these passages, the problem lies in our *theology*, not in the the text of Scripture! We dare not allow our theology to determine our translation, which, sadly, is what we have in many KJV Only presentations.

Finally with reference to the Gospel itself, we note the allegation of one KJV Only advocate[4] that illustrates how we must look closely at the material that is presented to us to see if it is well researched and sensible. Note this section of a chart presented as evidence that the new versions "present a progressive, tentative salvation."

NIV or NASB et al.		KJV
And you were dead in your trespasses and sins	Eph. 2:1	and you hath he quickened, who were dead in trespasses and sins

At first glance it *seems* as if the modern versions are missing something, that being the wonderful truth that God has "quickened" or made alive believers in Jesus Christ. Yet, is this the case? Not at all. Instead, the KJV *translation* is rather unusual, since it borrows a phrase that is not found until verse 5 in the Greek and transposes it into verse 1. All the modern translations have the relevant phrase in its proper place in verse 5. Nothing has been "left out," and certainly the unwillingness of modern versions to engage in the same creative translation as the KJV indicates nothing about their alleged lack of orthodoxy.

AGE OR WORLD?

The KJV will often use one English word to translate two different Greek terms that may not be referring to the same thing. A good example of this is found in the KJV's use of the term "world." Two Greek terms[5] are translated by the same word "world" in the KJV, even though the two terms do not always refer to the same thing. The term that often gives rise to allegations of heresy on the part of KJV Only advocates is the Greek term *aion,* which the AV consistently translates as "world." Note a comparison of the NASB and KJV:

NASB	*aion*	KJV
age	Matthew 12:32	world
age	Matthew 28:20	world
age	Mark 10:30	world
age	Luke 18:30	world
age	Luke 20:35	world
age	Galatians 1:4	world
age	Ephesians 1:21	world
age	Titus 2:12	world

Those who look for "New Age conspiracies" get a lot of mileage out of the use of "age" in the modern translations, seemingly ignoring the fact that the *misuse* of a term by a false religious group does not in any way mean that the *proper* use of the term should be avoided. What is more, the most basic, literal translation of the term *aion* from the Greek in these contexts is "age." The most common use of the term is in the phrase that is translated "for ever and ever," where it refers to eternity itself. But its other use is to refer to a specific *age,* a specific period of time. Note the Lord's use of the term at Matthew 12:32:

> Anyone who speaks a word against the Son of Man, it will be forgiven him; but whoever speaks against the Holy Spirit, it will not be forgiven him, either in this age or in the *age* to come. (NKJV)

"This age" is differentiated from "the age to come," that is, the eternal state. The Lord said elsewhere,

> So it will be at the end of the age; the angels shall come forth, and take out the wicked from among the righteous (Matthew 13:49, NASB).

This age ends at the coming of Christ, as Matthew 24:3 indicates,

> And as He was sitting on the Mount of Olives, the disciples came to Him privately, saying, "Tell us, when will these things be, and what *will be* the sign of Your coming, and of the end of the age?" (NASB)

It is the Lord's promise that He will be with His people throughout this present age (Matthew 28:20), which Paul describes as this "present evil age" (Galatians 1:4). In these passages, then, "age" refers to a definite period of time, one in which we now live (this present evil age), and one which is yet future. The KJV's use of "world" is certainly less clear than the modern "age," for it allows for confusion between the intended meanings of the authors of Scripture. One must consult lexicons and concordances to discover if the text is speaking of the world around us (the other Greek term, *kosmos*) or the present evil age (*aion*). This ambiguity is cleared up in modern translations.

HELL OR HADES?

One of the most obvious differences in translation focuses upon the use of the word "hell" in the KJV. Unfortunately, cultic groups such as Jehovah's Witnesses have made great use of the KJV's ambiguous rendering of words that have to do with the afterlife, both in the New Testament and the Old. Surely any person examining the facts without a vested interest in defending the KJV has to admit that this is one place in which many modern translations far surpass the KJV in accuracy.

The word "hell" appears 54 times in the text of the King James Bible, 31 times in the Old Testament, and 23 times in the New. In each of the Old Testament passages the KJV is translating the Hebrew term *sheol* as "hell." In the New Testament the KJV translates two main terms, *hades* and *gehenna,* by the one word "hell." The term *gehenna* is translated as "hell" twelve times, and the term *hades* ten times.[6] The word *sheol* in the Hebrew is best translated by the Greek term *hades*. Both terms refer to the "realm of the dead," which at times can refer simply to the grave, or at times to the world of shadows as seen in Isaiah 14:9-15 in the Old Testament, or more clearly to the place of departed spirits in Luke 16:19-31. KJV Only advocates will often attack the use of the term "grave" by modern translations, yet the KJV translators themselves recognized that the Hebrew term *sheol* did not always refer to "hell," for they often translated it by other terms. Note Genesis 37:35 in the KJV:

> And all his sons and all his daughters rose up to comfort him; but he refused to be comforted; and he said, For I will go down **into the grave** unto my son mourning. Thus his father wept for him.

The phrase "into the grave" is the KJV's rendering of "into *sheol*." The problem that arises from the inconsistency of the KJV can be seen in the fact that *sheol* and *hades* are not synonyms for the Greek term *gehenna,* which really *does* mean "hell" in the traditional sense. This is rather obviously seen in Revelation 20:13-14 where death and *hades* are cast into the lake of fire. What is the lake of fire if it is not hell itself? And how does one cast hell into hell? Instead, in this example we have *hades*, the realm of the dead, being differentiated from the lake of fire by the biblical text itself.

As we noted earlier, groups that deny the existence of hell have utilized the KJV's rendering of passages that obviously are referring to the grave, not the lake of fire, as "hell" to obscure the Scripture's testimony to the reality of everlasting punishment.[7] While the KJV's translation of these terms is certainly unfortunate, should we cast blame upon them and accuse them of all sorts of evil and heresy for their actions? Certainly not. Yet, again we have to point out that much of the argumentation presented by KJV Only advocates, if it were consistently applied, would force them to do just that!

JEROME AND LUCIFER

How deeply we are influenced by our traditions can be seen in Isaiah 14:12:

KJV	NASB	NIV
How art thou fallen from heaven, **O Lucifer**, son of the morning! *how* art thou cut down to the ground, which didst weaken the nations!	How you have fallen from heaven, **O star of the morning**, son of the dawn! You have been cut down to the earth, You who have weakened the nations!	How you have fallen from heaven, **O morning star**, son of the dawn! You have been cast down to the earth, you who once laid low the nations!

The term "Lucifer," which came into the biblical tradition through the translation of Jerome's *Vulgate,* has become so entrenched (even though it does not come from the original authors of Scripture) that if one dares to translate the Hebrew by another term, such as "star of the morning" or "morning star" (both of which are perfectly acceptable translations of the Hebrew word[8]), one will be accused of "removing Lucifer" from the Bible! Such a "change" surely "preaches" well, and this example is often used as the "capper" to prove the true intention of the "devilish modern versions." Yet, a person who stops for a moment of calm reflection might ask, "Why should I believe Jerome was inspired to insert this term at this point? Do I have a good reason for believing this?" Given that Jerome's translation is certainly not inerrant itself, one would do well to take a second look and discover that the very translations being accused of "hiding Lucifer's name" refer to Satan, the accuser, the "old serpent," the devil, each and every time the terms appear in Scripture. Again, the inconsistency of the argument is striking.

"But," someone is sure to retort, "isn't Jesus the 'morning star' at Revelation 22:16?" Yes, He certainly is. "So doesn't translating Isaiah 14:12 with 'morning star' identify Jesus with Lucifer? Aren't the modern translations trying to connect Jesus with the devil?"[9] Only if one does not read things in context very well. The person under discussion in Isaiah 14 is obviously not the Lord Jesus Christ, and how anyone could possibly confuse the person[10] who is obviously under the wrath of God in that passage (note verse 15) with the Lord Jesus is hard to imagine. Further, aren't the terms being used in Isaiah 14 sarcastic in nature? Didn't this person claim lofty titles that were proven to be misapplied? Doesn't the Scripture speak of his "pomp" (v. 11) and his inward boasting (v. 13)? Should we not recognize that the terms that are applied to him in verse 12 are meant to be taunts rather than actual descriptions of his person? And doesn't this differ dramatically from the personal description that Jesus applies to *himself* in Revelation 22? All of these considerations make it obvious that there is no logical reason to take offense at the proper translation of Isaiah 14:12 in the NIV or NASB.

THE ROOT OR A ROOT?

Another favorite passage of KJV Only adherents is found in Paul's first letter to Timothy:

1 Timothy 6:10		
KJV	**NASB**	**NIV**
For the love of money is **the root** of **all evil**: which while some coveted after, they have erred from the faith, and pierced themselves through with many sorrows.	For the love of money is **a root** of **all sorts of evil**, and some by longing for it have wandered away from the faith, and pierced themselves with many a pang.	For the love of money is **a root** of **all kinds of evil**. Some people, eager for money, have wandered from the faith and pierced themselves with many griefs.

Two issues are readily seen by comparing these translations. First, is the love of money *the* root of evil, or *a* root of evil? Secondly, is it a root of *all* evil, or of *all kinds* of evil? Once again we encounter a situation in which something can be said for each translation. The word for "root" in the Greek does not have the article before it, hence the more literal translation in this case would be "a root," not the definite *the* root. The text is not saying that the love of money is the *only* origin or source of evil, but that it is *one* of great importance. And is it *all evil*, or *all kinds of evil*? Literally the Greek reads, "of all the evils," the terms being plural. The modern translations see this as referring to all *kinds* of evil, while the KJV takes all evil as a whole concept. The KJV translation is a possibility grammatically speaking, but it seems to miss Paul's point. The love of money gives rise to all *sorts* of evil things, but there are, obviously, evils in the world that have nothing to do with the love of money. A minister friend of mine pointed out with reference to this passage that it is difficult to see how rape, for example, can be blamed on "the love of money." Such is surely a good question for a person who would insist upon the KJV rendering.[11] In any case, the modern translations are certainly faithful to the text of Scripture and adequate in their translation of the passage.

STUDY OR BE DILIGENT?

Those of us who grew up in Christian homes early learned Paul's exhortation to Timothy found at 2 Timothy 2:15:

KJV	NASB
Study to show thyself approved unto God, a workman that needeth not to be ashamed, rightly dividing the word of truth.	**Be diligent** to present yourself approved to God as a workman who does not need to be ashamed, handling accurately the word of truth.

Are we to "study to show thyself approved" or "be diligent" to do so? The term under consideration is a part of a family of related terms that first and foremost refer to haste and speed, therefore by extension to eagerness, earnestness, and zeal, and finally to taking pains and making every effort to accomplish something. Therefore, the NASB's "be diligent" is right on the mark. The NIV's "do your best" seems to miss some of the force of the term, and the KJV's "study" limits the meaning of the word far too much for the modern reader who might not understand "study" to refer to a concerted effort at diligence and effort. Paul is exhorting Timothy to have an attitude that is marked by zeal, enthusiasm, and determination in his ministry. This attitude may well include the aspect of study, but in no way is Paul's admonishment to be limited solely to that activity.

QUICK AND POWERFUL

One passage that illustrates the evolution of language over time in a better way than most is Hebrews 4:12. Note the translation of this passage:

KJV	NASB	NIV
For the word of God *is* **quick**, and powerful, and sharper than any twoedged sword,	For the word of God is **living** and active and sharper than any two-edged sword,	For the word of God is **living** and active. Sharper than any double-edged sword,

I remember as a youth wondering what "quick and powerful" meant when applied to the Bible. My Bible did not move particularly fast, and I wasn't sure how "powerful" related to the speed of my Bible. Neither term that is used by the KJV means today what it meant nearly four hundred years ago. The first term, "quick," *never* means "fast" when used by the KJV. Normally "quick" refers to "living" or "alive" in the AV, and that is what it means here as well. The second term, rendered "powerful" here by the AV (but rendered "effectual" at 1 Corinthians 16:9 and Philemon 1:6), refers to something that is active and effective in its task. Therefore, the writer is asserting that the Word of God is alive and active over against being dead, sterile, and ineffective. Surely no one can seriously argue that the modern translations are in any way *inferior* to the KJV at this point. Any honest person must admit that the modern translations provide a much needed element of clarity and precision that is lacking in the AV.

LET'S BE HONEST

Another term that does not always mean what it did back in the days of James I of England is the word "honest." The KJV uses this term to translate a couple of Greek words. Note some passages:

NASB		KJV
honorable	2 Cor. 8:21	honest
honorable	Phil. 4:8	honest
excellent	1 Pet. 2:12	honest

In a number of instances the writer of Scripture is referring to that which is "honorable" and "excellent," not to that which is "honest" as we use the word today. When we are exhorted to think on that which is "honorable" or "noble" as the NIV has it (Philippians 4:8), we are being called to consider higher things, not merely things that are honest over against dishonest. Surely it is a greater thing to be called to think on "excellent" or "noble" things than merely "honest" things, for that which is noble and excellent will at the very least be honest, but there are many honest things that are hardly noble or excellent. Again we find the modern translations quite *honestly* surpassing the KJV in clarity and exactitude.

ANGELS, HEAVENLY BEINGS, OR GOD?

A very interesting difference in translations arises in the Old Testament's use of the Hebrew word *elohim*. This word can be translated as "gods," "God," or "angels," depending on its context and its usage. It appears in Psalm 8:5 in a context that produces some level of controversy:

KJV	NKJV	NIV	NRSV	NASB
For thou hast made him a little lower than **the angels,**	For You have made him a little lower than **the angels,**	You made him a little lower than **the heavenly beings**	Yet you have made them a little lower than **God,**	Yet Thou hast made him a little lower than **God,**

The KJV and NKJV opt for "angels," the NIV for "heavenly beings," and both the NASB and NRSV for "God," though the NRSV provides a footnote giving the other possible translations. The simple fact is that you can find the term *elohim* used in each of these ways somewhere in the Old Testament, so the issue is one of interpretation more than it is translation. What makes this passage more significant than most, however, is the fact that the writer to the Hebrews cites the passage as it appears in the Greek translation of the Old Testament known as the Septuagint, mentioned in a previous chapter with reference to Jerome. The Septuagint understands this passage to be referring specifically to *angels*, and hence uses the specific term *angelos* which is then found at Hebrews 2:7[12] in the New Testament. Scholars may argue over whether we should allow New Testament usage to determine Old Testament translation. What seems certain, however, is that the New Testament *application* should be made the norm for our understanding of the Old Testament's *meaning.*[13]

A POTPOURRI OF PASSAGES

As noted at the beginning of this chapter, we cannot possibly examine every single difference in translation between the KJV and the modern translations. Instead, we are seeking to examine the citations that are most commonly advanced by KJV Only advocates, as well as important passages that represent various elements of the process of translation. To conclude this section let us look at a number of passages that illustrate the fact that the modern translations are both *accurate* and *without a diabolical agenda* in their providing alternative readings to the KJV.

| Colossians 2:14 ||
KJV	NASB
and took it out of the way, nailing it to **his cross**;	and He has taken it out of the way, having nailed it to **the cross**.

Here the KJV has "his cross," while the NASB (and NIV, RSV, etc.) have "the cross." In this case the modern versions are giving the more literal rendering, seemingly finding no reason in the text itself to translate the Greek article "the" with the possessive pronoun "his." There are many places in the New Testament where the article does function possessively, so the KJV rendering is proper, but it is not as literal as some others. There is, of course, no effort being made to hide the identity of the cross or in any way separate Christ from His work at Calvary.

1 Peter 2:9		
KJV	**NKJV**	**NIV**
But ye *are* a chosen generation, a royal priesthood, an holy nation, **a peculiar people**;	But you *are* a chosen generation, a royal priesthood, a holy nation, His **own special people**,	But you are a chosen people, a royal priesthood, a holy nation, **a people belonging to God,**

This is another passage that struck me as rather "peculiar" as a young person. I could see how Mr. Peabody (who always sat in the third row over on the right side of the pulpit) could be described as "peculiar," but I didn't like being lumped in with Mr. Peabody at all! Again we note how language has changed, for "peculiar" does not mean "strange" but "a possession," just as the KJV translates the very same term at Ephesians 1:14.[14]

Many KJV Only individuals see shades of Roman Catholicism in the NASB and NIV at Romans 15:16:

KJV	**NASB**	**NIV**
That I should be the minister of Jesus Christ to the Gentiles, **ministering** the gospel of God, that the offering up of the Gentiles might be acceptable, being sanctified by the Holy Ghost.	to be a minister of Christ Jesus to the Gentiles, **ministering as a priest** the gospel of God, that *my* offering of the Gentiles might become acceptable, sanctified by the Holy Spirit.	to be a minister of Christ Jesus to the Gentiles **with the priestly duty** of proclaiming the gospel of God, so that the Gentiles might become an offering acceptable to God, sanctified by the Holy Spirit.

The use of the term "priest" is what causes the charges to be made against the modern versions. Yet, again, we find the Greek text in full support of the modern readings. In fact, the entire passage is placed in "priestly" language, for Paul is purposefully drawing from familiar terms from the Old Testament to make a point. Note that even the KJV has the word "offering" in its translation with reference to the Gentiles. Paul is picturing himself as a priest, offering up the Gentiles as an *acceptable* sacrifice to God, being *sanctified* by the Holy Spirit. The term translated "minister" at the beginning of the verse is the very same term used in the Greek version of the Old Testament to describe the ministering of the priests in the Temple. The word translated "ministering as a priest" by the NASB and "the priestly duty" by the NIV comes from the very Greek term for "priest," which is found in one Apocryphal work meaning "priestly service." The modern translations recognize the context in which this word is found and translate it accordingly, bringing out the meaning that is, quite simply, obscured in the KJV. This passage in no way even *hints* at a sacramental priesthood, as found in Roman Catholicism. The use of the term by modern translations in no way lends credence to the establishment of the entire edifice of a sacramental priesthood.

For those seeking a translation that continues to have the "flavor" of the KJV, the NKJV often provides an excellent alternative. Many times obscure or unclear translations in the KJV are updated and corrected in the NKJV. Note the following examples:

Reference	KJV	NKJV
Ephesians 4:12	For the perfecting of the saints,	for the equipping of the saints
2 Timothy 3:17	That the man of God may be perfect,	that the man of God may be complete,
Hebrews 13:21	Make you perfect	make you complete
2 Timothy 3:12	all that will live godly in Christ Jesus	all who desire to live godly in Christ Jesus
Romans 12:8	he that giveth, *let him do it* with simplicity;	he who gives, with liberality;
Luke 3:14	Do violence to no man,	Do not intimidate anyone
2 Timothy 3:3	despisers of those that are good,	despisers of good,
Titus 1:8	a lover of good men,	a lover of what is good,

The first three references deal with the KJV's use of the term "perfect" in translating a number of different Greek terms, at times obscuring the intention of the author in so doing. The NKJV makes the sense much clearer with its use of "equipping" and "complete." Second Timothy 3:12 is an example of a very unfortunate KJV rendering, for here the entire concept of the *desire* of the individual to live a godly life is passed over in the AV translation, or possibly rolled into the one word "will." Romans 12:8 uses "simplicity" for a term that today means "generosity" or "liberality," while Luke 3:14 uses a term that is best understood as referring to intimidation, not to direct physical violence. In both 2 Timothy 3:3 and Titus 1:8 the KJV is a little more "interpretive" than the modern versions. The texts are better understood as referring to the general concept of "good" being despised or loved. The KJV limits this to good *men,* though the term "men" is nowhere in the Greek text but is assumed from the form of the Greek term.

NO GRAND CONSPIRACIES

It seems fair to say that, in a majority of the passages examined in the preceding pages, translations such as the NASB and NIV have been seen to *surpass* the KJV with reference to clarity and ease of comprehension far more often than the reverse. No grand conspiracies have been uncovered, no attempts to hide doctrines or beliefs by mistranslating the text have been found. What we have discovered is that the comparison of various translations of the Bible is often very useful in ascertaining the meaning of the passage being studied, and that the KJV is one of those many fine translations available for just that task. When used in conjunction with such fine modern translations as the NKJV, NIV, and NASB, the KJV adds a noble rendering to the list and is often helpful in grasping the literal meaning of the terms involved.

We hope it has also become clear that we must be very careful to look *closely* at the claims of those who would attack the work of Christian scholars as found in the NKJV or NIV. Most of the time a translation that differs from the KJV is just as valid and reliable as the one found in the AV itself, and frequently, it is more clear and understandable. When differences are examined in a context of seeking to understand the reasons for the differences, rather than in one of fear and emotion, we *learn* more about the Word and the original intents of the authors. This is how Christian dialogue and discussion *should* take place. Whenever you encounter a supposed "change" in the Bible's text, take the time to look carefully at the available information. You will discover that there are reasons for the differences, and that there is no rationale at all for running to theories of conspiracies or evil intentions on the part of modern translators.

Their goal is not to corrupt God's Word but to preserve it and accurately pass it on to future generations.

Endnotes

[1] Note Dr. Samuel Gipp's words, "God has always given His word to **one** people in **one** language to do **one** job; convert the world. The supposition that there must be a perfect translation in every language is erroneous and inconsistent with God's proven practice." *The Answer Book* (Bible & Literature Missionary Foundation: 1989), p. 32.

[2] I have used the edition of *New Age Bible Versions* that is identified as "Second Printing, 1993." However, for this chart I was forced to use the third printing, identified as "October, 1993," due to errors in this chart that would have been confusing to the reader.

[3] The KJV is used as the "official" version by the Church of Jesus Christ of Latter-day Saints (the Mormons), who present a very works-oriented system of salvation. See my *Letters to a Mormon Elder* (Bethany House: 1993), pp. 249-282.

[4] Gail Riplinger, *New Age Bible Versions*, p. 256.

[5] κόσμος and αἰών.

[6] The other term translated "hell" is *tartarus* at 2 Peter 2:4.

[7] A glowing example of this is found in the Watchtower publication *You Can Live Forever in Paradise on Earth* (Watchtower Bible and Tract Society: 1982), pp. 81-89.

[8] The Hebrew term used here, הֵילֵל, *does* mean "shining one" or "morning star." The standard lexicon in the field, Brown, Driver, and Briggs, states,

> הֵילֵל **n.m. appell.** shining one, epith of king of Babylon, נָפַלְתָּ מִשָּׁמַיִם הֵילֵל בֶּן־שַׁחַר אֵיךְ Is 14 [12] *how art thou fallen, shining one, son of dawn! i.e. star of the morning.*

[9] As amazing as it sounds, this is the exact argument of Gail Riplinger, *New Age Bible Versions,* pp. 40-55.

[10] Christian scholars are divided over the identity of the person in Isaiah 14; most clearly the initial application must be made to the king of Babylon (see verse 4), but there is a long tradition, seen in Jerome's translation as well, of seeing in Isaiah 14 a reference to the banishment of Satan to "the pit."

[11] KJV Only advocate William Grady focuses upon this passage to accuse any and all modern version publishers of only seeking to make a profit. See his *Final Authority* (Grady Publications: 1993), p. 283.

[12] In the plural form *angelous.*

[13] Some KJV Only advocates such as Peter Ruckman and Samuel Gipp

deny the Septuagint existed before the Christian era. See Ruckman's "The Mythological LXX" in *The Christian's Handbook of Manuscript Evidence* and Gipp's "What is the LXX" (Question #9) in his *The Answer Book*.

[14] A very sad example of the utter lack of charity in the writings of KJV Only advocates presents itself with reference to this passage. We have already noted how Gail Riplinger mercilessly attacked Dr. Edwin Palmer (the executive secretary of the NIV Committee on Bible Translation until his death) in her book *New Age Bible Versions*, connecting Palmer with people like Charlie Manson and Madam Blavatsky (p. 91). The character of these kinds of writings is seen in her comments on Palmer's defense of the NIV's rendering of 1 Peter 2:9, found on pages 170-171 of her book:

> A lifestyle driven by verses not vogue, will brand one as "peculiar" (NERD, in the vernacular). Unwilling to bear "his reproach," the NIV's Edwin Palmer pushes the "peculiar people" of Titus 2:14 and 1 Peter 2:9 into the closet— already crowded with the 'righteous' and 'the perfect'. Palmer writes:
>
> . . .a peculiar people. Today that means odd. It should be. . . .
>
> It meant odd when Peter and Paul wrote it and when Moses wrote it 4000 years earlier.

Gail Riplinger neglects to mention the translation of the very same term by the KJV as "possession" at Ephesians 1:14.

Textual Differences | 7

We come now to the major portion of our investigation of the claims of the KJV Only movement. The largest portion of the alleged "changes" in the text of the modern versions has to do with differences in the underlying Greek texts. We have already discussed how such "textual variants" arose, and how it is not necessary to assume malevolent, evil motivations on the part of "Alexandrian scribes" to understand why manuscripts and manuscript families differ from one another. We have already looked at a number of textual variants in examining the *Textus Receptus* as well.

To this point I have attempted to stay as "general" as possible, recognizing that the material being presented can be difficult to follow at times. Even in discussing translational differences there has been an attempt to keep away from overly technical discussions. But once we address textual matters there is no substitute for a deep seat in the saddle, a firm grip on the reins, and a strong desire to master the materials that simply *must be* discussed.

This chapter will be organized in such a way as to allow it to be referenced in an "encyclopedic" fashion. That is, the variants will be organized into groups sharing common features. Then the passages addressed will be organized in canonical (biblical) order so that particular verses can be found quickly. When the situation warrants, more in-depth information will be presented in Part Two of this work, and an endnote will be attached indicating the treatment of the passage in full at a later point. The majority of KJV Only publications focus upon the New Testament, and I shall follow that lead. Also please note that the variants that are specifically relevant to the topics of the deity of Christ and the virgin birth are addressed in chapter 8.

At times it may seem that the subject has become quite complex. It is admittedly much easier to ignore the many issues that go into the study of the text of the Bible and pass over them with a simple allegation that "they" have "changed" or "deleted" this or that. But those who really want to know the truth must invest the time and effort to be sure they have indeed found it and are not merely following after another human tradition or belief.

The two largest textual variants in the New Testament, Mark 16:9-20 and John 7:53-8:11, are addressed in Part Two. The most famous textual variant, 1 John 5:7-8, has already been addressed in chapter 4.[1] We will begin by briefly describing the means by which modern Christian scholars go about their task of studying, collating, and analyzing ancient manuscripts. Then we will look at certain verses that do not appear in the modern texts (note we did not say "deleted" or "added," but will leave that decision to the reader to make). Examples of passages showing "parallel-influence" will be examined, drawn primarily from the Gospels. Then we will examine variations where there is a fairly "even" split in the manuscript evidence, or where the modern texts follow a small minority of the extant (existing) Greek manuscripts, and explain why at times it is best to go with the minority when those manuscripts carry the greatest weight. We have already examined a number of passages where the *Textus Receptus* follows either a very tiny number of very late manuscripts, or goes so far as to import passages from other sources such as the Latin *Vulgate*. Those passages will not be repeated here. Finally, the reader is referred to Part Two for a "mini-glossary" of textual terms and symbols for a brief explanation of some of the terms and symbols often used in discussions of the text of the New Testament.

THE PROCESS OF DETERMINING A READING

My desire is to lay out the general principles upon which the textual choices of the modern texts have been made so that the form of those modern texts, and the translations based upon them, will be understood by everyone, even if they choose not to accept the underlying principles that guided the work of collation or translation. It is vitally important that anyone concerned with the text of the New Testament have at least a working understanding of why the modern texts do what they do. I have found KJV Only advocates not only ignorant of the most basic principles of textual criticism (the vast majority of Christians are unaware of the same things!), but much worse, *unwilling* to learn.

There are differences of opinion among scholars in the area of textual criticism. The vast majority of scholars follows the perspective that has given rise to such modern Greek texts as the United Bible Societies' 4th Edition and the Nestle-Aland 27th edition. This approach would basically be characterized as "eclectic," in that each reading is examined on its own merits and no absolutely overriding rule is used to artificially decide every variant.[2] Representatives of this viewpoint include Dr. Kurt Aland, Dr. Bruce Manning Metzger, Dr. Gordon Fee, and Dr. Daniel B. Wallace. A small minority of scholars prefer the "Majority Text" approach, believing that the reading found in the majority of manuscripts has the most right to be called the original. And even within each of these camps there are disagreements and discussions about methodology and specifics, *as there should be.* Those who think that scholars should walk lock-step on all matters don't seem to realize that it is disagreement and discussion that almost always lead to better insights and understandings. It should be axiomatic among Christian scholars that open discussion and liberty should prevail. That is one reason why KJV Onlyism has found no true proponent amongst Christian scholars: it denies anyone the freedom to examine the KJV on the very same basis as any other translation. The position is, by its nature, anti-intellectual, anti-scholarship, and anti-freedom.[3]

The most puzzling aspect of the entire debate for most people is to be found in the reliance of modern texts upon what seems to be a minority of the Greek manuscripts. Majority rules, does it not? Isn't that how we determine the laws in our land? We have the right to vote, and it seems downright anti-democratic to let the minority decide for the majority! Yet, there is a very good reason for this.

We have already noted the historical facts regarding the transmission of the text of the New Testament. We have briefly pointed out that historical events shaped the history of the written text in such a way as to make the text-type found in the area around Byzantium the "majority" text. The largest number of handwritten manuscripts that exist today contains the Byzantine text-type. But, of course, the majority of handwritten manuscripts that exist were made long after the writing of the New Testament, too. Because Erasmus used these later manuscripts, the TR is a Byzantine text, and hence the KJV's New Testament reflects this same manuscript tradition.

Why then utilize other texts that differ from the Byzantine? The answer is fairly simple. It is plainly evident that the majority of textual variations arose quite early in the history of the New Testament, during that period of time when the Christian faith was still illegal, persecution was common, and most of those engaged in copying the Scriptures were not professional scribes but simple laypeople who hungered to have a copy of any portion of the inspired writings for themselves. After the faith became legal at the beginning of the fourth century, more accurate methods of copying and more professional copyists helped to "freeze" the readings of the text, keeping variation that was due to unprofessional scribal work down to a minimum in the centuries that followed. The Alexandrian, Western, and Caesarean "text-types" that we described in chapter 3 were already in existence at this time. They arose in those first few generations of the Christian church.

The Byzantine text-type, however, arose later. This is the great area of conflict. The question we must ask the proponents of the Byzantine text-type is this: upon what basis should we believe that the Byzantine text, simply because it ended up being the majority text later in history, was in fact the best representative of the original writings during that vital period of the first few centuries? If we were to transport ourselves to the year A.D. 200 and look at the text of the New Testament at that time, ignoring for the moment what was to come later, what would we find? The evidence right now indicates that the text that existed at that time looked most like the Alexandrian text-type. How do we know this? Every one of the papyrus manuscripts we have discovered has been a representative of the Alexandrian, not the Byzantine, text-type.[4] The early Fathers who wrote at this time did not use the Byzantine text-type. In fact, the Byzantine text-type is not found in full form until the fourth century, and does not become the "majority" until the ninth century. Graphically we can compare the number of Alexandrian manuscripts to the Byzantine manuscripts found over the first centuries of the Christian era:[5] the chart provided on the next page gives us a view of the *relative* relationship of the Alexandrian and Byzantine text-types. Of course, if we were to graph the *total* number of manuscripts up to the sixteenth century the Byzantine manuscripts would dwarf the Alexandrian.[6] But the fact remains that the closer we get to the original writing of the New Testament, the less prevalent is the Byzantine manuscript tradition.

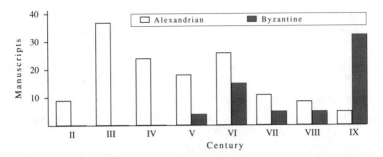

This fact is borne out by other historical considerations. An examination of the early translations of the New Testament reveals that they were done on the basis of Alexandrian type manuscripts, not Byzantine type manuscripts. And the early church fathers who wrote during the early centuries give no evidence in their citations of a familiarity with the Byzantine text-type.[7]

Finally, when we apply sound methods of examining the readings of the texts themselves, taking into consideration the concepts presented above regarding scribal errors of sight or hearing, harmonization, parallel influence, and the "expansion of piety," we discover a remarkable thing: almost all the time these "internal criteria" point us to the Alexandrian, Western, or Caesarean, not the Byzantine, reading.

There are, of course, exceptions to the rules. Daniel Wallace, for example, cites Philippians 1:14 as an example of a uniquely Byzantine reading that is found in the papyri manuscripts. This exception, however, proves the rule, as there are not more than eight such examples to be found.[8] And, we might note that the modern critical texts, the UBS 4th and the Nestle-Aland 27th, both adopt the Byzantine reading! Why is this significant? It proves that these texts are not engaged in some kind of conspiracy to deny the Byzantine text *any* place in textual choices, and that when faced with plain evidence, the modern texts will follow that evidence and adopt the proper readings.

It is common for KJV Only advocates to assert that modern textual scholars simply believe that "the older manuscripts are the better manuscripts." While it is not true in *every* instance that the older a manuscript is the better it is, it is *generally* true. Surely it is easy to understand that a manuscript that comes from only a century after the writing of the original, such as $\mathfrak{P}^{66}$ or $\mathfrak{P}^{75}$, should be given more "weight" in examining a variant reading than a manuscript from the fourteenth century. Unless that later manuscript was somehow copied from a *very* ancient manuscript, it is probably the result of a long series of transcriptions. It may well be a fourth- or tenth- or fifteenth-generation copy. Obviously a manuscript from A.D. 200 is not a tenth-generation copy; there simply isn't enough time between the date of its production and the writing of the original. All of this demonstrates why we cannot simply "count" manuscripts, but must *weigh* them, looking at their general character, age, and text-type. Some manuscripts are simply more "important" in helping us to find the original text than others.

In light of these things we can understand why there are many times when the modern Greek texts will adopt a reading that is found in a minority of the Greek texts. When we look at these instances, we find that either those minority texts carry great weight, or they are coupled with internal considerations that add to the weight of the manuscripts themselves. We will see many examples of this as we look at passages that are in dispute between the modern texts and the KJV.

ADDED OR DELETED?

Just as Erasmus was accused of "deleting" a verse from the Bible when he did not include the *Comma Johanneum,* so too modern versions are accused of "deleting" a number of verses from their text. If one does not include blocks of text such as the longer ending of Mark, there are sixteen single verses that are either marked by brackets or completely removed from the text of modern versions such as the NIV. In three of these instances the verse itself is attested by a *minority* of Greek manuscripts; that is, the Majority Text (symbolized hereafter by the letter $\mathfrak{M}$) does not include that verse. These verses are Luke 17:36; Acts 8:37; and Acts 15:34. The other verses are found in the majority of Greek manuscripts, yet they are not found in the text of modern critical editions of the Greek New Testament.[9] Of course, they are noted in the textual apparatus of these texts, so they have not actually been "deleted" or removed without notification. But the issue is, why would anyone not include these passages when they are in the majority of the Greek manuscripts?

In some instances it is fairly obvious that a verse has been either repeated or imported from another place in the text. In both Mark 9:44 and 46 the phrase "where their worm dieth not, and the fire is not quenched" has been inserted in later manuscripts in both places, repeating the very same phrase that is found in verse 48. The manuscripts that do not contain the phrase, while the minority, make up a wide range of witnesses against these verses. There is no reason for these verses to have been accidentally omitted, and obviously they were not *purposefully* omitted because all the manuscripts contain the very same words at verse 48. Hence, both of these verses are rightly removed from the text as not being part of what Mark originally wrote. The Gospel of Mark also provides a good example of a verse being imported from elsewhere. Mark 7:16 is not found in modern texts due to its being absent from a rather small number of ancient manuscripts,[10] yet again there is a good reason for this. The passage is derived from Mark 4:9 and 23, where it functions as the "conclusion" to an important teaching of the Lord. It is much easier to understand how the passage would be inserted elsewhere when appropriate than to understand why it would be deleted in the important ancient witnesses. But we point out again that since the material in the verse appears elsewhere in all the Greek manuscripts, it is impossible to say that someone was *purposefully* trying to "hide" or "change" anything. What is more, modern translations include such verses either in brackets (NASB) or include the verse in a footnote (NIV). Such is hardly what conspirators do when trying to "hide" something. And remember, the KJV translators included similar notes about verses being absent in certain manuscripts.

Other passages that fall into the same category of inserted text from other places in the Gospel accounts include Matthew 17:21 (borrowed from Mark 9:29); Matthew 18:11 (from Luke 19:10); Matthew 23:14 (from Mark 12:40 and Luke 20:47); Mark 11:26 (from Matthew 6:15); Mark 15:28 (from Luke 22:37 or Isaiah 53:12); Luke 17:36 (from Matthew 24:40); and Luke 23:17 (from Matthew 27:15 or Mark 15:6). In fact, nearly every verse that is displaced from the modern texts is a "copy," so to speak, of a verse that is found in all the Greek manuscripts. Obviously, then, there is no purposeful agenda to "remove" any of these verses *for doctrinal reasons*.

One of the more interesting verses that has been displaced by research into the earliest forms of the New Testament text is John 5:4 in the KJV, "For an angel went down at a certain season into the pool, and troubled the water: whosoever then first after the troubling of the water stepped in was made whole of whatsoever disease he had." This verse provides a classic example of how a marginal note explaining something in the text can end up as part of the text somewhere down the line. John's reference to the pool of Bethesda and the sick lying about it would be confusing to some. A marginal note explaining the traditional belief of the Jews regarding the angel stirring the waters could have easily been accidentally inserted into the text by a later copyist, thinking that it was actually a part of the text that had accidentally been left out and placed in the margin.[11]

The question that we will ask over and over again in looking at textual issues such as these is, "What did the original author write?" That must be our controlling thought. We wish only what was inspired by the Holy Spirit, without deletions, *and without additions, either.* Additions are just as dangerous as deletions. When we encounter a passage like John 5:4 we should not ask, "Why do modern versions *delete* this passage?" but, "Is this passage an addition on the part of some later texts, or a deletion on the part of earlier ones?" This illustrates one of the main problems with KJV Only writings. Any examination of these works will find the consistent use of terms like "omitted," "deleted," and "removed" when discussing such issues. There is no effort to determine the *original* text because the KJV is *assumed* to be the standard by which all others are to be judged. This involves, again, *circular reasoning* on the part of the KJV Only group.

Parallel Influence, or, "It SHOULD Say . . ."

We have already noted the very understandable tendency on the part of scribes to "harmonize" passages of Scripture, especially where there is a parallel passage, such as the one we noted at Ephesians 1:2 and Colossians 1:2. This is most evident in the Gospels where parallels exist quite often between Matthew, Mark, and Luke, and once in a while with John. In the preceding section we saw how entire verses could make the "trip" from one Gospel to another and find a place even in a majority of the Greek texts. Since verses have done this it is obvious that phrases and words can do the same thing.

So prevalent is the occurrence of parallel influence that it is unnecessary to examine each and every example. Instead, we offer the following chart that provides the KJV rendering with the textual variant in bold typeface, the NIV translation, and then a listing of the parallel passage in which we find the same wording or material. Some passages, due to their importance or frequent citation by KJV Only advocates will be discussed in fuller detail, either following the chart or in Part Two.

KJV	NIV	Background
Matthew 1:25: And knew her not till she had brought forth her **firstborn** son: and he called his name JESUS.	Matthew 1:25: But he had no union with her until she gave birth to a son. And he gave him the name Jesus.	"Firstborn" borrowed from Luke 2:7, "and she gave birth to her firstborn, a son." (NIV)
Matthew 8:29: And, behold, they cried out, saying, What have we to do with thee, **Jesus**, thou Son of God? art thou come hither to torment us before the time?	Matthew 8:29: "What do you want with us, Son of God?" they shouted. "Have you come here to torture us before the appointed time?"	"Jesus" is borrowed from the similar passage[12] in Mark 1:24, "What do you want with us, Jesus of Nazareth? Have you come to destroy us?" (NIV)
Matthew 20:16: So the last shall be first, and the first last: **for many be called, but few chosen**.	Matthew 20:16: "So the last will be first, and the first will be last."	Phrase is borrowed from Matthew 22:14, "For many are invited, but few are chosen." (NIV)
Matthew 25:13: Watch therefore, for ye know neither the day nor the hour **wherein the Son of man cometh**.	Matthew 25:13: Therefore keep watch, because you do not know the day or the hour.	Phrase is found in Matthew 24:44: "because the Son of Man will come at an hour when you do not expect him." (NIV)
Matthew 27:35: And they crucified him, and parted his garments, casting lots: **that it might**	Matthew 27:35: When they had crucified him, they divided up his	Quotation borrowed from parallel passage in John 19:24, "This happened that the

KJV	NIV	Background
be fulfilled which was spoken by the prophet, They parted my garments among them, and upon my vesture did they cast lots.	clothes by casting lots.	scripture might be fulfilled which said, 'They divided my garments among them and cast lots for my clothing.' " (NIV)
Mark 6:11: And whosoever shall not receive you, nor hear you, when ye depart thence, shake off the dust under your feet for a testimony against them. **Verily I say unto you, It shall be more tolerable for Sodom and Gomorrha in the day of judgment, than for that city.**	Mark 6:11: And if any place will not welcome you or listen to you, shake the dust off your feet when you leave, as a testimony against them.	Phrase comes from Matthew 10:15: "I tell you the truth, it will be more bearable for Sodom and Gomorrah on the day of judgment than for that town." (NIV)
Mark 10:21: Then Jesus beholding him loved him, and said unto him, One thing thou lackest: go thy way, sell whatsoever thou hast, and give to the poor, and thou shalt have treasure in heaven: and come, **take up the cross**, and follow me.	Mark 10:21: Jesus looked at him and loved him. "One thing you lack," he said. "Go, sell everything you have and give to the poor, and you will have treasure in heaven. Then come, follow me."	Phrase comes from Mark 8:34: "If anyone would come after me, he must deny himself and take up his cross and follow me." (NIV)
Colossians 1:14: In whom we have redemption **through his blood**, *even* the forgiveness of sins:	Colossians 1:14: in whom we have redemption, the forgiveness of sins.	Phrase comes from Ephesians 1:7: "In him we have redemption through his blood, the forgiveness of sins . . ." (NIV)

The first thing to note of relevance to the KJV Only controversy is the fact that in each instance where the NIV lacks a phrase in its text that is found in the KJV, *that same material is found elsewhere in the NIV New Testament.* The importance of this should be clear: if the NIV (or any other modern translation) is attempting to "hide" something, why include the very same material in another place? Such a translation procedure simply makes no sense at all, and yet this is the constant accusation of KJV Only materials against modern translations.

Some of the preceding passages touch upon doctrinal issues. For example, Matthew 1:25 is often cited by critics of modern translations as an attempt to deny the virgin birth of Christ. Yet if a modern translation wished to do this, why not remove the parallel occurrence of the term at Luke 2:7 where all the modern translations contain the disputed term? In reality, we have here another example of parallel influence that caused a scribe, undoubtedly zealous for orthodox doctrine, to insert the term "firstborn" here so as to protect a sacred truth and bring this passage into line with Luke's account. Modern translations, far from seeking to denigrate such divine truths, are simply seeking to give us what was written by the original authors.

Mark 10:21 provides us with an excellent example of how simple textual variants that arose from easily understandable sources can be turned into grand conspiracies by KJV Only advocates. On page 22 of Gail Riplinger's *New Age Bible Versions*, we find an attempt to contrast the KJV with "New Version/New Christianity." In this chart Riplinger alleges that while the KJV calls believers to "take up the cross," the new versions "OMIT" this call. Though she does not give a specific citation to back up her claim, she is referring to Mark 10:21.[13] Let's look at the verses:

KJV	NIV
Then Jesus beholding him loved him, and said unto him, One thing thou lackest: go thy way, sell whatsoever thou hast, and give to the poor, and thou shalt have treasure in heaven: and come, **take up the cross**, and follow me.	Jesus looked at him and loved him. "One thing you lack," he said. "Go, sell everything you have and give to the poor, and you will have treasure in heaven. Then come, follow me."

Many believers are troubled by charts such as the one above. At first glance, it would appear that the NIV is somehow "deleting" or "removing" the phrase "take up the cross" from Mark 10:21. But is this the case? Is there reason for not including the phrase in Mark 10:21? And is there some bias *against* the call to take up the cross in the modern translations, as some KJV Only advocates would have us to believe?

We begin by pointing out that the NIV and other modern translations do not include this phrase because the Greek texts they utilized in their work do not contain the words "take up the cross." The text utilized by the NIV translation committee was virtually identical with the Nestle-Aland text. It is the judgment of the scholars who compiled this text that the phrase was not a part of the original Gospel of Mark.

Next, it is important to note that the phrase "take up the cross" appears four times in the King James Version of the Bible: Matthew 16:24; Luke 9:23; Mark 8:34; and the disputed passage at Mark 10:21.[14] The first three all recount the same incident in the teaching ministry of the Lord Jesus. If there is indeed some "conspiracy" on the part of the modern translators to get rid of the call to take up the cross, surely they will delete this phrase in these passages as well, will they not? And yet the modern translations have all three occurrences in their translations. Note, as an example, Mark 8:34 in the NIV (emphasis added):

> Then he called the crowd to him along with his disciples and said: "If anyone would come after me, he must deny himself and **take up his cross** and follow me."

It is difficult to see how a charge of "conspiracy" can be made against the modern translations, unless one believes that theology is based upon how often the Bible repeats a command. That is, if the Bible says "take up the cross" only three times, rather than four, this somehow makes the command less important or binding than if it were said four or five times. But surely we all can see that this kind of thinking is muddled. God's truth is not decided by counting how many times He says the same thing. When God says, "Before me no god was formed, nor will there be one after me" (Isaiah 43:10, NIV), we do not ask that He repeat himself three or four more times before we will accept the great truth of monotheism: there is but one true God. In the same way,

Scripture records Jesus' call to take up the cross in three places, and this is sufficient.

Why, then, does the KJV contain the phrase at Mark 10:21? Again, we note that it is because the TR contains the phrase in the Greek. In point of fact, the majority of Greek texts contain the phrase. So why omit it? Here are the reasons.

First, and foremost, the oldest manuscripts of the New Testament do not contain the phrase. This includes not only the two manuscripts, Sinaiticus and Vaticanus (‭א‬ and B) that are so often vilified by KJV Only advocates, but many others. Not only this, but entire translations into other languages lack the phrase.

Remember how Mark records the one time the Lord Jesus spoke of taking up the cross in chapter 8, verse 34:

> Then he called the crowd to him along with his disciples and said: "If anyone would come after me, he must deny himself and **take up his cross** and follow me."

Notice that Jesus says that those who would come after Him must deny themselves and "follow me." When we come to Mark 10:21, we again find that phrase "follow me." Seemingly an early scribe, familiar with the phraseology of Mark 8:34 and its use of "follow me," upon encountering the same thing in Mark 10:21, either mistakenly, or even on purpose, inserted the phrase "take up the cross."

But this is not the only fact that points to the correctness of not including "take up the cross" at Mark 10:21. There is another good reason. Mark 10:21 is part of a story that is found in both Matthew and Luke as well, specifically, in Matthew 19:21 and Luke 18:22. Note that neither Matthew nor Luke records the phrase "take up the cross" in their Gospels at this point:

| Jesus said unto him, If thou wilt be perfect, go *and* sell that thou hast, and give to the poor, and thou shalt have treasure in heaven: and come *and* follow me (Matthew 19:21, KJV). | Now when Jesus heard these things, he said unto him, Yet lackest thou one thing: sell all that thou hast, and distribute unto the poor, and thou shalt have treasure in heaven: and come, follow me (Luke 18:22, KJV). |

The fact that the parallel passages in Matthew and Luke omit the phrase in *all* manuscripts further verifies the propriety of not including it in Mark 10:21. Indeed, those who would charge the modern texts with "heresy" for not including the later insertion at Mark 10:21 are hard pressed to explain why they do not make the same charge against both Matthew and Luke! Nearly all the charts produced by KJV Only advocates suffer from this same kind of double standard.

Colossians 1:14 provides KJV Only advocates with one of their "strongest" arguments against modern versions. I say "strong" only in that the alleged "deletion" on the part of modern texts *preaches well.* For example, I was leading a group of volunteers who were passing out tracts and witnessing to people at a large gathering of people who follow a major pseudo-Christian religion. I noticed another man passing out tracts, so I approached him. It only took a moment before I realized that this gentleman belonged to a KJV Only church in the local area. His first question was, "Do you use the Authorized Version?" When I informed him that our volunteers used a variety of translations he said, "Well, you don't use the NIV, *do you?*" I informed him that we did indeed use the NIV along with the NASB and NKJV and others. This quickly led to a number of comments on his part regarding how bad the modern versions were, and then he identified the NIV as "the bloodless Bible." He made reference to Colossians 1:14 and said, "How can you tell people about the blood of Jesus when your Bible doesn't have the blood?" I knew what he was referring to:

Colossians 1:14	
KJV	**NIV**
In whom we have redemption **through his blood**, *even* the forgiveness of sins:	in whom we have redemption, the forgiveness of sins.

I did not feel that it was the right time or place to attempt to help the man understand the concept of parallel influence, so I simply let him know that the NIV and all the others presented the Gospel with a clarity equal to or better than the KJV itself. He was obviously not satisfied, but I moved on to sharing with other people.

We have noted the very similar situation that arose around

Colossians 1:2 and Ephesians 1:2. There are a number of parallels between Colossians and Ephesians, hence it is natural to expect there to be some "harmonization" of the two epistles through normal scribal activity. This is why the NIV and others do not have the phrase "through his blood" at Colossians 1:14. It is missing not only in the dreaded "Alexandrian" manuscripts such as ℵ and B, but from the *majority* of Greek manuscripts, including the majority of the Byzantine tradition![15] According to the information cited by the UBS 4th edition Greek text, the earliest Greek manuscript to contain it is from the ninth century, and the earliest Father to cite it in this way is from the late fourth century. In any case, even a brief examination of the situation, coupled with a minimal familiarity with the facts, demonstrates plainly that there is no "conspiracy" involved in the modern readings.

One variant reading that involves *double* parallel influence is Luke 9:35:

Luke 9:35	
KJV	**NIV**
And there came a voice out of the cloud, saying, This is my **beloved** Son: hear him.	A voice came from the cloud, saying, "This is my Son, whom I have **chosen**; listen to him."

The modern versions have "chosen" here, following the most ancient witnesses to the text.[16] The KJV's reading, "beloved," most probably comes from Mark 9:7. But there is a third reading to be found in the manuscripts that is of most interest to us here. Some manuscripts have "beloved, in whom I am well pleased," drawing from yet another parallel source, Matthew 3:17 or 17:5. The two variant readings, both drawing from parallel sources, show how pervasive this kind of harmonization of passages in the Gospels can be.

Another kind of "parallel influence" is seen in the expansion of Old Testament quotations by later scribes. Feeling that the authors of the New Testament should have been complete and thorough in every citation of the Old Testament (how often do we give partial quotations?), later scribes were quick to "harmonize" an incomplete citation of the Old Testament that appeared in the new. For example, note Matthew 15:8:

Matthew 15:8	
KJV	**NASB**
This people draweth nigh unto me with their mouth, and honoureth me with *their* lips; but their heart is far from me.	This people honors Me with their lips, but their heart is far away from me.

The expansion of the quotation in the KJV is based upon the Greek Septuagint's reading of Isaiah 29:13. In fact, it is a common trait of the 𝕸 texts that Old Testament quotations will be harmonized to the form that is familiar to the scribe. This tendency is quite understandable. How often would we ourselves do the same thing? If one reads an author who, in citing a familiar passage like John 3:16, gives only a partial citation, such as "For God so loved the world that he gave his only-begotten Son, that whosoever believes in him might not perish," is it not natural for us to add the final clause even in our thinking? And if we are copying such a text, it is even easier to harmonize it to the fuller, more complete form of the citation. Even if a person were to disagree and insist that the biblical authors would never cite a passage from the Old Testament in an incomplete form, the fact remains that the modern translations are obviously not attempting to "tamper" with anything, or "remove" anything. Their translations are determined by the texts they are using, and those texts recognize the natural tendencies of scribes to expand and harmonize in the copying process. Many modern translations indicate citations of the Old Testament either by highlighting the text itself using italics or boldface, or indicate the source of the citation in a footnote. This would be a strange thing to do if there was some "conspiracy" afoot to "hide" some aspect of the text.

Variants Not Due to Parallel Influence

We now come to those variants that are not explainable as instances of parallel influence. Here we encounter all those readings that are due to scribal errors and oversights, as well as those that flow from the "expansion of piety" that we have discussed earlier. I have chosen to address those variants that I have most often encountered in the writings of KJV Only advocates. We will have occasion to illustrate many of the principles we noted earlier in this chapter as we work through the following material.

Matthew 16:20	
KJV	**NIV**
Then charged he his disciples that they should tell no man that he was **Jesus** the Christ.	Then he warned his disciples not to tell anyone that he was the Christ.

At times the "expansion of piety" led scribes to insert a name in such a way as to create a problem. Matthew 16:20 provides us with such an instance. After the great confession of faith by Peter in Caesarea Philippi, the Lord instructs His disciples to keep His identity as the Messiah secret. Yet the KJV, following the Byzantine reading,[17] reads, "Jesus the Christ." Not only is this phrase unusual in the Gospels, but it makes little sense here. Plainly it is the Lord's identity as the Messiah that is to be kept from the general public, not the name "Jesus," which is well known at the time, nor the combination "Jesus the Christ."

Matthew 17:20	
KJV	**NIV**
And Jesus said unto them, Because of your **unbelief**:	He replied, "Because you have so **little faith**.

In this instance we may be looking at a simple instance of scribal error. Here we have two words that look very much alike. Note the Greek terms:

unbelief	ἀπιστίαν
little faith	ὀλιγοπιστίαν

"Unbelief" is the more common term and had appeared just a few verses earlier (v. 17), therefore it is easier to understand how the switch could be made to it than the other way around. This text pretty much pits the Alexandrian reading ("little faith") against the Byzantine reading ("unbelief").

Matthew 21:12	
KJV	**NASB**
And Jesus went into the temple **of God**, and cast out all them that sold and bought in the temple, and overthrew the tables of the moneychangers, and the seats of them that sold doves,	And Jesus entered the temple and cast out all those who were buying and selling in the temple, and overturned the tables of the moneychangers and the seats of those who were selling doves.

Matthew 21:12 illustrates how a textual variant can be utterly irrelevant to the meaning of the passage: the 𝔐 text has "of God," while earlier texts do not. But then again, what other temple could be referred to? Yet, someone might urge that this "change" is somehow meant to de-emphasize the role of God in the Bible.[18] Yet, we have here a situation that is quite similar to Mark 10:21 and the insertion of "take up the cross." When we look at the parallel passages in Mark 11:15 and Luke 19:45, we have only "the temple" in both places, not "the temple of God." Note how again the internal evidence (derived from the parallel passages) coincides with the external evidence (the earlier, non-Byzantine manuscripts).

Mark 1:2	
KJV	**NIV**
As it is written in **the prophets**, Behold, I send my messenger before thy face, which shall prepare thy way before thee.	It is written in **Isaiah the prophet**: "I will send my messenger ahead of you, who will prepare your way"

Mark 1:2 is one of the most commonly cited passages in KJV Only literature, which in itself is quite instructive. The very same motivations that one finds in the writings of the defenders of the AV undoubtedly prompted the scribal alteration from "Isaiah the prophet" to "the prophets." Note the words of D.A. Waite:

> Instead of **"IN THE PROPHETS,"** the B/ALEPH texts and the English versions have **"IN THE PROPHET ISAIAH."** Though Mark 1:3 does refer to Isaiah 40:3, this verse 2 is found in Malachi 3:1 and NOT Isaiah! The way it stands in these false texts, it makes the Bible out as false and in error.[19]

Peter Ruckman is even more direct,

> 1. Mark 1:2,3. Using Origen's corrupt "Septuagint,"
> Eusebius, Augustine, and Jerome conjectured that the
> quotation which followed was from Isaiah the Prophet. Having
> made this conjecture, *without reading Malachi*, all of them
> changed the verse *from* "Καθως γεγραπται εν τοις
> προφηταις" to "Καθως γεγραπται εν τω Ησαια τω
> προφητη." The reader will find this Bible "boner" preserved in
> the RV, ASV, RSV, Catholic Bible (any edition), and 95% of all
> the "new" Bibles.[20]

In answer to the question, "Which is correct?" he writes,

> Well, if you are a conceited linguist who thinks that he can sit
> in judgment on the Scripture, you will go to books written by
> Trench, Driver, Gesenius, Delitzch, A.T. Robertson, Casper
> Gregory, Deissmann, Nestle, Westcott and Hort. If you are a
> Bible believing Christian, you will turn to the Book.

I only note again the circularity of Ruckman's position: we are asking
a question about a reading in the Bible, whether it is "in Isaiah the
prophet" or "in the prophets." Ruckman says that if you are a Bible-
believing Christian (which means, for him, if you believe only in the
KJV) you will turn "to the Book," i.e., to the KJV. So how does one
know the KJV is right? Because the KJV says so, of course. Later in
the same work he refers to this passage as a "famous scholarly 'boo-
boo,'" and says, "Here the only Bibles that maintain the correct
reading (which a 6th-grade pupil could understand!) are Tyndale,
Young, the Geneva Bible, the Bishop's Bible, and the A.V. 1611."[21]

Why are KJV Only advocates so confident that "the prophets" is
the only possible reading? The argument is that since part of the
quotation given by Mark is from Malachi, Mark *couldn't* have written
"in Isaiah the prophet," for this would be a "mistake" on the part of the
inspired writer. Even though Mark 1:3 is from Isaiah, the preceding
section is from Malachi, hence, it *must* be "in the prophets."

It is quite certain that some scribes early on in the transmission of
the text of the New Testament had the very same thought. In fact, the
reason why modern scholars are so confident that the proper reading is

"in Isaiah the prophet" stems partly[22] from this very fact: it is *much* easier to understand why a scribe would try to "help Mark out," so to speak, and correct what *seems* to be an errant citation than to figure out why someone would change it to "Isaiah the prophet."[23] But as in so many instances where a scribe *thought* he had encountered an error in the text, the error was, in fact, the scribe's, not the text's.

The problem with the KJV Only argument at this point is simply one of ignorance of the common forms of citation at the time of the writing of the New Testament. We have at least two instances recorded for us by the apostles where a conflated citation of two different Old Testament prophets is placed under the name of the more important or major of the two prophets. One of these instances is found in Matthew 27:9, where Matthew attributes to Jeremiah a quotation that is *primarily* drawn from Zechariah. We note in passing that the KJV has "Jeremiah" at Matthew 27:9, and hence must make reference to this phenomenon of citing a conflated Old Testament passage by the name of the more major of the two authors to explain this. Also, we find the very same attempt on the part of some later scribes to change "Jeremiah" to "Zechariah" at Matthew 27:9, though in this case their attempts did not become the majority reading of the manuscripts. The other instance is here at Mark 1:2-3, where a conflated reading, combining Malachi 3:1 with Isaiah 40:3, is cited under the single name of the more major of the two prophets, Isaiah. This was, as we said, common practice in that day, and we cannot fault the apostolic writers for using the conventional means of expressing themselves. The "error" exists when modern readers try to force the ancient writers into modern standards of citation and footnoting.[24]

We see, then, that Mark was quite accurate in his original wording and did not need the editorial assistance of later scribes, nor of KJV Only advocates, at all.

Mark 10:24	
KJV	**NIV**
But Jesus answereth again, and saith unto them, Children, how hard is it **for them that trust in riches** to enter into the kingdom of God!	But Jesus said again, "Children, how hard it is to enter the kingdom of God!"

This variant gives us an instance where the modern texts follow a very small minority of Greek texts. The UBS 4th edition Greek text lists all of four uncial texts, dating from the fourth to the ninth centuries, that lack the reading "for them that trust in riches." Why would scholars follow only four manuscripts and go against the reading in the vast majority? In this instance both ℵ and B do not contain the reading.[25] While these two manuscripts carry a great deal of weight, there is another reason why most would accept their reading over the majority text. Mark 10:25, in all manuscripts, records the Lord saying, "It is easier for a camel to go through the eye of a needle than for a rich man to enter the kingdom of God" (NIV). The appearance of the "rich man" in verse 25 called for a smoother transition into this topic than provided by verse 24 in the form found in ℵ and B. What is more, the words of verse 24, without the added limitation, seemed too harsh to many readers. Again we see that it is easier to understand how the phrase could be *added* than to understand why it would have been *deleted*. Of course, someone might argue that the omission in such a small number of manuscripts could have been due to simple scribal error, and such is, of course, a possibility. Hence we see the importance and benefit of having good textual notes in any translation being used. The reading should be noted if it is not contained in the text; or, if it is contained in the text, its absence in ℵ and B should be noted as well. In either case, the reader should be given all the information available.

Luke 2:14		
KJV	NIV	NASB
Glory to God in the highest, and on earth peace, **good will toward men**.	"Glory to God in the highest, and on earth peace to **men on whom his favor rests**."	"Glory to God in the highest, And on earth peace **among men with whom He is pleased**."

This variant involves the difference between the nominative form of the word *eudokia* (εὐδοκία) and the genitive form, *eudokias* (εὐδοκίας). The KJV follows the large majority of Greek texts in having the nominative *eudokia*, while the modern versions follow a minority of texts in reading *eudokias*. Dr. Metzger notes[26] that there is a possibility that the move from the genitive to the nominative could have taken place by simple oversight: in the uncial texts at the end of a line the genitive would have looked like this: ΕΥΔΟΚΙΑ᷎. The final sigma (᷎) would have been much smaller than usual, and hence could easily have been missed in copying. Furthermore, the nominative makes an "easier" reading than the genitive, which speaks of God's peace seen in the birth of the Savior resting on those that *God* has chosen to be the recipients thereof.

Edward F. Hills cites Theodore Beza, who, though retaining the nominative reading in his text, felt the genitive was the more likely reading: "Nevertheless, following the authority of Origen, Chrysostom, the Old (*Vulgate*) translation, and finally the sense itself, I should prefer to read *(men) of good will.*"[27] Compare this insight from Beza, whose readings were preferred by the KJV translators more than anyone else's, with the words of KJV Only advocate Gail Riplinger on the same passage:

> The former has the genitive *eudokios* [*sic*], while the latter has the nominative *eudokia*. Watch out for the letter 's'—sin, Satan, Sodom, Saul (had to be changed to Paul). The added 's' here is the hiss of the serpent. . . . In their passion to give space to Satan's sermon, they follow four corrupt fourth and fifth century MSS while ignoring a total of 53 ancient witnesses including 16 belonging to the second, third and fourth centuries and 37 from the fifth, sixth, seventh and eighth centuries.[28]

The difference between textual criticism done on the basis of facts and evidence, and that done on the basis of conspiracies and prejudgment, is plainly evident.

John 6:47	
KJV	**NASB**
Verily, verily, I say unto you, He that believeth **on me** hath everlasting life.	Truly, truly, I say to you, he who believes has eternal life.

The double standard that is inherent to the KJV Only position is well illustrated in the citation of John 6:47. The difference between the KJV and the NASB is readily seen. The modern Greek texts do not have "in me" following the term "believe."[29] As a result, serious charges of "tampering with the Gospel" are lodged against all translations that would not include this later addition to the text. Note the strong words of D.A. Waite:

> This is, perhaps, one of the CLEAREST theological errors in these three versions. To make salvation only a matter of **"believing"** rather than solely, as Christ said in this verse, **"believing on Me,"** is truly **"ANOTHER GOSPEL"**! If you were trying to lead someone to Christ with the NIV or NASV, using this verse, they could "believe" in anything and still have "everlasting life"—whether in Santa Claus, in the Easter Bunny, in the Tooth Fairy, in Rudolph the Red-nosed Reindeer, or in any of the false world religions! This is **SERIOUS THEOLOGICAL PERVERSION! This is certainly a matter of doctrine and theology.**[30]

Does the modern rendering of John 6:47 allow for faith in Santa Claus or the Easter Bunny for salvation? Do we have here a patent denial of the Gospel?

John 6:35 in the NASB reads,

> Jesus said to them, "I am the bread of life; he who comes to Me shall not hunger, and **he who believes in Me** shall never thirst."

And John 6:40 says,

> For this is the will of My Father, that everyone who beholds the Son and **believes in Him**, may have eternal life; and I Myself will raise him up on the last day.

Here, a scant few verses prior to John 6:47, the NASB (and all other modern versions) plainly present the Lord Jesus defining for all who would hear the object of the faith about which He was speaking. "He who believes **in Me**" the Lord says. As usual, we have to wonder why the modern versions would seek to hide faith in Christ in John 6:47 and not do the same thing only twelve verses earlier. Quite seriously, could anyone read John 6:35 through 6:47 and *not* know what the object of "faith" in verse 47 is to be? One would have to be a very poor reader not to understand what the Lord is talking about. But to pursue this thought just a bit further, why does the NASB have the following passages in the Gospel of John, if, in fact, it is trying to allow people to believe in any old thing, but not in Christ alone for salvation?

> John 7:38: **He who believes in Me**, as the Scripture said, "From his innermost being shall flow rivers of living water."

> John 11:25-26: Jesus said to her, "I am the resurrection and the life; **he who believes in Me** shall live even if he dies, and everyone who lives and **believes in Me** shall never die. Do you believe this?"

> John 12:44: And Jesus cried out and said, "**He who believes in Me** does not believe in Me, but in Him who sent Me."

> John 12:46: "I have come *as* light into the world, that everyone **who believes in Me** may not remain in darkness."

It seems too obvious to mention that the entire idea that the modern translations have some doctrinal impurity for not having "in Me" at John 6:47 falls flat upon the most basic examination. But, there is more. What happens if we apply Dr. Waite's standard to the KJV? Does the KJV *always* clearly define the object of faith? Not always. A quick perusal of the text reveals the following passages:

> Mark 9:23 (KJV): Jesus said unto him, If thou canst believe, all things *are* possible to him that believeth.

Him that believeth *what*?

> Romans 1:16 (KJV): For I am not ashamed of the gospel of Christ: for it is the power of God unto salvation to every one that believeth; to the Jew first, and also to the Greek.

Everyone that believeth *what*?

> Romans 10:4 (KJV): For Christ *is* the end of the law for righteousness to every one that believeth.

The end of the law for everyone that believeth in *what*?

> 1 Corinthians 7:12 (KJV): But to the rest speak I, not the Lord:
> If any brother hath a wife that believeth not, and she be pleased
> to dwell with him, let him not put her away.

What does the wife not believe? The KJV doesn't say.

It is hard to understand how anyone can possibly look at John 6:47 and seriously think that there is some malevolent purpose behind the reading in the modern translations. Surely the information as to *why* "in Me" is not found in the NASB or NIV is easily obtainable.

Yet KJV Only advocates do not address this, but rather focus attention upon an issue that is, in fact, self-contradictory: the idea that if you don't define the object of belief in *every instance*, you are somehow opening the door to all kinds of problems, even though the KJV does the same thing in many other places. This is a classic example of the use of a double standard. Here KJV Only advocates are found misusing the Gospel message itself to enlist people to their side, frightening people into thinking the modern versions are somehow attacking faith in the Lord Jesus Christ.

John 7:8	
KJV	**NASB**
Go ye up unto this feast: I go not up **yet** unto this feast; for my time is not yet full come.	"Go up to the feast yourselves; I do **not** go up to this feast because My time has not yet fully come."

Dr. Waite insists that the modern translations at this point place in the mouth of the Lord Jesus "a lying falsehood."[31] Certainly one can see his point: the Lord Jesus says in verse 8 that he is "not" going up to the Feast in the NASB, yet in verse 10 He does so. Does this not involve dishonesty on His part?

The problem here is that again we are trying to determine the reading of the text not on the basis of external and internal criteria, but upon what we *think* the text *should* say so as to fit our preconceived notions. There is a perfectly logical explanation of the NASB's reading that does not involve the Lord Jesus in dishonesty. When saying that

He was not going up to the feast, this should be understood as referring to the public procession to Jerusalem that was part of the regular celebration. Large groups of pilgrims would gather together, singing and celebrating (and sharing more safety in numbers I might add). The Lord indicates that He is not going up *openly* because His time is not yet come. However, He does then go up to the feast, but "secretly" as the NASB says, not openly and publicly. Hence, the reading of the NASB does *not* involve Jesus in dishonesty if it is understood properly.

Many modern scholars feel that quite early on in the transmission of this section of John the very same concern that motivates Dr. Waite to object to the reading "not" (in Greek, οὐκ) prompted them to change it to "not yet" (in Greek, οὔπω). In this case, however, the external evidence is greatly in favor of the reading "not yet." In fact, the UBS 4th edition gives the reading "not" a {C} rating, and for good reason. The reading "not yet" is supported by an awesome array of witnesses: $\mathfrak{P}^{66}$ $\mathfrak{P}^{75}$ B L T W Δ Θ Ψ 070 0105 0141 0250 f^1 f^{13} 28 33 157 180 205 597 700 892 1006 1010 1243 1292 1342 1424 1505, most lectionaries, a number of early versions, Basil, and the 𝔐 text! One cannot dismiss the reading "not yet" without going against the *vast* majority of the external evidence. Hence, given that the reading of "not yet" is a strong possibility, and that the reading "not" does not necessitate any dishonesty on the Lord's part, we see yet again that the modern texts do not denigrate the Lord Jesus.

Acts 4:25	
KJV	**NIV**
Who by the mouth of thy servant David hast said, Why did the heathen rage, and the people imagine vain things?	You spoke by **the Holy Spirit through** the mouth of your servant, our father David: "Why do the nations rage and the peoples plot in vain?"

Here we find a variant that is not normally cited in KJV Only material, and I believe the reason is fairly obvious. Here we find the unusual situation of the modern texts, following the most ancient manuscripts,[32] including a reading that has fallen out of the majority of Greek manuscripts, including those utilized in producing the TR. The phrase is not only eminently orthodox, it is theologically significant as well. It is an important verification of the role of the Holy Spirit in the inspiration of the writings of David in the Old Testament. One would think that writers who constantly assert that the KJV is "theologically superior" in similar situations, would embrace such a reading with joy. Yet such is not the case. I could not find a single reference to this passage anywhere in D.A. Waite's 307-page work, for example, though it is obviously "theologically significant." It is not cited, perhaps, because it raises a point that KJV Only literature does not wish to admit: even on the basis of their own standards, there are places where the modern texts are theologically superior to the KJV, and this is one of them. Another is found in Acts 16:7:

Acts 16:7	
KJV	**NIV**
After they were come to Mysia, they assayed to go into Bithynia: but the Spirit suffered them not.	When they came to the border of Mysia, they tried to enter Bithynia, but the Spirit **of Jesus** would not allow them to.

Here the modern texts again enjoy the support of the best ancient manuscripts. The identification of the Spirit as the "Spirit of Jesus" is theologically significant, of course. This passage should interest those KJV Only advocates who cite the variant at Romans 14:10, where modern texts speak of the "judgment seat of God," while the KJV has the "judgment seat of Christ." If reading "God" at Romans 14:10 indicates a theological bias against Christ by modern translations, doesn't *not* reading "Jesus" at Acts 16:7 prove the same thing regarding the KJV? Of course, neither accusation is true.

Acts 22:16	
KJV	**NASB**
arise, and be baptized, and wash away thy sins, calling on **the name of the Lord**.	Arise, and be baptized, and wash away your sins, calling on **His name**.

We have seen examples of this kind of variant in the chart we presented in chapter 2. I note it here out of fairness. Why? One will search in vain through the 25th, 26th, and 27th editions of the Nestle-

Aland text, and through the UBS 2nd, 3rd, 3rd corrected, and 4th editions, for even the slightest indication that this variant even exists, despite the fact that "the name of the Lord" is the reading of the majority of Greek manuscripts! Other older Greek texts, such as Von Soden[33] and Tregelles,[34] note the variant. Von Soden points out that it is probably another example of parallel influence from Romans 10:13 and 1 Corinthians 1:2. However, very few people have access to a resource such as Von Soden's text. Surely a reading like this, despite the fact that it is probably secondary, should at the very least be noted for the sake of all those who wish to do textual studies.

Romans 1:16	
KJV	**NIV**
For I am not ashamed of the gospel **of Christ**: for it is the power of God unto salvation to every one that believeth;	I am not ashamed of the gospel, because it is the power of God for the salvation of everyone who believes:

Here is another place where KJV Only advocates insist that the modern versions are trying to denigrate Christ by removing His name from the Scriptures. Actually, the modern versions are following the most ancient manuscripts[35] while recognizing the tendency toward expansion that is found in the Byzantine manuscripts. However, we must point out that the modern versions use the phrase "the gospel of Christ" elsewhere (it appears eight times in the NIV translation of the New Testament), so again there is no logical reason to impute evil motives to these translations.

Romans 8:34	
KJV	**NASB**
Who *is* he that condemneth? *It is* Christ that died, yea rather, that is risen again, who is even at the right hand of God, who also maketh intercession for us.	who is the one who condemns? Christ **Jesus** is He who died, yes, rather who was raised, who is at the right hand of God, who also intercedes for us.

Turning the tables a bit we here encounter a variant that "bucks the trend" so to speak. Here ℵ, A, and C (and possibly 𝔓[46]) have the name "Jesus" at Romans 8:34, while the 𝔐 text and B do not have it.

Despite its early presence in the manuscripts, the Nestle-Aland 27th edition places the term in brackets, questioning its inclusion in the text. This is due, of course, to the possibility of the "expansion of piety" even in the most ancient texts. Its importance to the KJV Only issue should be readily apparent: is the NASB "superior" to the KJV at Romans 8:34 simply because it has "Christ Jesus" rather than "Christ"? Is the KJV trying to "hide" the name of Jesus here? Of course not, and yet this is, again, a further example of the inconsistency in the application of arguments on the part of KJV Only advocates.

Romans 11:6	
KJV	NASB
And if by grace, then *is it* no more of works: otherwise grace is no more grace. **But if *it be* of works, then is it no more grace: otherwise work is no more work**.	But if it is by grace, it is no longer on the basis of works, otherwise grace is no longer grace.

Here we have a variant that demonstrates a tendency in later scribes that we have not yet had occasion to examine. Scribes tended to "balance" statements. Romans 11:6 is an example of this. Some early scribe[36] either felt that the statement needed to be expanded, or he himself had heard someone preach or teach about the passage so as to lead him to think that this passage contained the longer ending. In reality, the addition is not wholly in line with Paul's thinking, for while the term "grace" carries within it the freedom and "unmeritedness" that marks its use in Paul's theology, the term "work" does not communicate the same kinds of ideas. Another example of this kind of "balancing" of passages is found just a little later, at Romans 14:6:

Romans 14:6	
KJV	NASB
He that regardeth the day, regardeth *it* unto the Lord; **and he that regardeth not the day, to the Lord he doth not regard *it*.** He that eateth, eateth to the Lord, for he giveth God thanks; and he that eateth not, to the Lord he eateth not, and giveth God thanks.	He who observes the day, observes it for the Lord, and he who eats, does so for the Lord, for he gives thanks to God; and he who eats not, for the Lord he does not eat, and gives thanks to God.

Here the impetus for the addition is even clearer than in 11:6. The second section of the verse contains a balanced statement by the Apostle. The first, however, contains only one side of the statement. The insertion of the added material "balances" the entire passage out.

Romans 15:29	
KJV	**NIV**
And I am sure that, when I come unto you, I shall come in the fulness of the blessing **of the gospel** of Christ.	I know that when I come to you, I will come in the full measure of the blessing of Christ.

The reading "of the gospel" at Romans 15:29 is yet another place where KJV Only advocates can make an accusation against modern texts. Yet, we must point out again that the modern translations are merely following the Greek texts at this point. The phrase is not found in a wide variety of manuscripts, primarily of the Alexandrian text-type.[37] Many scholars would say that the later reading is an expansion, but there is another possibility that must be pointed out: the phrase "of the gospel" could have been accidentally skipped over early on due to "homoeoteleuton" (similar endings).[38] In either case, no malicious intention can be asserted one way or the other.

1 Corinthians 10:28	
KJV	**NASB**
But if any man say unto you, This is offered in sacrifice unto idols, eat not for his sake that showed it, and for conscience sake: **for the earth is the Lord's, and the fulness thereof:**	But if anyone should say to you, "This is meat sacrificed to idols," do not eat *it*, for the sake of the one who informed *you*, and for conscience' sake;

This passage is not very popular in KJV Only materials, but it does illustrate yet again the tendency toward *expansion* that is found in the New Testament manuscripts. The phrase "for the earth is the Lord's, and the fulness thereof" appears in all Greek texts in verse 26 immediately after the phrase, "for conscience sake." The repeated use of the phrase "for conscience sake" in verse 26 led a later scribe[39] to repeat the phrase yet once again in verse 28, though in all honesty the phrase simply does not fit at this point, while it made sense in verse 26.

Ephesians 3:9	
KJV	**NASB**
And to make all *men* see what *is* the **fellowship** of the mystery, which from the beginning of the **world** hath been hid in God, who created all things **by Jesus Christ**:	and to bring to light what is the **administration** of the mystery which for **ages** has been hidden in God, who created all things;

There are two textual variants at Ephesians 3:9, and one difference in translation of the same term. We have already noted the fact that the TR has a very unusual reading of "fellowship," found only in the margin of minuscule manuscript 31 and a few other very late manuscripts, rather than the reading of all ancient manuscripts including the uncials, 99% of the minuscules, and all the early Fathers, which have "administration."[40] We then note the more accurate rendering of the NASB, "ages" over against the KJV's "world." Finally the modern versions do not contain the phrase "by Jesus Christ" with reference to the creation of all things. Regarding this final variant, we quote Dr. Metzger's comments:

> The Textus Receptus, following D^c K L P many minuscules syr^h $^{with\,*}$ *al*, adds δια Ἰησου Χριστου. Since there is no reason why, if the words were original, they should have been omitted, the Committee preferred to read simply κτισαντι, which is decisively supported by $\mathfrak{P}^{46}$ ℵ A B C D* F G P 33 1319 1611 2127 and most versions and early patristic quotations.[41]

Yet this passage is frequently quoted by KJV Only advocates as evidence of the corruption of modern versions. It is a favorite of Gail Riplinger, who writes,

> The Greek *Textus Receptus* has the word for "fellowship," while other Greek texts use a word which could easily be translated as such. The words "by Jesus Christ" are in the majority of Greek manuscripts and are out in only a few Egyptian manuscripts. Ephesians 3:9 is a microcosm of the new versions. They have: (1.) no comforting fellowship, (2.) a New Age world that had no beginning, but is cyclical and (3.) no Jesus Christ.[42]

We note that: (1) Riplinger seems to recognize, but fails to acknowledge, the fact that the TR's reading of "fellowship" is pitted against 99.5% of all the Greek manuscripts; (2) the term "administration" is not, as she seems to indicate, a synonym for "fellowship"; (3) the manuscript evidence against the reading goes far beyond a "few Egyptian manuscripts" as Metzger's quotation indicates; (4) one could turn the argument around and say the KJV has "no administration of the mystery" as well, but that is hardly a meaningful argument; (5) correctly translating the term for "age" has nothing to do with the New Age; and (6) the "new versions" present Jesus Christ fully, accurately, and without compromise. Riplinger's accusations are simply groundless.[43]

Philippians 1:14		
KJV	NASB	UBS 4th / NA 27th
And many of the brethren in the Lord, waxing confident by my bonds, are much more bold to speak the word without fear.	and that most of the brethren, trusting in the Lord because of my imprisonment, have far more courage to speak the word **of God** without fear.	Omits "of God"[44]

This passage is one of only a very few that can be rightly used to assert that the Byzantine text-type has at least *some* readings that are both ancient and unique. The phrase "of God" is found primarily in Alexandrian manuscripts. It is deleted primarily in Byzantine manuscripts, with the notable exception of $\mathfrak{P}^{46}$. This is one of the few places where the Byzantine text rightly claims the support of an early papyrus manuscript for a unique, significant reading. The NASB follows an earlier edition of the Nestle text. The Nestle-Aland 27th edition has placed "of God" in the reference notes and gives the reading found in the KJV. There is some irony in the fact that when we do find a uniquely Byzantine reading that carries great weight, the reading goes against the general trend of KJV Only arguments! How so? First, the modern Greek texts adopt it, showing that they are willing to follow the data where it leads and are not on a crusade to do everything possible to "put down" the KJV. Secondly, the reading is one that is *away from* the normal "fuller" text of the Byzantine tradition. If the reverse were true, and the modern texts *removed* "of God" here in opposition to the Byzantine texts, we would certainly find modern KJV Only advocates using this passage as evidence of the "doctrinal inferiority" of modern texts.

Colossians 2:11	
KJV	**NASB**
In whom also ye are circumcised with the circumcision made without hands, in putting off the body **of the sins** of the flesh by the circumcision of Christ:	and in Him you were also circumcised with a circumcision made without hands, in the removal of the body of the flesh by the circumcision of Christ;

One of the arguments used by advocates of the Byzantine text is that Codex Sinaiticus (‭א‬) contains numerous corrections by later hands, hence demonstrating that it is "corrupt." We have already noted that what this really demonstrates is how highly the manuscript was esteemed that it would be used so often and for so long as to collect so many corrections. We have also noted that these corrections, coming later through the centuries, are generally *toward* the prevailing text of the day, the Byzantine. Colossians 2:11 provides us with an example of this kind of change.

The insertion of the phrase "of the sins" is cited in the Nestle-Aland 27th as having the support of "‭א‬[2]." This refers us to the second corrector of Sinaiticus, whose work is dated to the seventh century. We find the same manuscript cited, however, in support of the exclusion of the phrase, but in the form "‭א‬*." This refers to the original reading of the manuscript. The phrase is also not found in $\mathfrak{P}^{46}$ B C and others.

Colossians 2:18	
KJV	**NIV**
Let no man beguile you of your reward in a voluntary humility and worshipping of angels, intruding into those things which **he hath not seen**, vainly puffed up by his fleshly mind,	Do not let anyone who delights in false humility and the worship of angels disqualify you for the prize. Such a person goes into great detail about what **he has seen**, and his unspiritual mind puffs him up with idle notions.

Some have referred to this passage as evidence that modern scholars wish to lead believers to disobey God's Word by having "visions."[45] In reality, the support for the NIV's rendering encompasses manuscripts from both the Alexandrian and Western families.[46] What is more, it is hard to understand how anyone could present such an argument. Nothing in the passage *in either translation* asserts the reality of such "visions." The NIV translation is easily understood in the context of such a person *claiming* to have seen things, but it does not assert that they actually *have* seen such things. The translation does not require that particular *interpretation*. The point of the passage has to do with what men with "unspiritual minds" do, not that they actually *have* such visions, or that these visions correspond to reality.

| 1 Timothy 1:17 ||
KJV	NASB
Now unto the King eternal, immortal, invisible, the only **wise** God, *be* honour and glory for ever and ever. Amen.	Now to the King eternal, immortal, invisible, the only God, *be* honor and glory forever and ever. Amen.

Romans 16:27 may be the source of the insertion of the term "wise" into the phrase "only wise God," or it is quite possible that the term dropped out by accident again owing to scribal error and the similar forms of the words "only wise God" (in the uncial forms: ΜΟΝΩΣΟΦΩΘΕΩ). Obviously, however, there is no attempt to strip God of His wisdom in the modern versions, which include the term at Romans 16:27.

| James 5:16 ||
KJV	NASB
Confess *your* **faults** one to another, and pray one for another, that ye may be healed.	Therefore, confess your **sins** to one another, and pray for one another, so that you may be healed.

Here we see the difference between "faults" and "sins" in the modern translations. The support for "sins" comes from the ancient uncial texts, the reading "faults" arising later and becoming the majority reading. This passage is a favorite of KJV Only advocates. Note Peter Ruckman:

> You say, "What is the manuscript evidence?" The evidence is not listed. In the footnotes (on p. 582 of Nestle's) you will find Aleph, B, and A listed *every time they appear anywhere in James 5:11-20, but they are NOT cited for James 5:16!* "τας αμαρτιας" is a Roman Catholic interpolation, adopted by the ASV (1901) and the RSV (1952) to help the Ecumenical movement along, and the ASV is just as corrupt as its cousin, in this reading.[47]

This may well explain where Gail Riplinger derived her information on the same passage. I cite her chart from page 145 of *New Age Bible Versions:*

New Versions		KJV
confess your sins	James 5:16	confess your faults (All Greek texts have the word for faults here, —not sins.)

Neither Ruckman nor Riplinger is correct. Ruckman is referring to the 25th edition of the Nestle-Aland text. He is simply misreading the apparatus. ℵ, A and B are *not* cited in every variant, especially when they read as the text reads. At James 5:16 they read exactly as the text does, hence only the variant and its supporting manuscripts are cited. There is simply no basis for Ruckman's grand conspiratorial scheme. Seemingly Riplinger, following Ruckman's reading of the Nestle text, falls into the same trap, as her chart appears in a section where she is also asserting that modern versions are polluted by Roman influence. She is simply incorrect[48] in her assertion regarding the Greek texts.

1 Peter 2:2	
KJV	**NASB**
As newborn babes, desire the sincere milk of the word, that ye may grow thereby:	like newborn babes, long for the pure milk of the word, that by it you may grow **in respect to salvation,**

This passage is often cited as evidence that the modern texts teach a "works-salvation" system. Normally it is grouped together with the more accurate translation of the Greek participles that we discussed in chapter 6, such as "being saved."[49] The phrase "unto salvation" is found in a large portion of the more ancient manuscripts,[50] and represents a rather clear Alexandrian + Western reading against the Byzantine family reading. What is unusual, however, is the fact that it is the Byzantine that lacks the reading, not the other way around. The alleged theological problem is not a problem at all. Just as we are to "work out" our salvation with fear and trembling (Philippians 2:12—the fear and trembling being due to the fact that verse 13 tells us that it is God who is at work within us!), so we are to "grow in respect to salvation," that is, we are to increase in the knowledge of our Lord Jesus Christ, and we are to grow up in the faith, becoming mature believers. The possible *misuse* of a passage cannot be made the basis upon which we determine textual readings.

1 John 4:3	
KJV	**NIV**
And every spirit that confesseth not that **Jesus Christ is come in the flesh** is not of God: and this is that *spirit* of antichrist, whereof ye have heard that it should come; and even now already is it in the world.	but every spirit that does not acknowledge Jesus is not from God. This is the spirit of the antichrist, which you have heard is coming and even now is already in the world.

While it seems hard to believe, this passage is used by some KJV Only advocates as evidence that the modern versions wish to deny the centrality of Christ's coming in the flesh because the phrase is not found in verse 3 of the NIV, NASB, etc. I say "hard to believe" because anyone who reads the NIV has to get past verse 2 to get to verse 3:

> This is how you can recognize the Spirit of God: Every spirit that acknowledges that Jesus Christ has come in the flesh is from God (1 John 4:2, NIV).

The repetition of the phrase in verse 3 was prompted by the second use of "confess" or "acknowledge." This caused a number of variants, some reading simply "acknowledge Jesus Christ," some, "acknowledge that Jesus has come in flesh," "Jesus the Lord has come in the flesh,"[51] and the TR's "Jesus Christ has come in the flesh." Whenever one finds a number of different variants, one can be sure that the shorter reading (that of the modern texts) is the best, as it gave rise to all the others that are found in the manuscripts.

Despite the plain confession of the coming of Christ in the flesh that is found in all the Alexandrian and Western manuscripts at 1 John 4:2, and the faithful presentation of this truth in the NIV, NASB, RSV, NRSV, NEB, etc., KJV Only advocate Gail Riplinger can cite *only* verse 3, *never once mentioning verse 2,* and write,

> Bruce Metzger, author of the *Reader's Digest New Testament,* as well as co-editor of the *UBS Greek New Testament,* picked the wrong verse to help create a slimline bible. By omitting "Christ" and "is come in the flesh," new versions are *not* confessing that "Jesus Christ is come in the flesh"; as John says, "this is that spirit of antichrist." Readers, who subscribe to these "deceivers," may have full bookshelves instead of a "full reward."[52]

The "deception," it would appear, is being promulgated not by Dr. Metzger or any of the men who have faithfully translated *both* 1 John 4:2 and 3 into English, but by KJV Only advocates who fail to give the whole story and, hence, present an unbalanced picture.

Revelation 1:11	
KJV	**NASB**
Saying, **I am Alpha and Omega, the first and the last**: and, What thou seest, write in a book, and send *it* unto the seven churches which are **in Asia**[53] . . .	saying, "Write in a book what you see, and send *it* to the seven churches. . . ."

This variant demonstrates how even the 𝕸 text can split, though in this case not evenly. The TR's inclusion of the phrase is based upon a minority of the 𝕸 text,[54] while the rest of the 𝕸 text joins both ℵ and A in not containing the obvious addition, drawn from Revelation 22:13. But for KJV Only advocates the modern versions are again somehow "denying" the deity of Christ by having the phrase at 1:8 and 22:13 but not at 1:11.[55]

Revelation 19:1	
KJV	NASB
And after these things I heard a great voice of much people in heaven, saying, Alleluia; Salvation, and glory, and honour, and power, unto **the Lord our God**:	After these things I heard, as it were, a loud voice of a great multitude in heaven, saying, "Hallelujah! Salvation and glory and power belong to our **God**"

The final variant we will examine again finds the 𝔐 text splitting and the TR following one of the two possible readings. The Alexandrian text joins with part of the Byzantine text in having simply "our God," while the other section of the Byzantine has "the Lord our God." If someone were to assert that the modern texts are detracting from God's glory by not having "Lord," does it follow that all the Byzantine texts that likewise do not have "Lord" are also a part of this grand conspiracy?

Modern Texts Found Innocent

Conspiratorial thinking tends to see the "facts" in such a way as to *always* support one's preconceived notions. Once a person has accepted the idea that the "modern versions" are somehow in league with one another to "get" the KJV and to "hide" God's truths, every instance of variation between the KJV and those versions is filled with great importance. Rather than examining the facts and gaining a proper perspective on the issue, KJV Only advocates find in the most innocent scribal error a grand scheme to rob Christ of His deity or deny that salvation is by grace through faith. Yet, even a cursory examination of the *facts* is sufficient to make the reasoning behind the modern versions and their textual choices plain and understandable *for those who are willing to listen.*

Those who use a modern translation that was produced by godly men who were seeking simply to follow the best texts of the Hebrew Old Testament and the Greek New Testament, and to faithfully translate those texts into the English language, can have great confidence that they are reading God's Word in the best form in which it can be found in their language. The comparison of these translations against one another only serves to sharpen our understanding of the intention of the original authors. And when textual variants appear in footnotes or in comparison with the KJV, believers can be assured that these things arose not because of some attempt to hide the truth from them, but due to the very understandable actions of scribes down through the centuries who were themselves doing their best to accurately copy those precious manuscripts. Rather than being fearful that they can't be "certain" about what God has revealed, they should rejoice that God has made it possible for them to have and hold His Word, and they should seek to obey His will that is so clearly presented therein. The preacher and teacher can proclaim God's truth from the pages of such a translation with the full assurance that he is proclaiming the *whole counsel of God*, and can trust God with the results.

Endnotes

[1] Chapter 4, pp. 60-62.

[2] Dr. Bruce Metzger has given us an invaluable insight into how this process works in his book, *A Textual Commentary on the Greek New Testament,* Corrected Edition (United Bible Societies: 1975).

[3] Many KJV Only advocates glory in this fact. There is a strong element of anti-intellectualism in the Fundamentalist movement, and it is very popular to vilify "scholars" and "scholarship" as if being a prepared student of the Bible with a wide range of skills is somehow antithetical to Christian piety.

[4] Many critics of modern textual methods like to point out that there are variations between representatives of each "text-type," and hence any discussion based upon text-types is meaningless. Surely there are variations between representatives of each text-type. But text-types are used to describe groupings of manuscripts that contain common *types or patterns* of variation, not *identical* readings. Some defenders of the Byzantine text-type have pointed to Byzantine readings in the papyri (Harry Sturz, *The Byzantine Text-Type and New Testament Textual Criticism* [Thomas Nelson: 1984]). However, Dr. Daniel Wallace has well noted regarding this point:

> The difference between a reading and a text-type is the difference between a particular variant and a pattern of variation. For example, although both the NIV and KJV have identical wording in John 1:1, the pattern of variation of the NIV found over a whole paragraph will differ from the KJV. No one would argue that a handwritten copy of John 1:1 from c. AD 1775 was taken from the NIV—even though its wording would be identical with the wording of the NIV for that verse. Yet this is the same kind of argument that MT [Majority Text] defenders use for the primitiveness of the Byzantine text. Simply because isolated Byzantine readings are found before the fourth century is no argument that the Byzantine text existed before the fourth century. They have confused reading with text ("The Majority-Text Theory: History, Methods and Critique,"

Journal of the Evangelical Theological Society, June 1994, p. 209).

[5] Adapted from Wallace, p. 206.

[6] This can be seen by noting the total number of manuscripts by century, remembering that the Byzantine makes up at least 75% of the total number of manuscripts, and the *vast* majority of manuscripts after the ninth (IX) century. Below I reproduce a graph (adapted from Kurt and Barbara Aland, *The Text of the New Testament* (Eerdmans:1987), p. 82) that gives the reader a visual means of recognizing the relationship between the number of papyri, uncial, and minuscule manuscripts available to us today. The Roman numerals on the left side represent each century. As is clear, the minuscules far outnumber all others:

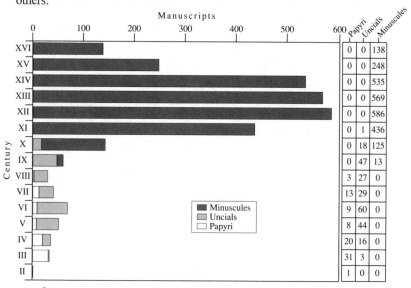

Century	Papyri	Uncials	Minuscules
XVI	0	0	138
XV	0	0	248
XIV	0	0	535
XIII	0	0	569
XII	0	0	586
XI	0	1	436
X	0	18	125
IX	0	47	13
VIII	3	27	0
VII	13	29	0
VI	9	60	0
V	8	44	0
IV	20	16	0
III	31	3	0
II	1	0	0

[7] Again we note that it is common for defenders of the Byzantine text to point to *instances* where early Fathers follow a Byzantine reading here or there, but individuals readings do not a text-type make. Gordon Fee noted,

> Over the past eight years I have been collating the Greek patristic evidence for Luke and John for the International Greek New Testament Project. In all of this material I have found one invariable: A good critical edition of a father's text, or the discovery of early MSS, *always* moves the father's text of the NT *away from* the TR and *closer to* the text of our modern critical editions (Gordon Fee, "Modern Textual Criticism and the Revival of the *Textus Receptus*" (*Journal of the Evangelical Theological Society,* March 1978), pp. 26-27).

[8] Wallace notes that of these eight, six are not "distinctively Byzantine," specifically, Luke 10:21; 14:3, 34; 15:21; John 10:38; 19:11. Ibid., p. 207.

[9] These verses are: Matthew 17:21; 18:11; 23:14; Mark 7:16; 9:44, 46, 11:26; 15:28; Luke 23:17; John 5:4; Acts 24:7; 28:29, and Romans 16:24.

[10] Specifically, ℵ B L Δ* 0274 and at least two early translations.

[11] That this is almost certainly the case can be seen from noting that the verse itself has many, many textual variants in the manuscripts in which it is included; other manuscripts place asterisks around the verse, indicating that the scribe who copied that manuscript realized that the verse was not present in all manuscripts available to him. What is more, the verse is not present in the two oldest manuscripts of John, $\mathfrak{P}^{66}$ and $\mathfrak{P}^{75}$.

[12] See the discussion of this variant in Part Two.

[13] Riplinger has confirmed in her second book, *Which Bible Is God's Word?*, that I was correct in assuming she was referring to Mark 10:21.

[14] The other three passages have "take up *his* cross" rather than "take up *the* cross," but even here the textual variant found at Mark 10:21 shows some manuscripts that have "take up *your* cross" as well.

[15] See the citation of textual evidence in Part Two, p. 272.

[16] Specifically, $\mathfrak{P}^{45,75}$ ℵ B L and others.

[17] The modern texts follow ℵ* B L Δ Θ f^1 f^{13} a number of minuscules, versions, and Fathers.

[18] Seemingly that is Gail Riplinger's thought when she cites this passage in her chart on page 260 of *New Age Bible Versions* (A.V. Publications: 1993).

[19] D.A. Waite, *Defending the King James Bible* (The Bible for Today: 1992), pp. 146-147.

[20] Dr. Peter Ruckman, *Handbook of Manuscript Evidence* (Pensacola Bible Press: 1970), p. 116.

[21] Ibid., p. 164.

[22] See the discussion of the textual data on this variant in Part Two, p. 254.

[23] Ruckman's rather entertaining theory that men like Origen and Jerome didn't bother to read Malachi and hence just jumped to a bad conclusion ignores the fact that both men quoted widely from all of the Scriptures and could not in the least bit be accused of ignorance of the conflation of Malachi and Isaiah in Mark 1:2-3.

[24] See Dr. Gleason Archer's discussion of this in *The Encyclopedia of Bible Difficulties* (Zondervan: 1982), p. 345.

[25] One might note that this fact favors the textual veracity of ℵ and B, given the early rise of ascetic piety in Egypt.

[26] Metzger, *A Textual Commentary*, p. 133.

[27] Edward F. Hills, *The King James Version Defended* (The Christian Research Press: 1984), p. 206.

[28] Riplinger, *New Age Bible Versions*, pp. 232-233.

[29] See the discussion of the textual evidence in Part Two, p. 261-262.

[30] D.A. Waite, *Defending the King James Bible* (The Bible for Today:

1992), p. 158.
   ³¹ Ibid., p. 163.
   ³² The phrase "Holy Spirit" is found in such sources as $\mathfrak{P}^{74}$ ℵ A B D E Ψ and many others.
   ³³ Hermann Freiherr Von Soden, *Die Schriften Des Neuen Testaments* (Göttingen: 1913), p. 586.
   ³⁴ Samuel Prideaux Tregelles, *The Greek New Testament* (London: 1879), p. 588.
   ³⁵ $\mathfrak{P}^{26}$ ℵ A B C D* G and others.
   ³⁶ The longer ending is not found in $\mathfrak{P}^{46}$ ℵ* A C D F G P 1739 1881 and others.
   ³⁷ The phrase is not found in $\mathfrak{P}^{46}$ ℵ* A B C D F G P 6 81 629 620 1506 1739 1881 and a few others.
   ³⁸ This can be seen by looking at the Greek phrase: εὐλογίας τοῦ εὐαγγελίου τοῦ Χριστοῦ. One might also note the similarity in the first two letters of εὐλογίας and εὐαγγελίου.
   ³⁹ The reading is found only in the third-hand correction of C, the final corrector of H, and in the original of the eighth- or ninth-century manuscript Ψ. From here, however, it became the 𝔐 reading.
   ⁴⁰ The Greek term in the TR is κοινωνία, while in the Greek manuscripts it is οἰκονομία. This is, arguably, the most obviously erroneous reading in the TR outside of the added words in the last six verses of Revelation.
   ⁴¹ Metzger, *A Textual Commentary*, pp. 603-604.
   ⁴² Riplinger, *New Age Bible Versions,* p. 456.
   ⁴³ For a full discussion of the passages relevant to the deity of Christ, please see chapter 8.
   ⁴⁴ The NASB follows an earlier edition of the Nestle-Aland text that contained the reading "of God." The 26th and 27th indicate changes in its textual choices by placing the " † " symbol before the reading in the textual apparatus. Hence this passage begins in the 27th edition, "**14** ᵀ † του θεου ℵ B" etc.
   ⁴⁵ Riplinger, *New Age Bible Versions*, p. 106.
   ⁴⁶ See the further discussion of the passage in Part Two, pp. 266-267.
   ⁴⁷ Ruckman, *The Christian's Handbook of Manuscript Evidence,* p. 101.
   ⁴⁸ The reading "sins" is found in ℵ A B K P 048ᵛⁱᵈ 33 81 614 630 1241 1505 1739 and others. Another KJV Only advocate, Samuel Gipp, former student of Peter Ruckman, makes the exact same mistake in his book, *An Understandable History of the Bible* (Bible Believers Baptist Bookstore: 1987), pp. 212-213:

> The Greek word for "faults" (paraptomata) is found in MSS E, F, G, H, S, V, Y, and Omega, plus the rest of the Receptus family and the *greater* number of all remaining witnesses. Nestle's text inserts "sins" (tax amartias) [*sic*] with *NO* manuscript authority, and the misguided men of the Lockman Foundation

accept it with no evidence. Perhaps there are more Jesuits lurking in the shadows than we think! Anyone accepting an alternate reading with *no evidence* CANNOT be credited with acting ethically or scholarly. [*sic*]

Dr. Gipp is not only completely in error in his assertion that there is no manuscript evidence, but he should apply his standards to the TR, which contains a number of readings that have "no evidence" to support them.

[49] See chapter 6, pp. 133-134.

[50] $\mathfrak{P}^{72}$ ℵ A B C K P Ψ 33 69 81 323 614 630 945 1241 1505 1739 and others.

[51] Interestingly this is the reading of ℵ.

[52] Riplinger, *New Age Bible Versions,* p. 351.

[53] The addition of "in Asia" is based upon *very* few manuscripts. Hoskier cites 57, 59, 141, and 187 as the only supporting manuscripts; 57 and 141 are almost certainly copies of Erasmus' text, hence, one is left with only two manuscripts in support of this reading. Even Reuchlin's text rejects this reading.

[54] Hodges and Farstad identify this group as the M^e text (the NA^{27} uses $\mathfrak{M}^a$). Hoskier lists a little more than a dozen manuscripts containing the phrase which is obviously borrowed, as Hodges and Farstad point out, from Revelation 22:13. See Hodges and Farstad, *The Greek New Testament According to the Majority Text,* 2nd ed. (Thomas Nelson: 1985), p. xxxvi.

[55] KJV Only advocate Texe Marrs attacked the name of my ministry, "Alpha and Omega Ministries," on the basis of this textual variant (although he thought the textual variant was at Revelation 1:1), saying that I was "ignorant and uninformed" about the existence of the variant.

The Son of God, the Lord of Glory 8

He was willing to die for his beliefs. He did not fear the faces of men. Five times he was forced to flee from the city and the people he loved. Each time he was brought back and restored to his position. He experienced a life of constant danger, constant difficulty, and all for one reason. He would not compromise his belief in the full and complete deity of his Lord and Master, Jesus Christ.

He was Athanasius, the great bishop of Alexandria. Almost single-handedly he stood against those who taught that Jesus was a creature, a being who came into existence at some point in the past; against the followers of a man named Arius. Athanasius understood that a Christianity without a divine Savior was just another of the world's religions. There could be no compromise on this crucial point. The Scriptures taught plainly the deity of Christ. Athanasius argued eloquently from the Bible, proving his opponents wrong at every turn.[1] And in God's providence, Athanasius, the great proponent of Christian truth, prevailed in the end.

Few topics bring out the depth of emotion in Christians more than a perceived attack upon the deity of Christ. We hear our Savior maligned every day in our world by those who hate Him and His cause. So when we hear those who profess religious faith denying His deity and denigrating His character, we respond quite often with righteous indignation and anger.

There are few doctrines that I as a Christian minister have studied more deeply or more intensely than the great truth of the deity of my Lord and Savior, Jesus Christ. I have defended this truth against those who have denied it for years. I have opened the Word of God with Jehovah's Witnesses, members of the Way International, and those who have come under the influence of such groups, too many times to remember. The Bible teaches that Jesus Christ is the eternal Word, the

Creator of all things, the mighty God, as the Nicene Creed states it so succinctly,

> . . . the only-begotten of the Father, that is to say, God from God, Light from Light, true God from true God, begotten, not made, consubstantial with the Father, through whom all things were made, the things in heaven and the things upon the earth.[2]

There is no Christianity where this truth is denied. Of this there can be no question.

It is just this doctrine of the Christian faith that is used as one of the primary tools of the KJV Only advocates who wish to impress upon Christians the importance of using only the KJV. Every KJV Only publication will make the same accusation: "The modern translations and the corrupted texts upon which they are based deny the deity of Christ and attack His Person." Entire lists of references are then provided, all of which use the KJV as the standard of comparison, that *allegedly* show that the modern translations are either weak in their affirmation of the deity of Christ, or seek to deny this truth.

We come then to examine the allegations that are made with great regularity against the modern translations. Is there a conspiracy to deny the deity of Christ by such translations as the NIV, NASB, NKJV, NRSV, etc.? Are the modern Greek texts, such as the Nestle-Aland 27th and the UBS 4th, corrupted so as to hide references to the deity of Christ? Such are vitally important issues to which we now turn.

Hundreds and Hundreds of Deletions

The single most common theme one will encounter in KJV Only materials is this: "There have been hundreds of deletions of terms relevant to the deity of Christ. Words like 'Lord' and 'Christ' disappear with regularity from the corrupted Alexandrian texts upon which modern translations are based." Often this claim will be followed by charts or lists similar to the following:

Reference	KJV: God's Word	New Versions
Matthew 4:18	Jesus	OMIT
Matthew 12:25	Jesus	OMIT
Mark 2:15	Jesus	OMIT

Reference	KJV: God's Word	New Versions
Mark 10:52	Jesus	OMIT
Luke 24:36	Jesus	OMIT
Acts 19:10	Lord Jesus	OMIT
1 Corinthians 16:22	Jesus Christ	OMIT
Acts 19:4	Christ	OMIT
1 Corinthians 9:1	Christ	OMIT
2 Corinthians 4:10	Lord	OMIT
Hebrews 3:1	Christ	OMIT
1 John 1:7	Christ	OMIT
Revelation 1:9	Christ	OMIT
Revelation 12:17	Christ	OMIT
1 Thessalonians 3:11	Christ	OMIT
2 Corinthians 5:18	Jesus	OMIT
Acts 15:11	Christ	OMIT
Acts 16:31	Christ	OMIT
1 Corinthians 5:4	Christ	OMIT
2 Cor. 11:31	Christ	OMIT
2 Thessalonians 1:8	Christ	OMIT
2 Thessalonians 1:12	Christ	OMIT
2 John 3	the Lord	OMIT

At first glance such a chart looks tremendously weighty and important. Why "omit" all these words regarding the Lord? Surely we can understand the concern of the Christian who first encounters this kind of information. And yet, appearances can be deceiving. In point of fact, does this chart look familiar? It should. It appeared, in a different form, on pages 45-46. But when you saw it that time, it was meant to communicate the real picture. There it was demonstrating how the Byzantine text-type has longer titles for the Lord Jesus in comparison with the Alexandrian or Western types. It made no judgments (the term "omit" assumes that the term is *supposed* to be there in the first place, and makes the KJV the standard by which all others are judged), and demonstrated that the terms "Lord" and "Christ" are used with great frequency in the non-Byzantine texts of the New Testament (a fact that KJV Only writers do not wish to communicate in their works). If it does nothing else, this chart shows that one should investigate a little further before making snap judgments, for one can always make the data appear to support your perspective by manipulating the *way* it is presented.

The reasons why modern texts follow the Alexandrian rather than the Byzantine manuscript tradition at this point have already been discussed.[3] As we noted, the later manuscripts show evidence of the "expansion of piety" that flowed from the understandable desire to maintain respect and reverence for the Lord Jesus. There is no "conspiracy" on the part of the modern Greek texts to hide or downplay the majesty or deity of the Lord Jesus through the "deletion" of His titles.

IS ONE TRANSLATION "STRONGER"?

Before we examine many of the passages that are in dispute regarding the deity of Christ and the modern versions, it would be good to take a step back and look at the issue in a little wider view. Is it true that some translations are "stronger" and others "weaker" on the doctrine of the deity of Christ? Yes, it is. In fact, one aspect of a translation that I check upon reviewing any new translation of the Scriptures is how it handles the classical passages on the deity of Christ. The "bent" of the translation committee can be rather quickly identified by checking how the translators handle key passages such as John 1:1-3; Acts 20:28; Romans 9:5; Philippians 2:5-11; Colossians 1:15-17; Titus 2:13; and 2 Peter 1:1. There are some modern translations that I cannot recommend due to their handling of various key passages.[4] But almost all of these differences are due to the *translation* chosen and are not due to any peculiarities or irregularities on the part of the underlying Greek texts.

Some KJV Only advocates are surprised to note that the KJV does not do as well as some modern versions when it comes to providing clear, understandable translations of the key, central passages in the New Testament that testify to the full deity of Jesus Christ. And yet anyone who has spent a great deal of time sharing the gospel with people who deny the deity of Christ, such as Jehovah's Witnesses, knows that using a modern translation such as the NIV makes one's work much easier. Why? The following chart will explain (specifics of many of these passages will be discussed later):

Comparison Chart of Passages on the Deity of Christ			
Reference	NIV	NASB	KJV
John 1:1	Clear	Clear	Clear
John 1:18	Clear	Clear	**Absent**
John 20:28	Clear	Clear	Clear
Acts 20:28	Clear	Clear	Clear
Romans 9:5	Clear	Ambiguous	Ambiguous
Philippians 2:5-6	Most Clear	Clear	Least Clear
Colossians 1:15-17	Clear	Clear	Clear
Colossians 2:9	Clear	Clear	Ambiguous
1 Timothy 3:16	**Absent**	**Absent**	Clear
Titus 2:13	Clear	Clear	Ambiguous
Hebrews 1:8	Clear	Clear	Clear
2 Peter 1:1	Clear	Clear	Ambiguous

We have chosen to use the terms "Clear" and "Ambiguous" to indicate the fact that at times it is not a cut-and-dried issue; some translations are clearer than others. For example, the NIV's "Who, being in very nature God, did not consider equality with God a thing to be grasped" at Philippians 2:6 is clearer than the KJV's ambiguous translation, "Who, being in the form of God, thought it not robbery to be equal with God." And the NASB's "our God and Savior, Jesus Christ" at 2 Peter 1:1 is clearer than the KJV's "of God and our Saviour Jesus Christ." In any case, we can see that the NIV provides the clearest translations of the key passages that teach the deity of Christ; the NASB just a bit less so, and the KJV the least of the three. Does this in the least indicate that there was some effort on the part of the KJV translators to be less than explicit in their belief in the deity of Christ? Surely not! And yet this is the exact argument that is used by KJV Only advocates against the modern translations, only in reverse.

If there was an effort on the part of modern translations like the NIV or NASB to downplay the deity of Christ, charts such as the above could not be constructed. Such a bias would be exhibited *throughout* a translation,[5] and such is simply not the case. Therefore, we can conclude that any and all arguments that are based upon the assertion of a bias against the deity or majesty of the Lord Jesus in the modern Greek texts or translations are without merit.

Having taken a broad picture of the issue, we will now look at the key passages that make up the bulk of the KJV Only materials on the deity of Christ. We will begin with passages that are, in fact, *less clear* in the KJV than in modern translations, and then move on to those passages that, allegedly, are "corrupted" by the modern texts.

The Only Begotten God

John 1:18	
KJV	**NASB**
No man hath seen God at any time; **the only begotten Son**, which is in the bosom of the Father, he hath declared *him*.	No man has seen God at any time; **the only begotten God**, who is in the bosom of the Father, He has explained Him.

The first eighteen verses of the Gospel of John form one long, beautiful testimony to the majesty of Jesus Christ. The apostle John works the Greek language with the passion of an artist and the fervor of one deeply concerned that men and women know the truth about his Lord and Master. The balance of this great prologue to the Gospel of John is magnificent in its intricacy. For example, John carefully distinguishes between the very verbs he uses of the eternal Word in the first thirteen verses and the verbs he uses of everthing else that is created. By so doing he makes sure to avoid any thought that the Word is a mere creature, a creation like all other things. Plain and obvious doctrinal bias must be demonstrated by a translation for it to avoid the glowing testimonies to the deity of Christ found in this passage.[6] John 1:1 confesses the eternal deity of Christ. John 1:3 asserts His creatorship in unmistakable terms. John 1:14 proclaims the marvelous fulfillment of the promise that God would be with us, Immanuel, as the Word becomes flesh and dwells among us.

The summary of the prologue of John is found in verse 18. It is just here that we have a reference to the deity of Christ that is tremendously important, for it not only speaks to the majesty of the Son, but it also reveals very plainly the truth of the Trinity as well. The NASB translation is given above; the NIV reads,

> No one has ever seen God, but God the One and Only, who is at the Father's side, has made him known.

And a striking, if a bit free, translation is provided by the *New Revised Standard Version*,

> No one has ever seen God. It is God the only Son, who is close
> to the Father's heart, who has made him known.

Here in the modern versions Jesus Christ is directly called God. He is the "unique" or "one and only" God, the term "only-begotten" referring primarily to *uniqueness* rather than *origination*. And a great truth of the very nature of God is presented in this passage through John's description of the Lord Jesus in these words.

Is it true that no one has ever seen God? Did not the elders of Israel see God in Exodus 24:10? And did not Isaiah see Jehovah in the Temple in Isaiah 6:1ff? Surely this is true. So what is John referring to? One cannot understand John 1:18 without interpreting the passage in a Trinitarian context. When he says, "No one has seen God," he is referring specifically to the Father. He then differentiates between the Father and the Son by identifying the Son as the "unique God." This unique God is in close fellowship with the Father, in the Father's "bosom," or to use more modern terminology, at the Father's side, or close to the Father's heart. This is the same truth that is presented at the beginning of John when we read that the Word was eternally "with" God, that is, face-to-face with Him, in personal contact. The Son has eternally been "with" the Father, in communion with Him, at His side, in His bosom.

It is the unique God, the Son, Jesus Christ, who has made the Father known. Since no one has seen God, the Father, He has chosen to make himself known in the unique God, the Son, Jesus Christ. This is vitally important, for this confirms John's own identification of Jesus as Yahweh[7] in John 12:39-41.[8] John 1:18 is one of the clearest, strongest affirmations of the deity of Christ.

Yet, we see that the KJV does not contain this reference to the deity of Christ. The difference between the AV and the modern translations is easily discerned, for here again we face a textual, rather than a translational, difference. As we discuss the textual information elsewhere[9] we will not go into the topic here. Suffice it to say that the most ancient texts, including the oldest existing copies of the book of John, $\mathfrak{P}^{66}$ and $\mathfrak{P}^{75}$, as well as a number of the early fathers of the church, refer to Christ as the "only-begotten God," or more accurately, the "unique God."

If KJV Only advocates are consistent, they should welcome this reading of the modern texts over against the *Textus Receptus*. Do they not often speak of their strong belief in the deity of Christ? And yet, we find just the opposite when we examine the books written by the defenders of the AV. For example, Dr. D.A. Waite writes,

1. The Denial of the Eternality (Past or Future) of Christ the Eternal Son of God.
(1) John 1:18
"No man hath seen God at any time; the Only Begotten *Son*, Which is in the bosom of the Father, He hath declared {Him}." (John 1:18)
Greek Texts: -B/ALEPH
English Versions: (-3) -NIV, -NASV, -NKJV -FN
The italicized portion is CHANGED in the Greek texts and English versions specified above. They take away the word, "**Son**," and change it to "**God**." This is pure HERESY! It is not possible to have an "Only Begotten God." This is an example of the Gnostic error that teaches Christ was only one of the many "gods" that were mere "emanations." You MUST have an "**Only Begotten Son**" to be doctrinally correct.[10]

In this critique Waite assumes a particular theological position, and on that basis rejects the reading "God," without reference to the merit of the reading. There is no discussion of the understanding of the passage that was presented above; there is no evidence given that gnostics had anything to do with "changing" the reading at John 1:18; and there is no discussion of the actual meaning of the term "only-begotten" or "unique."[11] Instead, the KJV is assumed to be the standard, and any reading that differs from that standard, even if it is one that is manifestly orthodox, is accused of being heretical and destructive. We should truly be concerned when maintaining allegiance to a *translation* causes us to weaken the case for a central doctrine of the faith, and this is exactly what we find here in the KJV Only camp. This leads us to another example of how far KJV Only advocates will go to defend their position.

OUR GOD AND SAVIOR, JESUS CHRIST

Twice the New Testament identifies Jesus Christ by the phrase "our God and Savior, Jesus Christ." The first reference is found at Titus 2:13:

> looking for the blessed hope and the appearing of the glory of
> our great God and Savior, Christ Jesus (NASB).

This is the consistent translation of nearly all of the modern translations. Note the NKJV and NIV renderings:

> while we wait for the blessed hope—the glorious appearing of
> our great God and Savior, Jesus Christ (NIV).

> looking for the blessed hope and glorious appearing of our
> great God and Savior Jesus Christ (NKJV).

In each instance we find the same great truth: Jesus Christ is our God and Savior. All these translations make it plain that both "God" and "Savior" are being applied to one person: Jesus Christ. The same is true for the second reference, 2 Peter 1:1:

> Simon Peter, a bond-servant and apostle of Jesus Christ, to
> those who have received a faith of the same kind as ours, by
> the righteousness of our God and Savior, Jesus Christ (NASB).

Again the NIV and NKJV agree with the NASB in speaking of Christ as our God and Savior. Yet the King James Version is at best ambiguous in its translation of both of these passages:

> (Titus 2:13) Looking for that blessed hope, and the glorious
> appearing of the great God and our Saviour Jesus Christ;

> (2 Peter 1:1) Simon Peter, a servant and an apostle of Jesus
> Christ, to them that have obtained like precious faith with us
> through the righteousness of God and our Saviour Jesus Christ:

The insertion of the second "our" in the AV translation makes it possible to separate "God" from "Savior," as indeed those who deny the deity of Christ would assert. But this is an error, as is demonstrated elsewhere.[12] The simple fact is that the KJV provides an inferior translation in these passages, one that unintentionally detracts from the presentation of the full deity of Jesus Christ. The willingness of KJV defenders to overlook this fact is most disturbing. Indeed, Barry Burton provides the following comments on Titus 2:13, and while he attacks the perfectly acceptable translation of the NASB at this point[13] he ignores the inferior translation of the KJV and writes:

> LOOK! LOOK! LOOK! LOOK! LOOK! LOOK! LOOK!
>
> Here they changed it from the "glorious appearing *of Christ* to . . .
> > the appearing of *"the glory".*
>
> What kind of "glory" are we supposed to look for? If *that* isn't CHANGING the Word of God, I don't know what is!!![14]

Such inconsistency is a hallmark of KJV Only materials.

PRAYER TO CHRIST

KJV	NASB
John 14:14 If ye shall ask any thing in my name, I will do *it*.	John 14:14 "If you ask **Me** anything in My name, I will do *it*."

In John chapter 14 the Lord Jesus speaks of things that are yet to come, after He has died and risen again. The future is in view. How will the believers relate to Him when He is no longer with them? How will the Holy Spirit work within them? It is in this context that Jesus speaks of His disciples' communication with Him, even after He has risen to heaven. "If you ask **Me** anything in My name, I will do it." How can the believers ask Christ for something after He has ascended to the Father? By prayer, of course. Therefore, we see that John 14:14 presents to us the concept of prayer to Christ. And as prayer is something that is reserved for deity alone, this passage is important in demonstrating another aspect of the deity of Christ.

The inclusion of the term "Me" in John 14:14 is based upon its being present in a large portion of the manuscripts, including the oldest manuscripts of the Gospel of John.[15] Yet the KJV lacks the term, following only one portion of the Majority Text.

We pause for a moment to illustrate how easy it is to create "conspiracies" out of partial information, using John 14:14 as our example. If someone were intent upon alleging that the King James Version has a bias *against* the deity of Christ, and is somehow in collusion with such groups as Jehovah's Witnesses, and that, in fact, the modern texts are the "true" texts to the exclusion of the KJV, one could produce the following kind of chart (W&H referring to the Westcott and Hort text and NWT referring to the Watchtower's *New World Translation*):

Against Prayer to Christ		For Prayer to Christ	
KJV	**NWT**	**W&H**	**NASB**
ask any thing in my name	ask anything in my name	ask me anything in my name	ask Me anything in My name

Such a chart, however, would be unfair and erroneous. Why? Because there is no evidence of such collaboration between the KJV and the NWT. *The mere fact of having the same reading proves nothing at all.* The KJV translators had no bias against the deity of Christ, just as the translators of the NIV or NASB have no such bias, either. Furthermore, similarities in text do not indicate similarities in theology. Even so, the above chart should look familiar to anyone who has read KJV Only materials, as it presents the very same kind of argument that fills page after page of their books, only this time it is presented in reverse! Since the same argument works both ways, we see that the KJV Only position is inconsistent when it utilizes this kind of polemic.

THE FULNESS OF DEITY

Colossians 2:9	
KJV	**NASB**
For in him dwelleth all the fulness of the **Godhead** bodily	For in Him all the fulness of **Deity** dwells in bodily form

I have often told believers that one of the best passages in the New Testament to commit to memory regarding the deity of Christ is

Colossians 2:9. Not only is it short and easily memorized, it is very clear in its teaching, and is not one of those passages that many anti-Trinitarians have studied in-depth. Yet, the KJV rendering of this passage is probably the least clear of almost all currently available translations. How does one explain what "Godhead" means? Who really uses this term any longer? And what about the fact that the KJV uses "godhead" in other places when it is translating a completely different Greek term?

The term translated "deity" by the NASB and NIV is a Greek term that is nowhere else used in the New Testament.[16] It is a very strong affirmation of the deity of Christ. The KJV, by using a term that it uses elsewhere in translating other words that are not as strong as the term here, unintentionally obscures the meaning of the apostle. Note the following chart:

NASB	Reference	KJV
the Divine Nature	Acts 17:29 (θεῖος)	the Godhead
divine nature	Romans 1:20 (θειότης)	the Godhead
Deity	Colossians 2:9 (θεότης)	the Godhead

Modern translations correctly recognize the differences in meaning between the three Greek terms all translated as "Godhead" by the KJV, and therefore differentiate between them in their translations. A person using the RSV or NIV or NASB will be in a better position to explain these passages than one utilizing *only* the KJV. Such is hardly consistent with the charges of conspiracy that are part and parcel of KJV Only writings.

Sanctify Christ as Lord

1 Peter 3:14-15	
KJV	**NRSV**
and be not afraid of their terror, neither be troubled; But sanctify the **Lord God** in your hearts: and *be* ready always to *give* an answer to every man that asketh you a reason of the hope that is in you with meekness and fear:	Do not fear what they fear, and do not be intimidated, but in your hearts sanctify **Christ as Lord**. Always be ready to make your defense to anyone who demands from you an accounting for the hope that is in you; yet do it with gentleness and reverence.

One of the most effective ways of sharing the deity of Christ with one of Jehovah's Witnesses is to demonstrate that the New Testament identifies Jesus as Yahweh. This can be done through the comparison of a number of passages in the Old Testament with others in the New. For example, the writer of Hebrews cites Psalm 102:25-27, which in its original context is specifically about Yahweh, of the Lord Jesus in Hebrews 1:10-12. Earlier we noted another such passage, that being John's use of Isaiah 6 in John 12:39-41. Another striking passage is found at 1 Peter 3:15. Here we find Peter drawing from Isaiah chapter 8, verses 12-13:

> Do not call conspiracy all that this people calls conspiracy, and do not fear what it fears, or be in dread. But the LORD of hosts, him you shall regard as holy; let him be your fear, and let him be your dread (NRSV).

A comparison of the Greek translation of this passage in the Septuagint version shows that when Peter uses this passage in his epistle, he replaces the Greek, which reads, "Lord of hosts" with "Christ as Lord." Just as the prophet Isaiah spoke of sanctifying (regarding holy) the Lord of hosts, so Peter speaks of sanctifying Christ as Lord, plainly identifying Christ as the LORD, Yahweh. This is further shown in Peter's use of the very next verse of Isaiah, 8:14, earlier in his epistle, in chapter 2, verse 8. Here Peter, citing a passage in which Yahweh is described as a "stumbling stone," applies this to the Lord Jesus, again making the same identification of Jesus as Yahweh. A person carrying the NASB, NIV, RSV, NRSV, or any number of other modern translations can show this passage to one of Jehovah's Witnesses. A person carrying the KJV or NKJV, however, cannot. Why? Because the Greek text utilized by the KJV and NKJV does not have "Christ" here at 1 Peter 3:15. Instead, following the majority of Greek texts, but ignoring the united testimony of the most ancient texts and translations, the *Textus Receptus* has "Lord God" as its reading, completely obscuring this wonderful testimony to the deity of Christ. Again, is this the result of some conspiracy? Surely not. But those who would invest the TR with infallibility force us to abandon this passage as evidence of the deity of our Lord.

Our Only Master and Lord

Jude 4	
NASB	**KJV**
For certain persons have crept in unnoticed, those who were long beforehand marked out for this condemnation, ungodly persons who turn the grace of our God into licentiousness and deny **our only Master and Lord, Jesus Christ**.	For there are certain men crept in unawares, who were before of old ordained to this condemnation, ungodly men, turning the grace of our God into lasciviousness, and denying **the only Lord God, and our Lord Jesus Christ**.

The last passage we will examine wherein the deity of the Lord Jesus is more plainly revealed in modern translations than in the KJV is Jude 4. Few KJV Only works address this passage,[17] though it would seem like consistency would demand at least some explanation of the difference between the KJV and the modern texts. The TR adds one word here, "God," which results in the disruption of the flow and the introduction of a second person into the text, "the Lord God," who is then differentiated from the Lord Jesus Christ. Most would feel that "Lord God" would be referring to the Father.

However, the modern texts contain a very clear testimony to the deity of Christ, for the term that is translated "Master" by the NASB is also translated "Sovereign" by the NIV in the same passage. It is a very strong term in the Greek language. In fact, we derive our English word "despot" from it. It can be used of human masters, but is also used of God as Master. Note Acts 4:24 (NIV):

> When they heard this, they raised their voices together in prayer to God. "Sovereign Lord," they said, "you made the heaven and the earth and the sea, and everything in them."

Jude tells us that there is only one "Sovereign Lord," and that is Jesus Christ. I have often pointed this passage out to Jehovah's Witnesses and asked, "Now, can you say with Jude that you have *only one* Sovereign Lord? Or do you have *two*, Jehovah, and Jesus Christ?" The point is rarely missed. But the KJV's rendering obscures this by following inferior manuscripts,[18] resulting in a reading that allows one to distinguish between the "Lord God" and the Lord Jesus Christ.

We now move to those passages that are consistently cited by KJV Only advocates as evidence that the modern translations are in point of fact specifically *attacking and denying* the deity of Christ. We begin with the most common passage, 1 Timothy 3:16.

GOD WAS MANIFESTED IN THE FLESH

1 Timothy 3:16	
KJV	**NIV**
And without controversy great is the mystery of godliness: **God** was manifest in the flesh, justified in the Spirit, seen of angels, preached unto the Gentiles, believed on in the world, received up into glory.	Beyond all question, the mystery of godliness is great: **He** appeared in a body, was vindicated by the Spirit, was seen by angels, was preached among the nations, was believed on in the world, was taken up in glory.

There is much to be said in defense of the KJV rendering of 1 Timothy 3:16 as "God was manifest in the flesh." In fact, I prefer this reading, and feel that it has more than sufficient support from the Greek manuscripts. I can agree with the majority of the comments made on the topic long ago by Dean Burgon.[19] But none of this requires us to believe that there is some conspiracy on the part of the modern translations with reference to their rendering of the disputed phrase in this passage as "He appeared in a body" (NIV) or "He who was revealed in the flesh" (NASB). There is a very clear, logical reason why these versions read as they do.

As we noted earlier, the first written manuscripts of the New Testament were "uncial" texts, that is, they were written in capital letters without spaces or punctuation. Another element of the uncial texts that is important to understand with reference to 1 Timothy 3:16 is known as the *nomina sacra*, the "sacred names."[20] Terms such as God and Jesus, which were used often in the text of the New Testament, were abbreviated. In the case of the term "God," the first and last letter of the Greek term would be written. To call attention to the abbreviation, a line would be written above the contraction. Hence, in Greek, the word "God" would normally be written like this in all capitals: ΘΕΟΣ. However, when abbreviated, it would look like this: Θ̄Σ̄.

Why is this important at 1 Timothy 3:16? The word that is translated "He who" in the modern versions in Greek looks like this: ΟΣ. Notice that this word looks almost identical to the abbreviated form of "God." When we put these two terms into their respective contexts, seeing how they would have appeared in an ancient uncial text of the New Testament, we can quickly grasp the problem faced by the modern texts of the New Testament. Here is how the first reading, "God was manifested in the flesh," would appear in an ancient manuscript:

ΚΑΙΟΜΟΛΟΓΟΥΜΕΝΩΣΜΕΓΑΕΣΤΙΝΤΟΤΗΣΕΥΣΕΒΕΙΑ
ΣΜΥΣΤΗΡΙΟΝΘ̅Σ̅ΕΦΑΝΕΡΩΘΗΕΝΣΑΡΚΙΕΔΙΚΑΙΩΘΗΕΝ

And the same text with the reading "He who was manifested" would look like this:

ΚΑΙΟΜΟΛΟΓΟΥΜΕΝΩΣΜΕΓΑΕΣΤΙΝΤΟΤΗΣΕΥΣΕΒΕΙΑ
ΣΜΥΣΤΗΡΙΟΝΟΣΕΦΑΝΕΡΩΘΗΕΝΣΑΡΚΙΕΔΙΚΑΙΩΘΗΕΝ

Rather hard to see the difference, isn't it? Indeed it is. Recall that these words were being written on animal hides (which often had small lines or creases that are normal parts of such materials), so it is easy to see how a Θ could be taken for an O and *vice versa*. Hence, we can see how a textual variant arose at this point merely by the fact that human beings with less than perfect vision were copying words that are liable to cause confusion on the part of a person who is not paying close attention, or even on the part of one who is doing his best, but is working with less than perfect materials. There simply is no reason to assume some great conspiracy on the part of a manuscript that reads ΟΣ rather than Θ̅Σ̅. A scribe who might believe fully and completely in the deity of Christ may still see ΟΣ and copy it as such. No theological bias needs to be asserted to understand how this reading could arise.

When we see, then, such claims as that provided by Barry Burton, "The NAS CHANGES it to . . . '*He* who was revealed in the flesh, *Was* vindicated in the Spirit . . .' "[21] we can recognize that there has not been a "change" at all, but that the particular translation being examined uses a Greek text that feels that ΟΣ is the stronger reading than Θ̄Σ̄. While we may disagree with their chosen reading, we need to realize that the translators did not just sit around and say, "Well, the Greek may say 'God,' but I think we should change that to 'He!'" Certainly not. And, we might note that such versions as the NIV and the NASB provide textual footnotes that indicate the reading of "God" in the Greek manuscripts (something that most KJV Only advocates would never want to see in their KJVs when the manuscripts provide a different reading that goes the other way, such as John 1:18, noted earlier).

MARK 1:1 AND THE SON OF GOD

Mark 1:1, NIV
The beginning of the gospel about Jesus Christ, the Son of God.[a]
[a]Some manuscripts do not have *the Son of God.*

Modern translations of the Bible as a matter of standard practice include textual footnotes to indicate to the reader where the Greek or Hebrew manuscripts contain variants. KJV Only advocates, generally, dislike such footnotes, feeling that they can "confuse" the reader, and that they are, in fact, faith-destroying. If a version dares to note that a word, phrase, or verse is questionable, it will be accused of "attacking" the Word of God by those who define the KJV as the Word of God. Unfortunately, many defenders of the AV seem to be unaware of the fact, noted previously,[22] that the King James Version contained 8,422 such marginal readings and notes when it was first published. High-quality printings of the King James to this day, such as those printed at Cambridge, contain these references, though many printed in America omit these items. Most of these notes gave alternative readings, but some indicated the fact that the KJV translators recognized the existence of textual variations in the Greek and Hebrew texts. One example should suffice to demonstrate that the dislike of textual notes on the part of AV Only advocates is more than slightly inconsistent. Note the KJV's own marginal reference at Luke 10:22:

> many ancient copies add these words, *And turning to his disciples, he said,*

If the KJV is not "attacking God's Word" with such marginal notes, why is the NASB or NIV?

With reference to Mark 1:1, the fact is that modern versions such as the NASB, RSV, NIV, and NRSV all have "the Son of God" in their main text. Each appends a textual note indicating the fact that some[23] ancient manuscripts do not contain the phrase. Since this is the case, one must wonder why anyone would want people to be ignorant of this fact. Surely one cannot seriously suggest (though many do) that there is some effort on the part of modern translations to deny that Jesus is the Son of God! As we have seen over and over again, the truth that is here proclaimed, that Jesus is the Son of God, is repeated over and over and over again in the modern translations, since, of course, this is a truth found all throughout Scripture. Obviously, therefore, if translators were trying to "hide" this truth, they have done a very, *very* bad job of it in the new translations!

Son of God or Son of Man?

Another of the favorite passages of defenders of the AV is John 9:35.

KJV	NIV
Jesus heard that they had cast him out; and when he had found him, he said unto him, Dost thou believe on the **Son of God**?	Jesus heard that they had thrown him out, and when he found him, he said, "Do you believe in the **Son of Man**?"

The modern texts read "Son of Man," while the TR has "Son of God." The textual background for this passage is addressed in the latter part of this work.[24] There is a very strong case to be made for the modern reading, "Son of Man." This passage is normally cited, however, as evidence of some bias against the deity of Christ by KJV Only advocates. But we must ask, "Is the phrase 'Son of Man' any less a title of deity than 'Son of God'?" Surely this is what is being suggested by the use of this passage in this debate, but such is far from the truth. Note just a few passages from Matthew's gospel:

> "But in order that you may know that the Son of Man has authority on earth to forgive sins"—then He said to the

paralytic—"Rise, take up your bed, and go home." (Matthew
9:6, NASB)

"For the Son of Man is Lord of the Sabbath." (Matthew 12:8,
NASB)

Is anyone going to suggest that when Jesus says that the Son of Man
has authority on earth to forgive sins that this involves an implicit
denial of His deity? And did not the Jewish people understand very
clearly what the claim, "The Son of Man is Lord of the Sabbath,"
meant with regard to *who* the Son of Man is? Of course. And the same
is true in John's own gospel. Note John 13:31 in the NASB:

When therefore he had gone out, Jesus said, "Now is the Son
of Man glorified, and God is glorified in Him;"

When the Lord himself uses terms such as "glorified" with reference
to the Son of Man, obviously there is no idea that the Son of Man is a
lesser title in His mind than "Son of God." Therefore, the use of "Son
of Man" at John 9:35 cannot logically be taken as in any way
diminishing a translation's testimony to the exalted character of the
Lord Jesus Christ. This *should* be plain to even the most die-hard
defenders of the KJV, especially when they are quick to point to another
passage, John 3:13,[25] which also uses the phrase "Son of Man," even in
their AV, and yet here they have no problem seeing Christ's deity in the
title! Inconsistency, we repeat, is not glorifying to God.

HE THOUGHT IT NOT ROBBERY

Philippians 2:6-7	
KJV	**NIV**
Who, being in the form of God, thought it not robbery to be equal with God: But made himself of no reputation, and took upon him the form of a servant, and was made in the likeness of men:	Who, being in very nature God, did not consider equality with God something to be grasped, but made himself nothing, taking the very nature of a servant, being made in human likeness.

Some might wonder why we would address such a passage as
Philippians 2:6-7 when addressing charges that the modern versions

have a bias against the deity of Christ. The NIV's rendering of this passage is one of the plainest, clearest available. And yet, despite this, KJV Only advocates insist that even here the modern versions are trying to deny the deity of Christ! How? Despite the plain affirmation made by the NIV that Jesus Christ was "in very nature God," these critics look at the phrase "did not consider equality with God something to be grasped" and understand it to mean that Christ did not have this equality, and gave no consideration to attempting to become equal with the Father. Of course, the very same idea could be attached to the rather awkward translation of the KJV as well, but that does not seem to concern those who have a dedication to the KJV. Is there merit in their accusation?

No, there is not. The issue raised by the KJV Only advocates is an issue faced by every translation, including the KJV itself. It involves the entire interpretation of this passage, and is not based upon any alleged "bias" in the modern translations. Briefly, the idea that Christ was not equal with the Father is contradicted by the very context of the passage. Paul is exhorting his readers to humility of mind. He is encouraging them to serve one another in love. Though they are all equals before God, they are to lay aside their privileges in humility and give their lives in service for the brethren. He introduces the Lord Jesus as the greatest example of this mindset. Here we have the preincarnate Lord, existing eternally in the very form of God, laying aside that equality that He had with the Father so as to give His life for His people. If one does not start with the Lord *having* equality with the Father, the entire example is destroyed. *Not* trying to exalt oneself and become equal with God is hardly an example of humility, but that is what one is left with if one does not recognize that this passage teaches that equality with God was already something that the Lord had prior to His incarnation. The translation of the NASB or NIV in no way suggests any kind of heretical idea.

Before looking at a couple of Old Testament passages that appear often in King James Only writings, I wish to note a particular *kind* of textual variation that often prompts charges of heresy and error on the part of the new versions. We often encounter variants in the New Testament that involve the names of God and of Christ. A good example is found at Romans 14:10:

Romans 14:10	
KJV	**NASB**
But why dost thou judge thy brother? or why dost thou set at nought thy brother? for we shall all stand before the judgment seat of **Christ**.	But you, why do you judge your brother? Or you again, why do you regard your brother with contempt? For we shall all stand before the judgment seat of **God**.

A number of times one will find variations involving the terms "God" and "Christ." Again the reason is found in the Greek texts themselves. One might well point out that these variations are, in and of themselves, silent testimony to the antiquity of the belief in the deity of the Lord, for if as various cultic groups assert, the doctrine of the deity of Christ was unknown among early believers, how could those believers make such an error in their copying of the Greek manuscripts? But this aside, do passages such as Romans 14:10 impact the New Testament's teaching on the deity of Christ?

Again we must answer in the negative. None of these passages materially impact the plain witness to the doctrine. What is more, one can provide counter citations showing the same kinds of changes in reverse! Note Acts 16:7:

Acts 16:7	
KJV	**NASB**
After they were come to Mysia, they assayed to go into Bithynia: but the Spirit suffered them not.	and when they had come to Mysia, they were trying to go into Bithynia, and the Spirit **of Jesus** did not permit them;

The phrase "of Jesus" has dropped out of the majority of Greek texts, but is retained in the greater number of the ancient witnesses to the book of Acts. As I have pointed out many times, *if* such passages as Romans 14:10 prove some kind of conspiracy on the part of the modern translations, then Acts 16:7 proves an anti-Trinitarian conspiracy on the part of the KJV. Of course, no such conspiracy exists in either case.

Prophecies of the Coming Messiah

It is a certainty that the early Christians believed that the Old Testament spoke much of the Lord Jesus in a prophetic manner. This conviction is found throughout the writings of the apostles. But what of how these prophecies are handled in modern translations? Can we discern a desire to hide passages that refer to Christ in the Old Testament?

We have to admit that much of the literature that has been written in the last century regarding the Old Testament has hardly maintained a conservative or fully biblically oriented perspective. It may be said that conservatives, generally, have allowed liberals to predominate in the field. As a result, there is indeed a large amount of scholarly writing that seeks to "naturalize" the Old Testament by removing any kind of supernatural or spiritual element. And, one might well note certain less-than-conservative translations that can be properly accused of being too free with the Old Testament. But as usual, the KJV Only movement is rarely concerned with the more liberal translations. Instead, conservative translations such as the NASB and NIV come in for the criticism. The primary focus of the critcism is often aimed (with reference to the deity of Christ) at Micah 5:2:

KJV	NIV
But thou, Bethlehem Ephratah, *though* thou be little among the thousands of Judah, *yet* out of thee shall he come forth unto me *that is* to be ruler in Israel; whose **goings forth** *have been* from of old, from everlasting.	But you, Bethlehem Ephrathah, though you are small among the clans of Judah, out of you will come for me one who will be ruler over Israel, whose **origins** are from of old, from ancient times.

The allegation often goes along the lines of Jay P. Green, "But in this OT passage, once again you see these new versionists denying the eternal existence of the Godman, making Him to have origins—but Jesus is God, and God has no origin."[26] Is this what the NIV translators were seeking to do? Do the NIV translators deny the eternal nature of Christ?

Dr. Kenneth Barker is the General Editor of the *NIV Study Bible* and is the Executive Director of the *NIV Translation Center*. In his book, *Accuracy Defined and Illustrated,* Dr. Barker responds to criticisms of the NIV's translation of Micah 5:2:

> The NIV translators were not careless in the handling of Old Testament Messianic prophecies or of any other doctrines, but good, godly, spiritual scholars differ on the interpretation of certain biblical passages. For example, the Hebrew text at the end of this verse can be translated either (1) "whose goings out are from of old, from days of eternity" or (2) "whose origins are from of old, from ancient times." Those who prefer the first rendering naturally use it to argue for the eternity of the Messiah. Those who prefer the second translation believe that the expression refers to the ancient "origins" of the Messiah in the line of David (as indicated in the Davidic covenant of 2 Sam. 7) and in the tribe of Judah (Gen. 49:10).
>
> The majority of the Committee on Bible Translation felt that the *context* favored the second view: "*Bethlehem . . . of Judah,* out of *you* [emphasis mine] will come for me one who will be ruler over Israel" (note the emphasis on the origins of the future Davidic Ruler in the Davidic town of Bethlehem). So we put the second rendering in the text and the first one in the footnotes as an alternative. Incidentally, those who favor the second translation still believe in the eternity of the Messiah (and so in the eternal Son of God) and believe that His eternality is clearly taught in other passages, particularly in the New Testament.[27]

I asked Dr. Barker if he had been contacted by any of the KJV Only advocates who are so quick to accuse him and the other NIV translators of heresy. Do any of these individuals take the time to actually determine if indeed the translators are anti-Trinitarian, Christ-denying heretics? No, they do not. Dr. Barker's explanation of the textual choice of the NIV at Micah 5:2 makes plenty of sense, *even if you do not agree with the viewpoint held by the majority of the Translation Committee.* Even if a person prefers the "first" rendering of the passage as given above, one must admit that the second interpretation, and hence the second rendering, is supported by solid arguments and has a firm basis in the Hebrew text itself. *Only a commitment to a "traditional" position can cause a person to bring charges of "heresy" in such a situation.* Dr. Barker referred to his own reference note in the *NIV Study Bible* at Romans 9:5, wherein he listed a number of passages that teach the deity of Christ. He noted that the NIV has been criticized by liberals for being too conservative and for being too strong on the deity of Christ. At this point he commented, "If they want to accuse me of being biased toward the deity of Christ, I'm honored!" [28] One will not find AV Only advocates reporting *that* kind of statement by an NIV translator, since it destroys the very root of the conspiratorial theories that are at the heart of the KJV Only position.

THE VIRGIN BIRTH OF CHRIST

The final aspect of the deity of Christ that we need to address is that of His virgin birth. Three primary passages are presented by AV advocates under the charge that modern translations are attempting to hide this teaching of Scripture: Isaiah 7:14; Matthew 1:25; and Luke 2:33.

The Virgin Birth		
Reference	**Modern Version**	**KJV**
Isaiah 7:14	Therefore the Lord himself will give you a sign. Behold, **a young woman** shall conceive and bear a son, and shall call his name Immanuel. (RSV)	Therefore the Lord himself shall give you a sign; Behold, **a virgin** shall conceive, and bear a son, and shall call his name Immanuel.
Matthew 1:25	and kept her a virgin until she gave birth to a Son; and he called His name Jesus. (NASB)	And knew her not till she had brought forth her **firstborn** son: and he called his name JESUS.
Luke 2:33	The child's **father** and mother marveled at what was said about him. (NIV)	And **Joseph** and his mother marvelled at those things which were spoken of him.

Both the NIV and NASB have "virgin" at Isaiah 7:14, but other translations have "young woman" or "maiden." The battle over the proper translation of the Hebrew term has waged for generations. It should be noted with reference to the KJV Only controversy that the

KJV is not consistent in its rendering of the Hebrew words that are translated variously as "virgin" or "maid." For example, the KJV renders the more technical term that specifically refers to a virgin, the Hebrew term *bethulah,* as "maid" in such places as Jeremiah 2:32 and 51:22. But, it also translates the less specific term, *almah,* which is the term in dispute at Isaiah 7:14, as "maid" in Exodus 2:8 and Proverbs 30:19. Hence, it is hard to defend the KJV from the charge of irregularity in rendering Hebrew terms. This aspect adds to the confusion over Isaiah 7:14.

Next, it should be noted that the Hebrew word *almah* can properly be translated "young maiden" or "young woman." The question is not of the translation, but of the meaning of the passage at Isaiah 7:14. Obviously, scholars who do not believe in the supernatural or the prophetic element of Scripture will not see a prophecy of the virgin birth no matter *how* they translate Isaiah 7:14.[29] But the person who accepts the supernatural origin and character of Scripture is in a position to see the *entirety* of the Bible and its message. In light of this, the New Testament's plain understanding that Isaiah 7:14 refers to a virgin is determinative with reference to the use of the passage as a prophecy of the Messiah. The physician Luke, who surely would know the specific meaning of terms such as "virgin," uses the Greek term that can *only* mean "virgin" when he speaks of Mary.[30] There is no attempt to "hide" this fact in modern translations, hence, there is no conspiracy to change this teaching. We would agree with the NIV and NASB rendering over against others, seeing the use of the passage in the New Testament as significant.

The issue at Matthew 1:25 is textual rather than translational in nature. We have already looked at Matthew 1:25 and noted that it is an example of "parallel influence,"[31] that is, of a passage being influenced by another parallel passage in another of the Gospels. In this instance the parallel passage is Luke 2:7, a very important passage that very early on had a central place in Christian liturgy. As such, the passage would naturally lend itself to influencing other passages, especially Matthew 1:25, which speaks of the same topic and uses similar terminology. As we noted earlier, Luke 2:7 has not been "tampered with," which in and of itself destroys the theories of conspiracy with reference to "heretics" somehow "changing" the manuscripts (why not remove *all* references to a doctrine you do not like, if you have your editorial scissors out anyway?). The modern translations all contain Luke 2:7, and all have the phrase "firstborn" right there in the text, a rather silly thing to do if, in fact, you are trying to hide a doctrine.

Likewise, Luke 2:33 is a textual issue as well, though this time it is not a matter of "parallel influence" as it is at Matthew 1:25. Here the charge that is leveled is obvious: the use of "father" rather than "Joseph" lends itself to a denial of the virgin birth, making Jesus the son of Joseph. Yet, given the plain teaching of Luke's gospel that Joseph was *not* the natural father of Jesus (Luke 1:34-35), is it not much more natural to take this term as referring to the *role* of Joseph in Jesus' life? Was not Joseph the husband of Mary? Are we to believe that Jesus never referred to, or thought of, Joseph as His earthly father, the head of His family on earth? Could this not be a perfectly plausible explanation? Surely it is. Yet, KJV Only advocates are not likely to accept such an explanation. Their certainty that the "modern versions" are up to no good keeps most of them from allowing for such clarifications. But in this case, they have no choice. Their own King James Version forces them to abandon Luke 2:33, *if* they are in the least bit consistent in their arguments:

> And when they saw him, they were amazed: and his mother said unto him, Son, why hast thou thus dealt with us? behold, thy father and I have sought thee sorrowing. (Luke 2:48)

Here, from the very lips of Mary, no less, we have the use of the term "father" of Joseph with reference to the Christ child, and that in the Authorized Version of 1611! This use of "father" by Mary is perfectly consistent with the use of "father" at Luke 2:33, where both Mary and Joseph are in view as a family unit. Also, the KJV itself refers to Joseph and Mary as "his parents" in Luke 2:41. There is absolutely no reason to read into the use of the term "father" a denial of the supernatural nature of the birth of the Messiah. Surely no KJV Only advocate who is the least bit concerned about being fair and accurate and honest in one's arguments can use Luke 2:33 as an example of "heresy" on the part of the modern Greek texts or the modern Bible translations.

MODERN TRANSLATIONS VINDICATED AGAIN

The doctrine of the deity of Christ is indeed a vitally important issue. But we have seen that KJV Only advocates are, in fact, guilty of using an important doctrine as a brickbat to further their promotion of the KJV. Their arguments have been found, again, to be utterly inconsistent and most often circular. Modern translations such as the NIV and NASB have been cleared of the accusations made against them, not by appeal to emotion or through use of insulting rhetoric, but by examination of the facts themselves. Surely we must decry the use of such a precious doctrine as the deity of Christ in the way we have seen it used by advocates of the AV. Such is surely not a proper use of such an important Christian belief. And what is worse, we have often seen that passages that do testify to the deity of Christ, and hence *should* be shared with those who have been deceived on this topic, are often translated more clearly in the modern translations than in the KJV. Followers of the prophets of KJV Onlyism are, therefore, less prepared to defend the faith than those who have not limited themselves to a single English translation from the seventeenth century.

Endnotes

[1] See especially his works, *Apology, Defense of the Nicene Council*, and *Against the Arians*, all found in Robertson, *The Nicene and Post Nicene Fathers II*, Philip Shaff, ed. (Eerdmans: 1983), volume IV.

[2] Translation of the author.

[3] See the discussion in chapters 4 and 7, especially pp. 150-154.

[4] For example, the *New American Bible* (NAB) (a Roman Catholic translation to be differentiated from the *New American Standard Bible*) provides poor translations of Romans 9:5 and Titus 2:13 (though correctly translating the exact same Greek construction at 2 Peter 1:1), and *Today's English Version* (TEV) likewise gives an inferior translation of Acts 20:28; Romans 9:5; and Philippians 2:6 (though giving a better reading in its textual footnote).

[5] This is what we see, for example, in the *New World Translation* of Jehovah's Witnesses. Each of the passages in the chart is mistranslated in the NWT so as to hide the deity of Christ. The doctrinal bias against the Trinity that is part of Watchtower theology forces them to mistranslate the Bible so as to support their beliefs. Obviously, then, the translators of such modern

versions as the NIV or NASB do not have the kind of bias that KJV Only advocates would have us to believe.

⁶ Such bias is found, of course, in the *New World Translation* of Jehovah's Witnesses, which mistranslates John 1:1 so as to attempt to hide its testimony to Christ's deity.

⁷ The divine name "Yahweh," which in Hebrew is made up of four letters, YHWH (יהוה) and hence called the "Tetragrammaton," is often badly mispronounced in the popular Anglicized form, Jehovah.

⁸ John quotes from Isaiah's Temple vision of Yahweh, found in Isaiah 6:1-13. Isaiah says he saw the glory of Yahweh himself (Isaiah 6:1). John says Isaiah saw the glory of Christ, thus identifying Christ as Yahweh.

⁹ See the discussion in Part Two on pp. 258-260.

¹⁰ D.A. Waite, *Defending the King James Bible* (The Bible for Today: 1992), p. 168. When this author debated Dr. Waite on KIXL radio in Austin, Texas, in August of 1994, he asked Dr. Waite for *evidence* that heretics had altered or changed certain manuscripts (the "Alexandrian" family of manuscripts). Dr. Waite cited no historical demonstration for alleged changes to specific biblical texts. William Grady simply assumes that Origen is the source of this reading as well. In doing so, however, he runs afoul of both church history as well as manuscript evidence. He writes on pages 95-96 of his book, *Final Authority* (Grady Publications: 1993):

> Having written, "μονογενης θεος," the only begotten GOD, Origen embraced the Arian position that Jesus was *created* by the Father, and therefore not total Deity.
>
> This heresy that Jesus Christ is a "god" (not Son) begotten somewhere in eternity is found in *Sinaiticus* and *Vaticanus*, and therefore in such modern perversions as the New American Standard Bible.

The first problem is that Arius arose after Origen, hence it is anachronistic to say that Origen embraced a position that developed later. Origen's theology tended toward subordinationism, but he did not take the system as far as Arius would years later. Second, as I discuss in Part Two, pages 258-260, "μονογενὴς θεὸς" is also found in 𝔓⁶⁶ and 𝔓⁷⁵, both of which *predate* Origen!

¹¹ See our discussion of this term in footnote 5 on page 259.

¹² For a full discussion of the grammatical structure of Titus 2:13 and 2 Peter 1:1, see the section on Granville Sharp's Rule in Part Two, pp 267-270.

¹³ The Greek of the passage can be translated either "the appearing of the glory" (the most literal rendering) or "the glorious appearing."

¹⁴ Barry Burton, *Let's Weigh the Evidence* (Chick Publications: 1983), p. 35.

¹⁵ This passage is addressed briefly in Part Two, p. 263.

¹⁶ The Greek term *theotes* (θεότης) is very strong and must be differentiated from a different term, *theiotes* (θειότης), which is found at Romans 1:20. Richard C. Trench wrote regarding these two terms in his *Synonyms of the New Testament* (Eerdmans, 1953), pp. 7-8:

. . . yet they must not be regarded as identical in meaning, nor even as two different forms of the same word, which in process of time have separated from one another, and acquired different shades of significance. On the contrary, there is a real distinction between them, and one which grounds itself on their different derivations; θεότης (*theotes*) being derived from θεός (*theos*), and θειότης (*theiotes*), not from τὸ θεῖον (*to theion*), which is nearly though not quite equivalent to θεός (*theos*), but from the adjective θεῖος (*theios*). . . . But in the second passage (Col. ii.9) St. Paul is declaring that in the Son there dwells all the fulness of absolute Godhead; they were no mere rays of divine glory which gilded Him, lighting up his person for a season and with a splendour not his own; but He was, and is, absolute and perfect God; and the Apostle uses θεότης (*theotes*) to express this essential and personal Godhead of the Son. . . .

[17] Gail Riplinger lists it as denying the deity of Christ, though no explanation is given as to how this comes from the text itself.

[18] The term "God" is not found in the papyrus manuscripts $\mathfrak{P}^{72,78}$ Sinaiticus (א) Alexandrinus (A) Vaticanus (B), numerous other texts and translations as well.

[19] See Burgon's *Proof of the Genuineness of God Manifested in the Flesh* in various editions of his works.

[20] Metzger gives a discussion of the *nomina sacra* on pages 13-14 of his work, *The Text of the New Testament* (Oxford: 1968). Such frequently used terms as God (θεός), Lord (κύριος), Jesus (Ἰησοῦς), Christ (Χριστός) and Son (υἱός) were abbreviated in the manuscripts.

[21] Burton, p. 20.

[22] See chapter 4, p. 77.

[23] We must agree that the NASB's "Many mss." is in error. Actually, very few manuscripts do not contain the phrase.

[24] See the discussion in Part Two, pp. 262-263.

[25] This passage is addressed in more depth in Part Two, pp. 260-261.

[26] Jay P. Green, Sr., *The Gnostics, the New Versions, and the Deity of Christ* (Sovereign Grace Publishers: 1994), p. 43.

[27] Kenneth Barker, *Accuracy Defined and Illustrated* (International Bible Society: 1995), p. 61.

[28] Personal conversation with the author, July 1994.

[29] We should also note that even many *conservative* scholars see in this passage a dual fulfillment, one that was relevant in the days of Isaiah that did *not* involve a virgin birth, and the greater fulfillment in the virgin birth of Christ centuries later.

[30] Matthew draws directly from the Septuagint's rendering of Isaiah 7:14, which uses παρθένος (*parthenos*), the specific term meaning "virgin," at Matthew 1:23; Luke likewise uses it at Luke 1:27.

[31] See chapter 7, p. 159.

Problems in the KJV

At the outset I emphasized the fact that this work is not "anti-KJV." I have no desire to "bash" the AV nor those who discover God's truth in its pages. No matter how strongly I assert this fact, however, I know that KJV Only advocates will find a way of discounting my protestations. It has been my experience that those who become deeply involved in the KJV Only movement have a very hard time believing that anyone who would say *anything* that strikes them as being less than fully supportive of the plenary verbal inspiration[1] of the KJV text could be anything other than "anti-KJV." Over and over again I have explained to individuals that I am not against the KJV, only to find them accusing me of dishonesty in return. And why? Because, from the KJV Only viewpoint, you are either with them, or you are against them. There is no middle ground.

For those who have not been indoctrinated into the AV Alone camp, the middle ground between being "anti-KJV" and being a KJV Only advocate is rather easily seen. As long as one does not make that fateful identification, "the KJV Alone = the Word of God Alone," one will recognize that it is quite possible to see the errors made by the KJV translators without at the same time attacking the Word of God. Surely we can count the very translators of the AV as taking our side on this issue, for they provided alternate renderings in the margins of their work, showing that they had no concept of infallible inspiration working in their behalf in their translation. Hence, they would be the first to allow for the need for revision and correction over time. Still it is vital to emphasize that demonstrating errors in the KJV in no way demonstrates errors in the "Bible." One involves recognizing the fallibility of human translators, the other questions the very inspiration of Scripture itself.

Someone might well ask, "Why bother dwelling upon the errors in the KJV at all?' It would be nice if we could avoid such a task, but such is simply not possible. KJV Only advocates make claims regarding the KJV that are simply untrue. Passing over the plain errors in the AV would allow their assertions to go unquestioned and unrefuted. When they claim the KJV is inspired and inerrant,[2] the demonstration of errors in that translation effectively (for anyone willing to follow the truth to its logical conclusions) ends the debate. And when a person will not accept the plain facts as they are presented, they are forced to engage in some rather obvious irrational argumentation, often taking the form of *ad hominem* attacks upon those who would point out the problems in the KJV, or an appeal to the emotions of the audience.

We have already noted the problems in the *Textus Receptus* in previous chapters. In this chapter we wish to focus upon the specific problems in the KJV *translation,* having already concluded our examination of the textual issues. And we repeat yet once again that we do not in any way believe that these errors were *purposeful* on the part of the KJV translators. Unlike many AV Alone defenders, we do not believe conspiracies are behind every aspect of the translational issue.

WELL NOBODY IS PERFECT

The men who worked on the translation of the AV nearly four hundred years ago were great scholars. No one can possibly dispute that fact. But all great scholars know their limitations. They recognize their fallibility. And I really doubt they would take the slightest offense to a reasoned critique of their work.

The first problem we will examine is to be found in Mark's gospel, chapter 6, verse 20:

KJV	NASB
For Herod feared John, knowing that he was a just man and an holy,[3] and **observed** him; and when he heard him, he did many things, and heard him gladly.	for Herod was afraid of John, knowing that he was a righteous and holy man, and **kept him safe**. And when he heard him, he was very perplexed; but he used to enjoy listening to him.

Did Herod "observe" John, as the KJV says, or "keep him safe," as the NASB says? The Greek term simply does not mean "observe," but instead means "to protect." One might possibly suggest that "observe" once meant "to protect," but such seems a long stretch, especially since the KJV renders the same word "preserve" at Matthew 9:17 and Luke 5:38. A similar less-than-perfect translation is found at Mark 9:18:

KJV	NASB
And wheresoever he taketh him, he teareth him: and he foameth, and gnasheth with his teeth, **and pineth away**: and I spake to thy disciples that they should cast him out; and they could not.	and whenever it seizes him, it dashes him *to the ground* and he foams *at the mouth*, and grinds his teeth, and **stiffens out**. And I told Your disciples to cast it out, and they could not *do it*.

It is difficult to get "stiffens out" or "becomes rigid" (NIV) from "pineth away." The KJV rendering is obviously less than adequate in comparison with the modern translations.

Another less-than-sterling translation is found at Luke 18:12:

KJV	NASB
I fast twice in the week, I give tithes of all that I **possess**.	I fast twice a week; I pay tithes of all that I **get**.

Did the Pharisee tithe on his *possessions* or his *increase*? The term means to "procure for oneself, acquire, get."[4] Some would find the difference quite significant.

Of more importance is this rendering offered by the KJV translators at Acts 5:30:

KJV	NKJV	NASB
The God of our fathers raised up Jesus, whom ye slew **and** hanged on a tree.	The God of our fathers raised up Jesus whom you **murdered by** hanging on a tree.	The God of our fathers raised up Jesus, whom you had put to death **by** hanging Him on a cross.

The NKJV corrects the problem seen in the KJV rendering. Peter did not say that the Jews had slain Jesus and then hung him on a tree.

Instead, they put the Lord to death *by* hanging Him upon the tree.[5] It is difficult to see exactly where the KJV derived its translation, as there is no "and" in the text to separate "slew" and "hanged on a tree."

The KJV translation of Hebrews 10:23 leaves most people wondering as well. The KJV has the phrase "the profession of our faith." Literally the first term should be translated "confession," but it is the KJV's very unusual translation of the Greek term "hope" as "faith" that is difficult to understand. The Greek term[6] appears thirteen times in the TR, and each time it is translated "hope" with this one exception.

Sometimes the KJV translation is misleading. For example, do we "offend all" or "stumble in many ways"? James 3:2 says:

KJV	NASB
For in many things **we offend all**. If any man offend not in word, the same *is* a perfect man, *and* able also to bridle the whole body.	For we all stumble **in many *ways***. If anyone does not stumble in what he says, he is a perfect man, able to bridle the whole body as well.

Do Christians offend all people? That's not what James is trying to communicate, that's for certain. Even the NKJV renders the phrase, "For we all stumble in many things." The same kind of ambiguity can be seen at 1 Corinthians 4:4:

KJV	NASB
For I know nothing by myself; yet am I not hereby justified: but he that judgeth me is the Lord.	**For I am conscious of nothing against myself**, yet I am not by this acquitted; but the one who examines me is the Lord.

The AV translation makes no sense in its context. Paul is talking about judging himself and his ministry, and in that context says that his "conscience is clear" (NIV), that is, he knows of no charge that could be laid at his feet. The AV rendering is unclear to say the least.

Sometimes an entire concept will simply disappear from the text due to a less-than-clear KJV translation. Note for example Hebrews 9:7:

KJV	NASB
But into the second *went* the high priest alone once every year, not without blood, which he offered for himself, and *for* the **errors** of the people:	but into the second only the high priest *enters*, once a year, not without *taking* blood, which he offers for himself and for the sins of the people **committed in ignorance**.

One may well look high and low for the idea that the sins being spoken of were "committed in ignorance" in the KJV, yet the Greek is very expressive.[7]

Our knowledge of the ancient world and the religious beliefs of the people who lived around the land of Israel has expanded greatly since the time of the KJV translators. This has influenced modern translations. For example, note Isaiah 65:11:

KJV	NKJV	NASB
But ye *are* they that forsake the LORD, that forget my holy mountain, that prepare a table for **that troop**, and that furnish the drink offering **unto that number**.	But you *are* those who forsake the LORD, Who forget My holy mountain, Who prepare a table for **Gad**, And who furnish a drink offering for **Meni**.	But you who forsake the LORD, Who forget My holy mountain, Who set a table for **Fortune**, And who fill *cups* with mixed wine for **Destiny**,

Readers of the AV might be left wondering just what "troop" and what "number" is being referred to, especially when it is plain that the people of Israel are preparing a sacrificial meal and making a drink offering to this "number" and to this "troop," unless they happened to have the 1611 marginal reading that indicated that the original Hebrew terms translated "number" and "troop" were "Gad" and "Meni." Some ventured to interpret it as referring to foreign armies in the land, but there is a much more logical understanding. The NKJV simply transliterates the Hebrew terms, "Gad" and "Meni." These were Babylonian or Syrian gods, specifically, the god of fortune (Gad) and the god of destiny (Meni). Isaiah is upbraiding the people for engaging in idolatrous worship of Gad and Meni, the gods of fortune and destiny. That's a fairly long way from "that troop" and "that number"!

A similar problem is seen in 1 Kings 10:28:

KJV	NASB
And Solomon had horses brought out of Egypt, and **linen yarn**: the king's merchants received the **linen yarn** at a price.	Also Solomon's import of horses was from Egypt and **Kue**, and the king's merchants procured *them* from **Kue** for a price.

"Kue" is a place in Egypt from which Solomon purchased horses, not "linen yarn." Another problem related to a name, this time of a king, is found in 1 Chronicles 5:26:

KJV	NASB
And the God of Israel stirred up the spirit of Pul king of Assyria, **and** the spirit of Tilgathpilneser king of Assyria, and he carried them away,	So the God of Israel stirred up the spirit of Pul, king of Assyria, **even** the spirit of Tilgath-pilneser king of Assyria, and he carried them away into exile,

As the NASB correctly notes, Pul *was* Tilgath-pilneser. The KJV rendering makes it look as if Pul is one king, and Tilgath-pilneser another, possibly a co-regent with Pul, when such was not the case.

In Other Words . . .

Most people who are not committed to the KJV Only position will admit that the AV needs some level of revision. No matter how strongly AV Only believers assert the alleged simplicity and clarity of the KJV, the fact remains that there are many passages that are anything *but* clear and understandable in this venerable old translation. And, at times, those ambiguities get in the way, and even give ammunition to those who would attack the Bible.

The first alleged "contradiction" that was ever shown to me was based upon the KJV translation. Two young LDS missionaries, Elders Reed and Reese, were sitting in my sister-in-law's home, explaining to me that I could not really trust the Bible because it had been "translated so many times." I was a young person at the time (I was the same age as the missionaries), and had not encountered too many real strong challenges to my faith, so I asked them for examples of the "errors" they were talking about. They took me to the KJV at Acts 9:7 and Acts 22:9.

Reference	KJV	NASB
Acts 9:7	And the men which journeyed with him stood speechless, **hearing a voice**, but seeing no man.	And the men who traveled with him stood speechless, **hearing the voice**, but seeing no one.
Acts 22:9	And they that were with me saw indeed the light, and were afraid; but they **heard not the voice** of him that spake to me.	And those who were with me beheld the light, to be sure, **but did not understand the voice** of the One who was speaking to me.

The alleged contradiction exists only in the KJV, not in modern translations such as the NASB or NIV. The good physician Luke did not contradict himself, as he differentiated the Greek terms he used to record Paul's story in Acts 9 and Acts 22.[8] However, the AV translation does not distinguish between the different uses of the Greek terms, leading to the alleged contradiction. Such ambiguity is, unfortunately, a common problem in the KJV. Years ago I engaged in a long written debate with a nationally known atheist who insisted that the Bible contradicts itself because of the KJV rendering of Matthew 19:18 and Romans 13:9. As with the example above, the alleged contradiction is due to the AV rendering, not the actual biblical text. Note the following chart.

Reference	Greek	KJV	NIV
Matt. 19:18	Οὐ φονεύσεις	Thou shalt do no murder	Do not murder
Rom. 13:9	Οὐ φονεύσεις	Thou shalt not kill	Do not murder

The reason why the KJV would render the very same Greek term "murder" at one place and "kill" at another is understandable. The KJV was translated by different committees, each entrusted with a particular section of Scripture. One committee chose "kill," while another chose "murder." The final editor simply did not catch such inconsistencies.[9] While this historical fact is obvious, those who view the KJV as inerrantly inspired are left with a problem. You can't speak of editors simply missing a small problem like this when you are endowing those editors with power from on high. There has to be a *reason* for the use of "murder" in one place and "kill" in another. Some go so far, as we have noted, to view this as "advanced revelation," superseding the Greek text itself. Such a position is, obviously, irrational at best.

One of the well-known problems in the AV is found at Acts 19:2:

KJV	NASB
He said unto them, Have ye received the Holy Ghost **since** ye believed? And they said unto him, We have not so much as heard whether there be any Holy Ghost.	and he said to them, "Did you receive the Holy Spirit **when** you believed?" And they *said* to him, "No, we have not even heard whether there is a Holy Spirit."

The King James Version has Paul asking the disciples in Ephesus if they received the Holy Ghost[10] *since* they believed, that is, subsequent to the act of believing. All modern translations, however, translate the passage, "*when* you believed." The difference is not a slight one. Entire theologies of a second reception of the Holy Spirit have been based upon this one rendering by the KJV. The doctrine of the Holy Spirit is materially impacted by how one translates this passage.

The rendering of the KJV is only marginally possible.[11] It involves a translation that is awkward, uncommon, and inconsistent with all of Paul's teaching on the subject. This author has been extremely frustrated in attempting to get KJV Only advocates to seriously interact with passages such as this one. The consistent response has been, "But what about all these deletions over here. . . ." The few who have attempted a response have utterly ignored the actual grammar and have, instead, relied upon a rather convoluted interpretation of the passage as their means of getting around a basic problem in translation on the part of the KJV translators.[12]

Another example of inconsistency can be found at Genesis 50:20:

KJV	NASB
But as for you, ye **thought** evil against me; *but* God **meant** it unto good, to bring to pass, as *it is* this day, to save much people alive.	And as for you, you **meant** evil against me, *but* God **meant** it for good in order to bring about this present result, to preserve many people alive.

The Hebrew text provides a plain parallel here that is obscured by the curious KJV translation. Joseph told his brothers that while they had *meant* their actions for evil ends, God had *meant* the same actions for good ends. The KJV introduces a distinction that is not to be found in the text it is translating.

Names cause no end of difficulty for the reader of the KJV as well. The translators sometimes use the Hebrew form, sometimes a Greek form, sometimes even a Latin form! Hence, one author lists for us,

> Sheth and Seth; Pua and Puah; Cis and Kish; Agar and Hagar; Jeremiah, Jeremias, and Jeremie; Enos and Enosh; Henoch and Enoch; Jered and Jared; Noe and Noah; Jonah, Jona, and Jonas; Jephthae and Jephthah; Balak and Balac; Sara and Sarah; Gidion and Gideon; Elijah and Elias;[13] Kora and Core; Elisha and Eliseus; Hosea and Osee; Isaiah, Esaias, and Esay; Hezekiah and Ezekiah; Zechariah and Zecharias; Judas, Judah, Juda, and Jude; Zera, Zara, and Zarah; Marcus and Mark; Lucas and Luke; Timothy and Timotheus; and Jesus and Joshua—both for the Old Testament character (Acts 7:45 and Heb. 4:8).[14]

Jack Lewis notes that the KJV is also well known for the large variety of ways in which it will translate the same word. Now certainly there are many times when one will wish to use synonyms to translate particular terms, and context is vitally important in determining the actual meaning of a word,[15] but the KJV goes beyond the bounds a number of times. For example, the Hebrew term for "word" or "thing"[16] is rendered by *eighty-four* different English words in the KJV! Another term, "to turn back,"[17] is rendered in one particular grammatical form by *sixty* different English words! Those who have attempted to follow the usage of a particular Hebrew or Greek term through the AV know how difficult such a task can be, and the inconsistency of the KJV in translating terms only makes the job that much harder.

One topic on which most KJV Only advocates are agreed is the use of "paraphrase" in modern translations. We have already discussed the issues of formal and dynamic equivalency.[18] The KJV is not free from "dynamic" translations. At times the translators were actually quite free with their terms. They translated the rather straightforward term "reviled" as "cast the same in his teeth" at Matthew 27:44 (there is no word "teeth" in the Greek text). Second Samuel 8:18 is rendered, "And Benaiah the son of Jehoiada *was over* both the Cherethites and the Pelethites; and David's sons were chief **rulers**." The term the KJV translates as "rulers" is actually the specific term for "priests,"[19] and is rendered as such at Exodus 19:6, "And ye shall be unto me a kingdom of priests." Another rather free rendering is found in the willingness of the AV translators to use the term "God" in familiar sayings. For example, the British mind certainly is accustomed to the saying, "God save the king," but the Hebrew mind never thought of such a thing. Despite this, it appears a number of times in the KJV in such places as 1 Samuel 10:24, where a literal rendering would be "Let the king live" or "Long live the king." The same free rendering is found in 1 Corinthians 16:2, where the KJV has "as *God* hath prospered him," though the term "God" is nowhere to be found (as the italics in the KJV indicate).[20] A more serious example will be found in the KJV's use of the phrase "God forbid" throughout Paul's epistles (Romans 3:4, 6, 31; 6:2, 15; 7:7, 13; 9:14; 11:1, 11, etc.). The Greek text nowhere has the word "God" in any of these passages. Instead, Paul is providing a very strong statement of denial, "may it never be" or "by no means!" And while "God forbid" is surely a strong negative statement, it is hardly an accurate translation of the Greek phrase that Paul uses with such frequency. Surely, if a modern translation used a similar phrase, the KJV Only advocates would jump on such a use *immediately* and with unparalleled fervor.[21]

At times the KJV attempts to "get around difficulties," so to speak. For example, at Amos 4:4 the KJV renders the Hebrew phrase "three days" as "three years," ostensibly so that the passage would remain in accordance with Jewish law, which required the gathering of certain of the tithes[22] each three years. Interestingly enough, the NIV also chose to translate the "three days" as "three years," probably for the same reason. While it may well be possible that both the KJV and NIV are correct in their understanding of this passage, the point should be made that neither is *strictly* translating the text. Both are engaging in a certain amount of "interpretation" at this point. Given the tremendously strong language that has been used by KJV Only advocates against such translations as the NIV for doing that very thing, we see here another example where the KJV itself makes the KJV Only position self-contradictory and inconsistent.

One might well include the KJV's unusual rendering of Acts 12:4 as more of a mistranslation than an ambiguous rendering, and it would be hard to argue against that assertion, given the facts. Note the text:

KJV	NASB
And when he had apprehended him, he put *him* in prison, and delivered *him* to four quaternions of soldiers to keep him; intending after **Easter** to bring him forth to the people.	And when he had seized him, he put him in prison, delivering him to four squads of soldiers to guard him, intending after the **Passover** to bring him out before the people.

The word that the KJV translates as "Easter"[23] appears twenty-nine times in the New Testament. In each of the other twenty-eight instances the KJV translates the phrase as "the passover." For example, in John 19:14, "And it was the preparation of **the passover**, and about the sixth hour: and he saith unto the Jews, Behold your King!" And there is no reason for confusion as to what Luke is referring to here, for the preceding verse said, "Then were the days of unleavened bread." The days of unleavened bread, of course, were connected with the Passover celebration. Yet in this one place the AV contains the anachronistic term "Easter." Luke's reference to the days of "unleavened bread" makes it clear that he is referring to the Jewish holiday season, not to some pagan festival that did not become known by the specific term "Easter" for some time to come.

Some KJV Only advocates have attempted to defend the anachronistic translation "Easter" at Acts 12:4, even using this as evidence of God's providential guidance of the KJV translators.[24] The argument is that the "days of unleavened bread" extended from the fifteenth to the twenty-first of the month, while Passover itself was the fourteenth. Hence, according to this line of reasoning, the Passover was already past, and hence Herod, a pagan, was referring to "Easter" in its pagan celebration, not the Passover. The problem, of course, is that (1) the term Easter would *still* be a misleading translation, since the celebration the English reader thinks of is far removed from the pagan worship of Astarte; (2) Herod Agrippa, according to the Jewish historian Josephus,[25] was a conspicuous observer of the Jewish customs and rituals, and since he was attempting to please the Jews (Acts 12:3), it is obvious that Luke is referring to the *Jewish* Passover, not a pagan celebration; (3) the argument depends upon making the "days of unleavened bread" a completely separate period of time from "the Passover." Unfortunately for the KJV Only position, the term "the Passover" is used of the *entire* celebration, *including* the days of unleavened bread after the actual sacrifice of the Passover, in other places in Scripture (note the wrapping up of the entire celebration under the term the "feast of the Jews" in John 2:13; 2:23; 6:4 and 11:55). Therefore, this ingenious attempt at saving the KJV from a simple mistake fails under examination.

THE CHANGING ENGLISH LANGUAGE

Languages change. They evolve and grow. Often this process involves the addition of new terms due to contact with other languages or from improving technology (the KJV translators would think we were speaking a foreign language if we spoke of astronauts, television, downloading, or CD-ROMs). Words change meanings over time due to use, first by small groups, then by the larger populace. Such common terms as "let," "prevent," and "communicate" all meant different things to English speakers only a few centuries ago.

The fact that languages change over time is one of the strongest arguments for either the revision of older translations of the Bible, or for completely new translations. It is difficult to understand how KJV Only advocates can resist the logic of the reality that the KJV is written in a form of English that is not readily understandable to people today. It is amazing to listen to people honestly asserting that they think the KJV is "easier to read" than the modern versions. Surely they must realize that this is so for them only because of their familiarity with the AV, not because it is, in fact, easier to read! But no, it is actually asserted that the KJV is the simplest, easiest to read version of the Bible.[26]

One could easily fill many pages with examples of unclear, difficult readings based upon archaic language from the KJV. We will limit ourselves to a small selection of examples. One interesting example appears in the following chart:

Reference	KJV	NASB
Joshua 15:3	and went up to Adar, and **fetched a compass** to Karkaa:	and went up to Addar and **turned about** to Karka.
2 Kings 3:9	So the king of Israel went, and the king of Judah, and the king of Edom: and they **fetched a compass** of seven days' journey:	So the king of Israel went with the king of Judah and the king of Edom; and they **made a circuit** of seven days' journey,
Acts 28:13	And from thence we **fetched a compass**, and came to Rhegium:	And from there we **sailed around** and arrived at Rhegium,

Surely "fetched a compass" is a phrase that few modern readers, even those skilled in such things, would understand. Some might even think that the expression refers to an actual *compass,* which, of course, did not exist at the times in which these passages were written. This kind of difficult reading is hardly a rarity, especially in the Old Testament portion of the KJV. Leviticus 14:10, for example, refers to "three tenth deals of fine flour *for* a meat offering." Flour is not a meat, of course, and the NASB has the proper rendering, "for a grain offering." First Samuel 27:10 has Achish saying to David, "Whither have ye made a road to day? And David said, Against the south of Judah." David was not a construction worker, and the NASB gets the wording right with "Where have you made a raid today?" Second Samuel 14:20 certainly defies attempts at rapid reading, "To fetch about this form of speech hath thy servant Joab done this thing." Compare the much easier NIV, "Your servant Joab did this to change the present situation." Certainly one of the most amusing examples is to be found in the description of the giant Goliath in 1 Samuel 17:6. The KJV says, "And *he had* greaves of brass upon his legs, and a target of brass between his shoulders." Why a mighty soldier would have a target of brass between his shoulders is surely a mystery, until, of course, one learns that the KJV's "target" actually refers to a javelin, hence the NASB's modern rendering, "a bronze javelin *slung* between his shoulders." This is almost as humorous as Song of Songs 2:12, "The flowers appear on the earth; the time of the singing *of birds* is come, and the voice of the turtle is heard in our land." Turtles are not known for their voices, and how these would be connected with flowers and the singing of birds is unknown. Of course, the passage is not referring to turtles at all, but to the *turtledove*, as the modern translations recognize.

The KJV New Testament is not without its intriguing passages as well. For example, Peter saw a vision that is described in the AV, "And saw heaven opened, and a certain vessel descending unto him, as it had been a great sheet knit at the four corners, and let down to the earth" (Acts 10:11). One could completely miss the point here, for the KJV has "knit" for a term that refers to the means by which the sheet was lowered, hence the NASB, "lowered by four corners to the ground." First Corinthians 10:24 seems to encourage looking after other people's money, "Let no man seek his own, but every man another's *wealth*." But Paul is not exhorting us to get involved in handling investments, but instead, "Let no one seek his own *good*, but that of his neighbor." And surely one cannot help but smile at the KJV rendering of 1 Thessalonians 5:14, "Now we exhort you, brethren, warn them that are unruly, comfort the feebleminded, support the weak, be patient toward all *men*." The term translated "feebleminded" has nothing to do with a weakness of the mind, but instead refers to those who are discouraged or "fainthearted." Hence the better rendering, "encourage the fainthearted" (RSV).[27]

Dr. Edwin Palmer in reviewing the KJV said,

> Just to drive the point home even more clearly, what is the meaning of "chambering" (Rom. 13:13), "champaign" (Deut. 11:30), "charger" (Matt. 14:8—it is not a horse), "churl" (Isa. 32:7), "cieled" (Hag. 1:4), "circumspect" (Exod. 23:13), "clouted upon their feet" (Josh. 9:5), "cockatrice" (Isa. 11:8), "collops" (Job 15:27), "confection" (Exod. 30:35—it has nothing to do with sugar), "cotes" (2 Chron. 32:28), "covert" (2 Kings 16:18), "hoised" (Acts 27:40), "wimples" (Isa. 3:22), "stomacher" (Isa. 3:24), "wot" (Rom. 11:2), "wist" (Acts 12:9), "withs" (Judg. 16:7), "wont" (Dan. 3:19), "suretiship" (Prov. 11:15), "sackbut" (Dan. 3:5), "the scall" (Lev. 13:30), "scrabbled" (1 Sam. 21:13), "roller" (Ezek. 30:21—i.e., a splint), "muffler" (Isa. 3:19), "froward" (1 Peter 2:18), "brigadine" (Jer. 46:4), "amerce" (Deut. 22:19), "blains" (Exod. 9:9), "crookbackt" (Lev. 21:20), "descry" (Judg. 1:23), "fanners" (Jer. 51:2), "felloes" (1 Kings 7:33), "glede" (Deut.

14:13), "glistering" (Luke 9:29), "habergeon" (Job 41:26), "implead" (Acts 19:38), "neesing" (Job 41:18), "nitre" (Prov. 25:20), "tabret" (Gen. 31:27), "wen" (Lev. 22:22)?

Additional examples include "quit you like men" (1 Corinthians 16:13), "superfluity of naughtiness" (James 1:21), and "he who now letteth *will let*" (2 Thessalonians 2:7—a passage that actually gives the opposite meaning in the modern context). Some defenders of the AV insist that all one has to do is have a good dictionary at hand and all will be well when encountering such terms. But we must ask, why should we always have to have a dictionary at hand when reading the Bible? Why make reading the Scriptures a laborious task when simply translating them into our modern tongue would do just as well? Again, we are not condoning the "dumbing down" of the Bible that can be seen in efforts to turn the Scriptures into a first-grade level piece of literature. But we are saying that there is no need to add *unnecessary* ambiguity to the scriptural text. Utilizing terms that are no longer a part of our language has no place in making the Scriptures available to all people.

Finally, Jack Lewis collected a number of KJV renderings that leave one confused at first glance. Here are just a few of them:

And Mt. Sinai was altogether on a smoke (Exod. 19:18).

Thou shalt destroy them that speak leasing (Ps. 5:6).

Nevertheless even him [Solomon] did outlandish women cause to sin (Neh. 13:26).

Solomon loved many strange women (1 Kings 11:1).

The ships of Tarshish did sing of thee in thy market (Ezek. 27:25).

We do you to wit of the grace of God (II Cor. 8:1).[28]

It needs to be emphasized one more time that the preceding information is not meant to "bash" the KJV, but to treat it as its translators would have desired. Any result of human effort will be, in some measure, flawed. And despite the strong assertions of some in the KJV Only camp, the AV is the result of human effort, human skill, human work. As a result, we are able to locate problems, ranging from unclear translations to simple *mis*translations, such as Acts 5:30. This is exactly what one would expect given the background of the KJV, but it is *not* what one would expect if the claims of KJV Only defenders regarding supernatural oversight or even inspiration are true. The presence of errors and mishaps in the text of the KJV is an insurmountable obstacle for those who wish to proclaim the KJV inspired, inerrant, and infallible.

Endnotes

[1] Some might object to the use of the term "inspiration" here, and certainly some KJV Only advocates differentiate between the inspiration of the originals and the "preservation" of the KJV translation. But the fact is that this hardly impacts the final conclusions. Note for example Question #58 in Dr. Samuel Gipp's *The Answer Book* (Bible & Literature Missionary Foundation: 1989), p. 154: "Question: How many mistakes are there in the King James Bible? Answer: None. Explanation: None." Gipp is the student of Dr. Peter Ruckman, as can be seen by Question #56 (p. 148), "What should I do where [*sic*] my Bible and my Greek Lexicon contradict? Answer: Throw out the Lexicon." This is just like Ruckman's statement, *"Where any version or text contradicts the A.V. 1611, THROW IT OUT"* (*The Christian's Handbook of Manuscript Evidence*, p. 172).

[2] When speaking of inerrancy, of course, I am not referring to the inerrancy of the Scriptures as they were inspired of God. Instead, I am speaking of the alleged inerrancy of an English translation, the King James Version. I fully believe the Word of God is inerrant (I have defended the inerrancy of Scripture against attacks by cultists and atheists in public forums for years), but I recognize that translations cannot (and do not) make that claim.

[3] We note in passing how inferior even this rendering by the KJV is. "He was a just man and an holy" makes little sense; what is "an holy"? Instead, the Greek phrase is quite easily translated as the NASB, "he was a righteous and holy man," both terms "righteous" and "holy" plainly describing John.

[4] F. Wilbur Gingrich, *Shorter Lexicon of the Greek New Testament*, Revised by Frederick W. Danker, 2nd ed. (Chicago: 1983), p. 114. Bauer, Arndt, Gingrich, and Danker, *A Greek-English Lexicon of the New Testament and Other Early Christian Literature* (Chicago: 1979) notes that this verb, κτάομαι, has the meaning "possession" when in the perfect form. The verb at

Luke 18:12 is in the present form, not the perfect. Interestingly, the KJV renders the same Greek verb at Luke 21:19 as an imperative (following the TR), "possess ye your souls," whereas most likely the verb is a future, "you will gain your lives" (NASB). This passage, however, involves a textual variant.

[5] The participle "hanging" is a circumstantial instrumental (or modal), expressing the means by which death was inflicted. Dana and Mantey list a syntactical category that would give us the KJV rendering; however, they indicate that this category should be utilized only when the participle does not "present in a distinct way any of the above functions" (H.E. Dana and Julius R. Mantey, *A Manual Grammar of the Greek New Testament* (Macmillan: 1955), p. 228). Since the participle clearly fits into one of those preceding categories, there is no reason to choose the category that would give us the KJV rendering.

[6] ἐλπίδος (*elpidos*).

[7] The text reads ἀγνοημάτων, "sins committed in ignorance."

[8] For a full discussion of this alleged contradiction, see my *Letters to a Mormon Elder* (Bethany House: 1993), pp. 33-37.

[9] This is not the only place where the KJV translates the *very same Greek phrase* in two different ways. Note Romans 12:19 in comparison with Hebrews 10:30; Romans 4:3 and 4:22, where within the same chapter the same citation from Genesis 15:6 is translated in two different ways; and James 5:20 in comparison with 1 Peter 4:8.

[10] I pause only to note that the translation "Holy Ghost" is not only inferior to the more proper rendering "Holy Spirit," but that the KJV is inconsistent in its rendering of the phrase in the New Testament. For example, while one finds the KJV translating the Greek phrase πνεῦμα ἅγιον at Luke 11:13 as "Holy Spirit," the very same phrase is translated "Holy Ghost" at Luke 2:25. It is interesting to note as well that the KJV always capitalizes Holy Ghost, but does not always capitalize Holy Spirit, i.e., Ephesians 1:13, 4:30, and 1 Thessalonians 4:8, where each time the KJV has "holy Spirit."

[11] For those wishing the specifics, the term in question is πιστεύσαντες, an aorist active participle. Aorist participles can be translated in two ways with reference to the time of the main verb, in this case, "received" (ἐλάβετε); they can refer to an action that is concurrent or simultaneous with the action of the main verb, that is, which takes place at the same time, or they can refer to an antecedent action, that is, one that takes place *prior to* the action of the main verb. See William Hersey Davis, *Beginner's Grammar of the Greek New Testament* (Harper and Row: 1923), p. 104; A.T. Robertson, *Word Pictures in the New Testament*, volume III (Baker: 1930), p. 311; and Robertson, *A Grammar of the Greek New Testament in the Light of Historical Research* (Broadman Press: 1934), pp. 860-861, 1112-1113. In this case, the translation "when you believed" is proper, marking the reception of the Holy Spirit as an action that takes place at the time of belief itself. The KJV rendering uses

antecedent action, the act of faith preceding the reception of the Spirit, making the reception of the Holy Spirit *subsequent* to faith. It is common to allege (I myself have made the error) that the KJV's rendering is not possible because it appears (due to a lack of clarity on the KJV's part) as if the participle is being made to refer to *subsequent* action, which it is not.

[12] It is highly informative to note the attempt of Dr. Peter Ruckman, the most vitriolic of the KJV Only advocates, to explain Acts 19:2. In his *Bible Believer's Commentary* on the book of Acts (pages 545-553) he provides the following amazing statements:

> Sensing that several drivers have lost a wheel (or at least a tire) at this point the New ASV (as the old one) has inserted "WHEN" for "**SINCE**" in verse 2. Then this necessitates altering "**HAVE YE**" to "did you?' And just to make sure the verse no longer bears any resemblance to the hated King James Bible, the word "**GHOST**" has been altered to "Spirit". . . .That is, if you don't interpret it wrong (as the Charismatic-Glossolalia – kerygma-synoptic-blubber, blabber, blubber people have it), then *change* it to read what you *think* it ought to teach! [Hello, Origen! Still writing "bibles" aye?] (p. 546)

> This finishes the matter for the real Bible believer who wisely ignores the faked sincerity of the ASV and New ASV in altering "**SINCE**" to "when." These two publications (with their promoters, translators, supporters, and users) could not solve the doctrinal problem with *ANY number of changes* and their inadeptness in expounding "sound doctrine" from "the words of truth" is as glaring at this point as the Charismatics who left the text standing as it stood in the AV (1611). (p. 549)

> The AV (1611) text is infallible absolute truth as it stands, and no "God-breathed originals" would shed any more light on it than the light it already has in the God-honored Reformation text of 1611. (pp. 549-550)

> Therefore, the alteration of "**since**" (vs 2) to "when" means absolutely NOTHING at all since the scriptural dumbbells who made this alteration could not expound the passage after they corrected it without referring to Cornelius Stam or C.I. Scofield (or the present work), if their lives depended on it. (pp. 550-551).

> If you can't handle verse 6 as it is written, *what is the point in changing verse 2,* unless you are trying to play "god" for a bunch of idol-worshipping suckers ("Christians") who are too stupid to check their speedometers? (p. 552)

Nowhere in this section does Ruckman even *attempt* to deal with the simple fact that the KJV translation chooses an unusual and inferior way of translating the Greek participle. Instead, he ignores the Greek, makes the KJV the standard, and in so doing, ignores the indications of the very grammar of an ancient language so as to maintain the myth of the inerrancy of an English language translation produced nearly 1,600 years after Paul uttered these words in Greek in a land half a world away.

[13] This particular irregularity led the Mormon prophet, Joseph Smith, to think that Elijah and Elias were two different people, hence allowing him to have a vision of both, which is now found in LDS Scripture (*Doctrine and Covenants* 110:12-16)!

[14] Jack P. Lewis, *The English Bible from KJV to NIV*, 2nd ed. (Baker Book House: 1991), p. 48.

[15] An *excellent* summary of this vital aspect of translation is provided by Moisés Silva, *Biblical Words and Their Meaning: An Introduction to Lexical Semantics* (Academie Books: 1983).

[16] *dabhar*, דָּבָר in Hebrew.

[17] *shubh*, שׁוּב in Hebrew.

[18] See chapter 3, pp. 23-26.

[19] It is possible the KJV translators here followed the LXX that attempts to get around the problem of calling David's sons "priests" by translating the Hebrew term with the Greek word αὐλάρχαι, "rulers," rather than the normal term used in the LXX to translate "priests," ἱερεῖς .

[20] Despite the obvious fact that "God" is a translator's addition as indicated by the use of italics in the KJV, some KJV Only advocates still accuse the modern versions with "removing God" on the basis of this passage. Note Gail Riplinger, *New Age Bible Versions*, p. 188.

[21] We note another inconsistency in the AV Only position. The KJV refers to the Holy Spirit with the neuter pronoun "it" in such places as Romans 8:26. While this is a technically correct rendering (the term "spirit" in Greek is neuter), modern translations use "him," recognizing the personality of the Holy Spirit. Surely the KJV translators were not attempting to deny the personality of the Spirit with their rendering, but one wonders about the double standard that is utilized by KJV Only advocates in attacking modern translations on similar grounds.

[22] There were three different tithes, adding up to about 20% of the income of the citizens of Israel.

[23] τὸ πάσχα (*pascha*).

[24] See Samuel Gipp, *The Answer Book,* pp. 3-8, and D.A. Waite, *Defending the King James Bible* (The Bible for Today: 1992), pp. 246-247.

[25] Flavius Josephus, *The Antiquities of the Jews* (XIX.7.3) in the *Works of Josephus* (Hendrickson Publishers: 1980), pp. 410-411.

[26] See D.A. Waite, *Defending the King James Bible,* pp. 50-52, and Riplinger, *New Age Bible Versions*, pp. 193-217.

[27] Just a few other examples include the KJV's "purchase to themselves a good degree" at 1 Timothy 3:13 (it is better, "obtain a high standing for themselves"). We note that the KJV never uses the word "quick" in the modern sense of "fast." See Psalm 119:25; John 5:21; and Hebrews 4:12. Finally we note the strange use of "cherubims" at Hebrews 9:5; "cherubim" is already in the plural.

[28] Lewis, *The English Bible from KJV to NIV,* p. 54.

Questions and Answers | 10 |

In this chapter we will provide short, concise answers to some of the most common questions that arise when discussing the King James Only controversy. Most of the questions have been answered in much more depth in the body of the book itself, but some present new information.

Q. Doesn't Psalm 12:6-7 promise that God will preserve His WORDS?

A: Psalm 12:6-7 is commonly cited by KJV Only advocates in their books and tracts. But note the differences of translation:

KJV	NIV
The words of the LORD are pure words: as silver tried in a furnace of earth, purified seven times. Thou shalt keep **them**, O LORD, thou shalt preserve **them** from this generation for ever.	And the words of the LORD are flawless, like silver refined in a furnace of clay, purified seven times. O LORD, you will keep **us** safe and protect **us** from such people forever.

My first question is, "Where does Psalm 12 say that the 'words of the LORD' refer to the King James Version of the Bible?" Of course, it doesn't. Secondly, nowhere does this passage tell us *how* God will preserve His words. Does this mean He will do so by ensuring that no one can ever change the substance of those words, or does it mean that He will always make sure that there is one infallible version in one or more languages or translations? The passage does not even begin to address such things. And finally, noting the NIV translation, it is quite possible that verse 7 does not refer back to "the words of the LORD" in verse 6, but instead back to those in verse 5 of whom the LORD says, "I will set *him* in the safety for which he yearns" (NKJV).

Q. Modern versions have copyrights. You can't copyright God's Word. The KJV has no copyright. Doesn't this prove the KJV is the best?

A: Even if it were true that the KJV has no copyright, it is hard to understand how this would be even slightly relevant to the topic at hand. There is nothing immoral about having a copyright on a translation. While it would be nice to have a king or a government provide all the funding for a Bible translation project, such is not to be expected in our day. One must pay for all the costs involved in such a large project.

But we should point out that the KJV carries what is called the *Cum Privilegio*. Technically the KJV belongs to the English crown, which authorized and paid for its translation nearly four hundred years ago. I pointed out earlier that the KJV was first printed by the royal printer, and that for a hundred years no one else could print it. Does this not sound pretty much like a modern copyright? It would seem so. So again we find the KJV Only argument to be inconsistent, involving a double standard.

Q: Weren't Westcott and Hort occultists (evil men, heretics, closet Roman Catholics, and any number of other accusations)?

A: B.F. Westcott and F.J.A. Hort were not fundamentalist Baptists. Then again, neither were any of the KJV translators. They were Anglicans, men influenced by their age. Both were professing Christians. Both professed faith in the deity of Christ, His saving death, His resurrection. Were they perfect men? No, they were not. Neither were the KJV translators. Were they influenced by events in their day, movements, and theological opinions that many would find objectionable? Yes, they were, more so than in the days of King James, and *far less* than we would find in Anglicanism today. Did they make statements that indicated that they had some leanings toward Roman Catholic piety? Yes, but far fewer than Desiderius Erasmus, who wrote in defense of the Mass and Transubstantiation. But were they terrible evil men, plotting with others in a grand conspiracy to overthrow God's truth and lead everyone down the path to destruction? Such is utterly ridiculous. Were they occultists? Westcott's involvement in a club called the "Ghostlie Guild" has led to all sorts of such charges, but the club was formed to *investigate* strange occurrences, not engage in devilish activity. Some of Westcott's friends called it the "Cock and Bull Club." Were they perfect saints then, infallible and inspired so that all modern scholars bow at their feet? Some defenders of the AV 1611 would like to think that this is just what modern scholars believe, but such is utterly untrue. They are remembered as men who, while not perfect, recognized particular truths about the transmission of the New Testament text that have been verified by many who have come after them. They are not idolized or worshiped, but are treated as all other scholars: their work is appreciated, reviewed, and where necessary, corrected.

Ⓠ: I've been told that there were homosexuals on the NIV translation committee. Is this true?

Ⓐ: No, it is not. But due to the consistent bearing of a false witness by many KJV Only advocates, Dr. Kenneth Barker, Executive Director of the NIV Translation Center, had to write a response to the accusation, which I quote below:

> It has come to my attention that false rumors are circulating, in both oral and written form, that the NIV is soft on sodomy (that is, homosexual sins). The alleged reason for this is that some NIV translators and editors were homosexuals or lesbians. These charges have no basis in fact. Thus they are simply untrue. And those who make such false charges could be legitimately sued for libel, slander, and defamation of character.

> Here are the facts. It is true that in the earliest stages of translation work on the NIV (in the late 1960s and early 1970s), Virginia Mollenkott was consulted briefly and only in a minor way on matters of English style. At that time she had

the reputation of being a committed evangelical Christian with expertise in contemporary English idiom and usage. Nothing was known of her lesbian views. Those did not begin to surface until years later in some of her writings. If we had known in the sixties what became public knowledge only years later, we would not have consulted her at all. But it must be stressed that she did not influence the NIV translators and editors in any of their final decisions.

Dr. Barker then went on to note some facts regarding the accurate rendering of terms in the NIV regarding homosexuality, and concluded by saying, "I want to go on record as affirming that the NIV translators are among the most spiritual and godly scholars I have ever had the privilege of knowing and working with."

The accusation of homosexuality on the part of KJV Only advocates shows us yet once again the obvious double standards that are characteristic of the entire movement. Scholars who are not involved in the entire Bible translation issue have noted the many facts that point to the conclusion that King James himself was a homosexual.[1] Is this supposed to demonstrate that the KJV is somehow a perverted translation that is soft on homosexuality? One might point out that the term itself nowhere appears on the pages of the KJV. Isn't this proof enough? Using KJV Only standards it is. But, of course, James' sexual behavior had nothing to do with the translation of the KJV, just as Virginia Mollenkott's views had no impact upon the NIV.

Q: You seem to feel that the "plain language" used by Dr. Peter Ruckman (and other defenders of the AV 1611) is unscriptural and simply wrong for a Christian minister. But the prophets of old spoke in strong terms, as did the Lord and the apostles. Why shouldn't Brother Ruckman speak in the same way?

A: Brother Ruckman is not the Lord, nor an apostle, nor a prophet. The Bible tells us how we are to respond to those who contradict us:

> And the servant of the Lord must not strive; but be gentle unto all *men*, apt to teach, patient, in meekness instructing those that

oppose themselves; if God peradventure will give them repentance to the acknowledging of the truth; and *that* they may recover themselves out of the snare of the devil, who are taken captive by him at his will (2 Timothy 2:24-26, KJV).

Blustery words and insulting invective are for those who have little substance to back up their position. A true Christian scholar is a lover of truth, and one does not need to adorn truth with mean-spiritedness. Calling it "plain speaking" does little to cover up the simple fact that it is behavior unbecoming a professing Christian.

Q: Doesn't the fact that God has blessed the KJV more than any other English translation prove that we should continue to use it as our only translation?

A: No, it does not. The very same argument was used against Erasmus long ago, except that time it was used to support the Latin *Vulgate* translation. A few centuries down the line we may have an "NIV Only" group that will use the same argument again. Who knows? The fact is that pragmatism is not the means by which we are to determine truth, whether that be in doctrine or in Bible translation.

God has indeed blessed the KJV, for which we can all be very thankful. And I do not doubt for a second that He will continue to bless those who read it and obey it. But God blessed the Septuagint, too. And the *Vulgate*. And translations in dozens of different languages as well. God has blessed the NASB, and the NIV, and many others. God blesses those who seek His will and follow it. Those who find His will in the NIV are just as blessed as those who find it in the KJV. *Limiting God's blessing to a particular translation of the Bible is historically untenable and spiritually dangerous.*

Q: Aren't you saying that we all have to know Greek and Hebrew to really know God's Word?

A: No, I am not. I have insisted throughout this work that English-speaking people today have access to the best translations that have ever existed, and by diligent comparison of these translations any

English-speaking person can study and know God's Word.

At the same time I *am* inveterately opposed to the "anti-intellectualism" that has become a part of the *tradition* of American fundamentalism. There is no inconsistency between Christian piety and a well-trained mind. There *should be* a desire on the part of many believers to be as prepared as they can be to be students of God's Word. Our local Bible colleges *should* have many applicants seeking a place in a beginning Greek or Hebrew class. When one thinks of the things upon which we spend our time (the hours many of us spend sitting in front of a television comes to mind), the pursuit of the biblical languages would be a *far* more noble thing! God is not honored by sloppy preaching and shallow interpretation of the Bible. Inconsistency in proclaiming His truth does not bring Him glory. Those who take pride in their *lack* of scholarship should rethink their priorities.

Q: Isn't using the phrase "KJV Only" or "KJV Onlyism" insulting and inaccurate?

A: It is neither. The phrase accurately represents those who seek to tell others that the King James is the only God-honoring English translation. It does not mean that KJV Only advocates do not "use" other English translations, but that they "use" them only to point out how bad and inaccurate they allegedly are. For worship and learning, the KJV is the only translation that is used in these groups. Any review of the writings of Peter Ruckman or Gail Riplinger or Samuel Gipp will demonstrate that the term "KJV Only" is perfectly accurate in describing the position being presented.

Endnote

[1] See Otto Scott, *James I: The Fool as King* (Ross House: 1976), pp. 108, 111, 120, 194, 200, 224, 311, 353, 382.

Let the Reader Understand...

This book has been a plea for understanding. It is my desire that the reader, upon completing this work, will first and foremost have a *desire* to understand *why* our English translations of the Bible read as they do. This is the one thing that I have found to be lacking in most KJV Only advocates with whom I have spoken: a desire to *truly know* why someone might be willing to use something other than the KJV, to *really understand* why some readings in the modern translations are, in fact, superior to those in the KJV. You cannot get far with a person who does not wish to travel with you. And I well know that many who are in the KJV Only camp will never set foot upon the path I have attempted to clear in the past pages.

I have written this work for the person who has a godly desire to know the truth. I have not attempted to convince the already convinced. I have written for those who are seeking answers, facts, explanations. I have been prompted by the honest inquiries, the concerned questions, of those who wonder about the claims made by KJV Only advocates. I have sought to be of assistance to the beleaguered pastor who does not need yet another problem cropping up in the congregation. And I admit to a desire to aid in the vindication of men of God who have labored diligently in the field of textual study and translation, a field hardly fraught with riches and glory. The constant denigration of their work, their spirituality, and even their intelligence cries out for a solid refutation and even rebuke, and I hope to have provided that in these pages.

King James Onlyism is a human tradition. It has no basis in history. It has no foundation in fact. It is internally inconsistent, utilizing circular reasoning at its core, and involves the use of more double standards than almost any system of thought I have ever encountered. And yet it is embraced by fellow believers, and as such must be addressed if I am to follow Christ's command, "Love one another."

The facts of the matter are now before you, the reader. Whatever you decide I pray that your deepest desire will be to believe only what is true, nothing that is false. I hope that you will be challenged to dig deeper, to become a student of the Word who is not dependent upon this writer or that "authority," but one who can draw from the rich supply of wisdom and knowledge that is available to us in our day, doing this solely and only to the glory of God.

Finally, as I said at the beginning, my desire is for the peace of Christ's church. I truly hope that this work will help to quell restless spirits in congregations who are by their zealousness for a human tradition (KJV Onlyism) causing dissension and discord. May the facts of the matter, rather than the emotions of the moment, convince such people to refrain from disturbing the brethren, and may the church focus instead upon the weighty and important issues that face her.

Part Two —
The Textual Data

Part Two is designed for those who wish to go "deeper" into the questions that have been addressed in the body of this book. The assumption on the part of the author at this point is that such a person is either proficient in *koine* Greek, and hence able to follow a discussion that utilizes some amount of that language in its text, or is able and willing to do the necessary "homework" to utilize the more in-depth data that will be presented here.

After providing a short mini-glossary, we will present, in canonical order, discussions of various textual variants and passages that have relevance to the KJV Only controversy. Those variants that were not addressed in the body of the work are marked with an asterisk.

A Mini-Glossary of Textual Terms and Symbols

TR	The *Textus Receptus*, so called in 1633, which goes back to Erasmus' work in the sixteenth century via the editions of Stephanus (1550) and Beza (1598).
𝔐	The "Majority Text," the text that is found in the majority of existing Greek manuscripts. This is most often the Byzantine textual reading.
ℵ	"Aleph," that is, Codex Sinaiticus, the great fourth-century uncial codex that is "Alexandrian" in text.
B	Codex Vaticanus, another great fourth-century uncial codex, also "Alexandrian" in text.
NA^{27}	The Nestle-Aland 27th edition Greek text, the current edition of the Nestle-Aland text. Earlier editions underlie such translations as the NASB and NIV.
UBS 4th	The United Bible Societies 4th Edition Greek text. The UBS 4th reads the same as the NA^{27} in its text, but has a different textual apparatus.
𝔊/LXX	The Septuagint, the Greek translation of the Old Testament.
𝔥	The "Hesychian" or "Egyptian" text

MATTHEW 6:13/LUKE 11:2-4: THE LORD'S PRAYER*

The "Lord's Prayer" of Matthew 6 is an excellent text for illustrating how scribal expansion took place in the context of a passage that was deeply ingrained in the Christian liturgy from the earliest times. Not only does the "long ending" in verse 13 provide a valuable insight into the habits of the scribes, but the many efforts at harmonizing Luke's much abbreviated version in Luke 11:2-4 are of great interest as well. Here is Matthew 6:13:

KJV	NIV
And lead us not into temptation, but deliver us from evil: **For thine is the kingdom, and the power, and the glory, for ever. Amen.**	And lead us not into temptation, but deliver us from the evil one.

As in the "longer ending" of Mark, the additional material in verse 13 gives us indications of its later origin in a number of ways. First we have the external evidence against its originality. The verse ends as in the NIV with the Greek term πονηροῦ in ℵ B D Z 0170 f^1 205 l 547, many Latin translations and numerous Fathers. Metzger notes regarding the reading,

> The absence of any ascription in early and important representatives of the Alexandrian (ℵ B), the Western (D and most of the Old Latin), and the pre-Caesarean (f^1) types of text, as well as early patristic commentaries on the Lord's Prayer (those of Tertullian, Origen, Cyprian), suggests that an ascription, usually in a threefold form, was composed (perhaps on the basis of 1 Chr 29.11-13) in order to adapt the Prayer for liturgical use in the early church.[1]

When we look at the longer ending we discover a number of variants. Some omit "and the power," one omits "and the glory," some omit "the kingdom and," and some add a Trinitarian formula, "of the Father, and the Son, and the Holy Spirit." This kind of "variant cluster" is a sure sign of a later addition. Yet verse 13 has become so traditional that to question its originality is often construed as engaging in the most rank kind of "liberalism."

Luke's version of the Lord's Prayer is highly abbreviated in its original form. Scribes sensed a problem and made a number of attempts at harmonization. The influence of Matthew's version is seen throughout the later Greek manuscripts and, hence, in the TR's reading of Luke's account. Entire phrases are imported into Luke, resulting in a much longer version in

---

[1] Metzger, *A Textual Commentary on the Greek New Testament* (United Bible Societies: 1975), pp. 16-17.

the King James Version. The comparison between the KJV and a modern translation such as the NIV is often disconcerting to someone who is not familiar with the reasons for the differences.

KJV	NIV
And he said unto them, When ye pray, say, **Our** Father **which art in heaven,** Hallowed be thy name. Thy kingdom come. **Thy will be done, as in heaven, so in earth.** [3] Give us day by day our daily bread. [4] And forgive us our sins; for we also forgive every one that is indebted to us. And lead us not into temptation; **but deliver us from evil.**	He said to them, "When you pray, say: " 'Father, hallowed be your name, your kingdom come. [3] Give us each day our daily bread. [4] Forgive us our sins, for we also forgive everyone who sins against us. And lead us not into temptation.' "

Each of the underlined phrases is found in Matthew's version of the Lord's Prayer. These additions were made quite early on, demonstrating that this prayer had an important part in the liturgy of the ancient church. As was the case with the longer addition in Matthew 6:13, so too we find a number of variants here as well. Most are to be traced directly to Matthew 6. One of the more interesting, however, that does not come from Matthew is the addition on the part of a few later minuscules of the phrase "Let Your Holy Spirit come upon us and cleanse us." This phrase was known to Gregory of Nyssa, so it goes back to a period earlier than its manuscript support would indicate (though it has insufficient attestation to be taken as original).

MATTHEW 8:29*

Another example of "parallel passage" corruption is seen at Matthew 8:29, where the term Ἰησοῦ is inserted by C^3 W Θ and $\mathfrak{M}$; it is deleted by ℵ B C^* and others. This phrase is most probably inserted from Luke 4:34 or Mark 1:24. Though these are not directly parallel passages, they each contain the very same phrase that would have prompted the insertion of the name of Jesus here at Matthew 8:29. Note the passages:

Mark 1:24	τί ἡμῖν καὶ σοί, Ἰησοῦ Ναζαρηνέ;
Luke 4:34	τί ἡμῖν καὶ σοί, Ἰησοῦ Ναζαρηνέ;
Matthew 8:29	τί ἡμῖν καὶ σοί, ..., υἱὲ τοῦ θεοῦ.

Familiarity with the phrase τί ἡμῖν καὶ σοί led an early scribe of Matthew to insert the name of Jesus, though he did not go so far as to add "Nazarene," a much less familiar term. We should note as well that there are other verbal parallels between Matthew 8:29 and both Mark 1:24 and Luke 4:34 that would merely add to the probabilities of the parallel corruption of the text.

MATTHEW 19:17*

Matthew 19:16-17	
KJV	NIV
And, behold, one came and said unto him, Good Master, what good thing shall I do, that I may have eternal life? And he said unto him, Why **callest thou me** good? there is none good but one, that is, God: but if thou wilt enter into life, keep the commandments.	Now a man came up to Jesus and asked, "Teacher, what good thing must I do to get eternal life?" "Why do you **ask me about what is good**?" Jesus replied. "There is only One who is good. If you want to enter life, obey the commandments."

This variant illustrates clearly the tendency toward scribal harmonization of parallel accounts, especially in the Synoptic Gospels. The problem arises in that Matthew does not record the words of the Lord in the exact same form as Luke and Mark. As a result later scribes, feeling a need to "smooth out" an apparent contradiction, alter Matthew's words to make them "fit." Specifically, Matthew records the Lord as saying, "Why do you ask me about what is good," rather than, "Why do you call me good?" (Luke 18:19). As there is, therefore, a readily available reason for the change to the "smoother" reading, and no apparent reason for the variant to arise otherwise, the reading of such witnesses as ℵ B L and Θ should be taken as the best.

MARK 1:2-3 AND "ISAIAH THE PROPHET"

The UBS 4th assigns to the reading "Isaiah the prophet" a rating of {A}, and that for good reason. The reading has the support of both the external and internal evidence. Externally the word "Isaiah" is found in various forms in ℵ B D L Δ Θ *f*[1] 33 205 565 700 892 1071 1241 1243 2427 *l* 253 arm geo Irenaeus[gr] Origen Serapion Epiphanius Severian Hesychius and numerous Latin manuscripts, which alone would be sufficient. But the internal considerations are even stronger. The desire to rescue Mark from an (misapprehended) error in citing Isaiah when the quotation is from Malachi and Isaiah together (see our discussion in the text above regarding this) is a strong argument in favor of the reading found in the modern texts.

We also note that in another place where a conflated OT reading is found, Matthew 27:9, we find scribal attempts to change "Jeremiah" to

"Zechariah," specifically in *l* 858[1/2] syr[hmg] Origen[latcom]; Jerome[com] Augustine[com], and by omitting any name at all in Φ 33 157 and others. If KJV Only advocates were consistent, they would need to adopt this reading as well!

MARK 16:9-20 AND THE ENDINGS OF MARK

It is found in nearly every manuscript of the New Testament ever written. It is the longest single textual variant in the New Testament. And it is the focus of much attention on the part of KJV Only advocates. It is the "long ending" of the Gospel of Mark, Mark 16:9-20.

It is easy to understand why this passage "preaches" so well. Only the dreaded and hated ℵ and B (and one other manuscript) do not have the passage, and even then, room is left for it in B. Surely nothing could demonstrate more clearly the destructive tendencies of the evil "critics" than their "attack" upon Mark 16:9-20!

It must first be admitted that the documentary evidence for the ancient existence of Mark 16:9-20 is admitted by all. No one claims that there is any similarity, for example, between the textual evidence for this passage and the near absence of such evidence for the *Comma Johanneum,* 1 John 5:7-8. In one case it is overwhelming, in the other nearly nonexistent. So why are modern textual scholars nearly unanimous in their rejection of Mark 16:9-20's claim to originality? Why do nearly all modern translations either set the section apart or even reduce it to footnotes?

The reasons can be summarized under three heads: external evidence, internal evidence, and content. Beginning with the external evidence we note the following items. First, the passage is excluded from ℵ, B, and 304. It is also not found in the Sinaitic Old Syriac, some manuscripts of the Sahadic Coptic version, manuscripts of the Armenian translation, and some versions of the Georgian translation. Jerome was aware of manuscripts that did not contain the passage. Secondly, the passage is included in a number of manuscripts *along with critical marks (such as asterisks or obeli) indicating that the scribe knew of the questionable nature of the passage.* These would include *f*[1], 205, and others. Quite significantly there is an alternative "shorter" ending that is found in the Latin "k", the Bobiensis version. This same shorter ending is combined with the longer ending in L Ψ 083 099 274[mg] 579 *l* 1602 syr[hmg] cop[samss,bomss] eth[mss,TH]. What is more, some Old Church Slavonic manuscripts (from as far along as the tenth century) include only verses 9 through 11 of the longer ending.

Another aspect of the problem comes from Codex W, which adds an entire paragraph to the longer ending between verses 14 and 15. Jerome not only knew of this addition, but indicated that it was popular in some places.

What does all of this mean? B.B. Warfield said, "The existence of the shorter conclusion . . . is *a fortiori* evidence against the longer one. For no one doubts that this shorter conclusion is a spurious invention of the scribes; but it would not have been invented, save to fill the blank."[2] It is the multiplicity of readings that causes so many experts to reject the originality of the longer ending, not merely the fact that it is not to be found in two uncials and a cursive. One must explain the existence of the shorter ending *and* the use of asterisks and obeli in some manuscripts to set verses 9 through 20 off *and* the inclusion of the long paragraph in W *and* the manuscripts that put both the long and short endings together. There simply would be no need for all these different endings if verses 9 through 20 were a part of the gospel when it was originally written.

One leaves strictly objective grounds when one begins to look at internal evidence. Here we are looking at the vocabulary and structure of the passage. Many have noted that the ending differs in many respects from the rest of the Gospel of Mark. Supporters of the TR have responded by pointing to other passages that, if isolated, would also appear "non-Markan." This area of debate seems unable to provide any clear direction on the matter.

The content of the passage has often been criticized, and rightly so. We do not, by pointing out the following items, wish to indicate that an orthodox interpretation of these passages is not possible. Many conservative scholars have provided such interpretations and we can stand by their work. Utilizing the principle of examining other passages that would help us understand or interpret these rather obscure verses does indeed yield a consistent viewpoint. However, the natural reading of these verses strongly suggests that the person who wrote them was *not* completely familiar with the entire Gospel of Mark itself and was utilizing apocryphal and unorthodox sources.

The first anomaly is found in verse 12. Jesus is said to appear in a "different form" (ἐφανερώθη ἐν ἑτέρᾳ μορφῇ) to two disciples, most probably the two on the road to Emmaus (Luke 24:13-35). It must be admitted that the phrase "different form" could refer to the fact that the two disciples were supernaturally kept from recognizing the Lord until He had broken bread with them (Luke 24:16, 31).[3] However, it seems unusual that this phrase would be used, as it tends to make one think that Jesus could change His form at will.

---

[2] B.B. Warfield, *An Introduction to the Textual Criticism of the New Testament* (New York: Whittaker, 1890) as cited by Walter Wessel in "Mark" in *The Expositor's Bible Commentary*, Frank Gaebelein, General Editor (Zondervan: 1984), p. 791.

[3] Beyer, in the *Theological Dictionary of the New Testament* (Eerdmans: 1964), II:702, notes another possibility for the phrase ἐφανερώθη ἐν ἑτέρᾳ μορφῇ, "i.e., not in the transfigured corporeality of the risen Lord as one might naturally suppose, nor in the form of a gardener . . . , but in the form of a traveller."

With the extreme care taken by the other Gospel writers to make sure that all would know that Jesus rose *physically* from the grave, this seems out of place and inconsistent.

The second problem crops up in verse 14, where we have eleven disciples reclining at the table. Aside from the possible numerical problem (was not Thomas absent?), we are here told that "Jesus reproached them for their unbelief and hardness of heart." This is quite out of character, given the other accounts of Jesus' dealings with the disciples after the resurrection. It is so strong that at least one scribe felt it needed toning down and introduced the ninety-word interpolation preserved today by codex W.

The next problem is seen in verse 16. The conjunction of baptism and belief is unusual to say the least. In no other passage does Jesus tie these things together so intricately. Now it is true that Jesus then goes on to say that the basis for condemnation is unbelief, not lack of baptism, and hence baptism does not, even on the basis of this passage, have saving power. But it still presents a phrase that is out of character with what we know of Jesus' teaching from Mark's gospel as well as the other accounts.

Verses 17 and 18 present yet another problem. The signs given here are said to accompany those who have believed, seemingly a promise to *all* who have believed. This again has no real counterpart in any other passage. Certainly Paul was bitten by a serpent and yet felt no ill effects. But even this story does not remove Christians from the natural consequences of life. Today a person can be bitten by a poisonous serpent and suffer no harm due to the snake not releasing any venom, which is not an uncommon occurrence. Possibly Paul's experience shows God's sovereignty over creation and His control of even animal life more than it shows Paul's ability to be poisoned and yet survive. These verses are reminiscent of many of the apocryphal writings that were circulating shortly after the close of the New Testament period.

What can we say, then, about Mark 16:9-20? We can speculate about how the longer ending arose. Did Mark issue two versions of his gospel, adding the longer ending later? No one can say, but that would certainly account for the various endings now in existence. More likely, early scribes felt the abrupt ending of Mark lacked the necessary proclamation of the resurrection, and hence some "parallel corruption" took place, drawing from oral stories and the other gospels to create the longer ending. Whatever the case may be regarding the genesis of the various endings of Mark, we can say that given the external evidence, we believe every translation should provide the passage. However, we also believe that every translation should note the fact that there is good reason to doubt the authenticity of the passage as well. Allow the readers of Scripture to "be diligent" (2 Timothy 2:15) in their own studies and come to their own conclusions.

JOHN 1:18 AND μονογενὴς θεός

A key passage that goes directly to the textual choices made by scholars is found in the prologue of the Gospel of John. The KJV reads at John 1:18:

> No man hath seen God at any time; the only begotten Son, which is in the bosom of the Father, he hath declared him.

The NASB, however, has:

> No man has seen God at any time; the only begotten God, who is in the bosom of the Father, He has explained Him.

Even more interpretive is the rendering of the NIV:

> No one has ever seen God, but God the One and Only, who is at the Father's side, has made him known.

One might well think that KJV Only advocates would welcome the modern renderings, concerned as they claim to be about the deity of Christ. Yet, this is surely not the case. One critic of most modern versions, Jay P. Green, has written under the topical heading, "EXAMPLES OF HOW THE 'BEST' MSS. ROB CHRIST OF GLORY,"

> 1. א in John 1:18 refers to Christ as the "only-begotten God." How can anyone claim that one that is begotten is at the same time essential God, equal in every respect to God the Father, and to God the Holy Spirit? This makes Christ to be a created Being. And it is a Gnostic twist given to the Bible by the heretic Valentinus and his followers, who did not regard the Word and Christ as one and the same; who thought of the Son of God and the Father as being one and the same Person. Therefore, they determined to do away with *"the only-begotten Son"* in order to accommodate their religion.[4]

We note that Mr. Green's reaction is based upon his understanding of theology, not upon the external evidence of the text. And while it is true that heretics down through the ages have appealed to this text or that, we must not allow the *misuse* of biblical texts to determine the readings we choose for the text of Scripture.

In reality we find five variant readings in the manuscript tradition at this point, two of which have obviously given rise to the others. Here is the textual evidence as given by the UBS 4th edition text:

---

[4] *Unholy Hands on the Bible, An Introduction to Textual Criticism*, edited by Jay P. Green, Sr. (Lafayette, Indiana : Sovereign Grace Trust Fund, 1990), p. 12.

μονογενὴς θεός	ὁ μονογενὴς θεός
$\mathfrak{P}^{66}$ ℵ* B C* L syr$^{p,h(mg)}$ geo^2 Origen$^{gr2/4}$ Didymus Cyril$^{1/4}$	$\mathfrak{P}^{75}$ ℵ^2 33 cop^{bo} Clement$^{2/3}$ Clement^{from} $^{Theodotus\ 1/2}$ Origen$^{gr2/4}$ Eusebius$^{3/7}$ Gregory-Nyssa Epiphanius Serapion Cyril$^{2/4}$

We note that when the definite article is passed over, the reading "only-begotten God" or more properly, "unique God,"[5] is found in the two oldest manuscripts, $\mathfrak{P}^{66}$ and $\mathfrak{P}^{75}$, as well as in both ℵ and B. Given the great antiquity of these manuscripts and the correlation with the great uncials, this reading bears great weight. We also note that the Syrian, Georgian, and Coptic translations support this rendering. The survey of the Fathers also shows the wide-spread nature of the reading, and the fact that such notably orthodox men as Gregory, the bishop of Nyssa, a staunch defender of the doctrine of the Trinity, knew this reading and found no objection to it; rather he utilized it often in his writings as evidence of the glory of Christ.[6]

The evidence for the reading ὁ μονογενὴς υἱός is very great indeed. It is, obviously, the majority reading of both the manuscripts, the translations, and the Fathers (though some Fathers show familiarity with more than one reading). The last two variants, μονογενὴς υἱὸς θεοῦ and ὁ μονογενής obviously arose from the preceding variants. They command little manuscript support.

The question that immediately faces the person desiring to know John's original wording is plain: given that both readings have ancient attestation, one commanding the earliest papyri ($\mathfrak{P}^{66}$ and $\mathfrak{P}^{75}$) and the other the majority of the manuscript tradition, how can we account for the rise of a variant at this point? Which reading gives us the most logical reason for the existence of the other?

It is difficult to see how the reading θεός could arise from υἱός. The terms are simply too far removed from one another in form to account for scribal error based upon morphology. However, it is easily understood how θεός could give way to υἱός, given the appearance of "the only-begotten Son" at John 3:16 and 18. "Only-begotten Son" is Johannine in character, and hence

---

[5] The translation "only-begotten" is inferior to "unique." It was thought that the term came from μόνος (*monos*), meaning "only" and γεννάω (*gennao*), meaning "begotten." However, further research has determined that the term is derived not from γεννάω but from γένος (*genos*), meaning "kind" or "type." Hence the better translation, "unique" or "one of a kind." See Louw and Nida, *A Greek-English Lexicon of the New Testament Based on Semantic Domains* (1988) p. 591; Newman and Nida, *A Translator's Handbook on the Gospel of John*, 1980, p. 24; and Moulton and Milligan, *The Vocabulary of the Greek Testament*, 1930, pp. 416-417.

[6] See relevant passages in *Nicene and Post-Nicene Fathers*, Second Series (Grand Rapids: Wm. B. Eerdmans Publishing Company, 1954), V:102, 104, 125, 140, 198, 240.

would naturally cause a scribe to write υἱός upon writing μονογενής rather than θεός.

Therefore, it is most logical to conclude that μονογενὴς θεός is the original reading that gave rise to all the other variants, including the reading that is found in the majority of Greek texts. The internal evidence, coupled with the ancient attestation of the reading in the papyri especially, leads one to take this reading with confidence. This decision is not arrived at due to gnostic or heretical beliefs or leanings, but simply due to the external evidence itself.

JOHN 3:13 — THE SON OF MAN WHO IS IN HEAVEN*

John 3:13	
KJV	**NIV**
And no man hath ascended up to heaven, but he that came down from heaven, *even* the Son of man which is in heaven.	No one has ever gone into heaven except the one who came from heaven—the Son of Man.

Critics of the "modern" texts are quick to pounce upon John 3:13, alleging that here we find the heretical denial of the omnipresence of Christ through the "deletion" of the phrase, "which (who) is in heaven." Nearly every KJV Only advocate who addresses the issue does so along with charges of "heresy" on the part of either the scribes who "corrupted" the text,[7] or the modern translators who would follow their lead. As normal, however, a calm examination of the facts demonstrates otherwise.

One may well prefer the reading of the 𝔐 text at this point. The external attestation for the reading is impressive, as cited by UBS 4th, without including patristic sources:

ὁ ὢν ἐν τῷ οὐρανῷ	OMIT
A[c] (A[*vid] omit ὢν) D Q Y 050 f^1 f^{13} 28 157 180 205 565 579 597 700 892 1006 1071 1243 1292 1342 1424 1505 *Byz* [E G H N] Lect it[a, aur, b, c, f, ff2, j, l, q, rl] vg	𝔓[66] 𝔓[75] ℵ B L T W[supp] 083 086 33 1010 1241 cop[sa, bopt, ach2, fay] geo[2]

The patristic material favors the inclusion of the phrase, though there are important witnesses against it. Still, it is always uncomfortable to go against both 𝔓[66] and 𝔓[75] when they are united in a particular reading. The wisest

---

[7] See Jay P. Green, *The Gnostics, the New Versions, and the Deity of Christ* (Lafayette, Ind.: Sovereign Grace Publishers: 1994), pp. 23-25. While Green alleges that the Gnostics tampered with the texts, he provides no direct evidence that this is so.

stance to take, it would seem, would be to make the reader aware of the reading through the use of textual footnotes. In either case, it is surely no sign of heresy or a desire to denigrate Christ to follow the lead of the two oldest witnesses to the Gospel of John in not including the reading. And, what is sad is that KJV Only advocates do not seem to recognize that the textual decisions made by scholars are not monolithic in nature; that is, one has the freedom to take either side of this particular variant reading without being ostracized by the scholarly community. One does not *have* to "delete" this phrase from John 3:13 to be in "good standing." Indeed, Dr. Metzger's comments on this variant are very instructional:

> On the one hand, a minority of the Committee preferred the reading ἀνθρώπου ὁ ὢν ἐν τῷ οὐρανῷ, arguing that (1) if the short reading, supported almost exclusively by Egyptian witnesses, were original, there is no discernible motive which would have prompted copyists to add the words ὁ ὢν ἐν τῷ οὐρανῷ, resulting in a most difficult saying . . . ; and (2) the diversity of readings implies that the expression ὁ υἱὸς τοῦ ἀνθρώπου ὁ ὢν ἐν τῷ οὐρανῷ, having been found objectionable or superfluous in the context, was modified either by omitting the participial clause, or by altering it so as to avoid suggesting that the Son of man was at that moment in heaven.
>
> On the other hand, the majority of the Committee, impressed by the quality of the external attestation supporting the shorter reading, regarded the words ὁ ὢν ἐν τῷ οὐρανῷ as an interpretative gloss, reflecting later Christological development.[8]

One can find good reason to agree with the minority viewpoint, and if one takes that position, one is not alone. Furthermore, given the openness of Dr. Metzger in relating this perspective, and of the UBS text in citing the variant in full, who can possibly think that there is, in fact, some "conspiracy" afoot to "hide" this passage from the average Christian reader of the Bible?

JOHN 6:47 AND "BELIEVE IN ME"

This KJV Only favorite again pits the oldest manuscripts against the 𝔐 text. NA[27] gives the evidence as follows:

Exclude εις εμε	Include εις εμε
𝔓[66,75vid] ℵ B C* L T W Θ 892 *pc* j ac²	A C² D Ψ *f*[1.13] 33 𝔐 lat sy[p,h] sa pbo bo; Did

---

[8] Metzger, *A Textual Commentary on the Greek New Testament,* pp. 203-204.

The conjugation of 𝔓⁶⁶ and 𝔓⁷⁵ together with ℵ and B, together with the internal evidence, is more than sufficient to substantiate the reading. The phrase ὁ πιστεύων εἰς ἐμε is classically Johannine in style (John 6:35; 7:38; 11:25, etc.). Therefore a shift to the "regular" phrasing is to be expected.

JOHN 7:53 - 8:11, THE "PERICOPE DE ADULTERA"

The evidence against the originality of this pericope is extensive and wide-ranging, including both external and internal elements. Externally we note that the passage is omitted by a truly diverse group of ancient manuscripts, including 𝔓⁶⁶ 𝔓⁷⁵ ℵ B L N T W Δ Θ Ψ 0141 33 157 565 1241 1333* 1424, the majority of lectionaries, Latin versions, and Syriac versions. Both A and C most probably did not contain the passage, though both are defective in this section of John and, hence, cannot be consulted directly. Other manuscripts that do contain the passage mark it off with asterisks or obeli. This amount of evidence alone would be sufficient, but there is more. In the manuscripts that contain the passage, it is normally found after John 7:52. However, in ms. 225 it is found after 7:36; in others after 7:44; in a group of others after John 21:25, and in f^{13} it is not even found in John, but after Luke 21:38! Such moving about by a body of text is plain evidence of its later origin and the attempt on the part of scribes to find a place where it "fits." Such is not the earmark of an original passage in the Gospel.

The primary internal consideration, aside from issues of vocabulary and style, is to be found in the fact that John 7:52 and John 8:12 "go together." The story of the woman taken in adultery interrupts the flow of the text and the events recorded by John regarding Jesus' ministry in Jerusalem (7:45-8:20).

All of these things taken together make it a near certainty that this passage was not originally a part of the Gospel of John. Yet, the story itself is certainly in harmony with the ministry and teaching of the Lord Jesus. Most feel it was an early oral tradition that was popular primarily in the West and that it came to have a part in the Gospel of John over time.

JOHN 9:35, SON OF GOD OR SON OF MAN?

The NA[27] text gives the following information regarding this variant:

υἱὸν τοῦ ἀνθρώπου	υἱὸν τοῦ θεοῦ
𝔓⁶⁶ 𝔓⁷⁵ ℵ B D W pc e bo^{ms}	A L Θ Ψ 070 0250 $f^{1.13}$ 33 𝔐 lat sy^{p.h} bo

The external evidence for Son of Man, υἱὸν τοῦ ἀνθρώπου is very strong, including the major uncials and papyri. It is very difficult to understand why θεοῦ would be replaced by ἀνθρώπου either intentionally or by mistake;

however, it is much easier to understand how the very common phrase υἱὸν τοῦ θεοῦ could replace the other reading, especially in this context. Hence, most textual scholars see "Son of Man" as the almost certain original reading.

JOHN 14:14 AND PRAYER TO CHRIST

The textual variant at John 14:14 illustrates again the fact that the Alexandrian text-type cannot be charged with some kind of bias against the deity of Christ, for here we find a reference to prayer to Christ in the Alexandrian as well as a portion of the Majority text-type. The UBS 4th gives the following textual data:

Include με	Exclude με
𝔓[66] 𝔓[75vid] א B W Δ Θ 060 *f*[13] 28 33 579 700 892 1006 1342 Byz[pt]	A D L Ψ 180 597 (1010) 1071 1241 1243 1292 1424 1505 Byz[pt]

Here the 𝔐 type splits, some joining the Alexandrian in supporting the reading. The TR excludes the reading, but it is retained by NA[27], UBS 4th and the Majority Text. Metzger noted,

> Either the unusual collocation, "ask *me* in *my* name" (yet it is not without parallel, cf. Ps 25.11; 31.3; 79.9, where the Psalmist prays to God for his name's sake), or a desire to avoid contradiction with 16.23, seems to have prompted (*a*) the omission of με in a variety of witnesses (A D K L Π Ψ *Byz al*) or (*b*) its replacement with τὸν πατέρα (249 397). The word με is adequately supported (𝔓[66] א B W Δ Θ *f*[13] 28 33 700 *al*) and seems to be appropriate in view of its correlation with ἐγώ later in the verse.[9]

Interestingly, the Jehovah's Witnesses' NWT, though allegedly following the Westcott and Hort text of 1881, which includes με, does not translate the term in its text, and that for theological reasons.

ROMANS 8:28*

KJV	NASB
And we know that all things work together for good to them that love God, to them who are the called according to his purpose.	And we know that God causes all things to work together for good to those who love God, to those who are called according to His purpose.

---

[9] Metzger, *A Textual Commentary on the Greek New Testament*, p. 244.

Surely Romans 8:28 is one of the most precious passages in all of Scripture, and yet even here we encounter a question: do we follow the vast majority of manuscripts (and even the most modern texts) and read as the KJV, "all things work together for good," or do we follow $\mathfrak{P}^{46}$ A B 81 and two translations in reading "God causes all things to work together for good"? The earlier editions of Nestle's text contained the phrase in brackets, and hence the NASB, following these texts, includes it in the translation. The NA^{27} has relegated the reading to the apparatus, going back to the earlier reading of the TR. Metzger notes that an early Alexandrian scribe may have felt that the majority reading was too impersonal, since συνεργεῖ seems to imply a personal subject. The KJV Only advocate who feels the modern texts are simply blindly following the Alexandrian text might wish to take note of the fact that here the chosen reading goes against the most ancient papyrus copy of Romans ($\mathfrak{P}^{46}$) as well as both A and B. The situation might be different, however, if ℵ had joined in this reading. We might note in passing as well that if one were to determine textual readings on the basis of theological "superiority," here the Alexandrian reading, which plainly presents God as the one who works all things together for the good, would be the "better" reading, but is absent from the KJV.

1 CORINTHIANS 11:22*

This passage provides an example of how modern eclectic texts take into consideration both external and internal evidence, and how this can sometimes lead to interesting results. The NA^{27} reads with the $\mathfrak{M}$ text here. The $\mathfrak{H}$ text is split, ℵ A^{vid} and minuscules 1739 and 1881 going with $\mathfrak{M}$, all reading ἐπαινέσω (aorist subjunctive or future indicative), "Shall I praise you?" But $\mathfrak{P}^{46}$ and B have the present indicative, ἐπαινῶ. Possibly the scribes of $\mathfrak{P}^{46}$ and B assimilated the first reading with the second appearance of ἐπαινῶ at the end of the verse? In any case, the split of the $\mathfrak{H}$ text is decided on the basis of internal criteria, the subjunctive or future indicative fitting Paul's use of τί εἴπω ὑμῖν;

1 CORINTHIANS 11:24, "TAKE, EAT"*

This textual variant, which presents a pretty much straight $\mathfrak{H}$ vs. $\mathfrak{M}$ split, shows how parallel influence can take place even between the Gospels and passages elsewhere in the NT, as long as a common event or saying is being related. Here the phrase, λάβετε φάγετε, "take, eat," comes from the more familiar passage in Matthew 26:26. One can recognize how something as important as the words of the institution of the Supper would be subject to a *strong* element of harmonization on the part of scribes of any period.

GALATIANS 5:21*

KJV	NIV
Envyings, **murders**, drunkenness, revellings, and such like: of the which I tell you before, as I have also told *you* in time past, that they which do such things shall not inherit the kingdom of God.	and envy; drunkenness, orgies, and the like. I warn you, as I did before, that those who live like this will not inherit the kingdom of God.

The modern texts do not have the term "murders" at Galatians 5:21. We noted earlier Erasmus' statement that textual variants were common in lists of sins like this because it is hard to copy lists as these things are "difficult to remember." This is a difficult reading, the UBS 3rd edition giving it a rating of {D}, the 4th a rating of {C}. The reason for the difficulty is readily apparent: the deletion of the phrase is supported by 𝔓[46] ℵ and B, together with a long list of early church Fathers. Also, the argument can be made that this passage has been "harmonized" with Romans 1:29, which has the terms "envy" and "murders" right next to each other. But on the other hand the term is included in A C D and others, and can be easily explained as an example again of *homoeoteleuton*, "similar endings." The two terms in Greek uncial letters appearing like this in direct sequence:

ΦΘΟΝΟΙΦΟΝΟΙ

EPHESIANS 3:14*

KJV	NIV
For this cause I bow my knees unto the Father **of our Lord Jesus Christ**,	For this reason I kneel before the Father,

Ephesians 1:3 begins, "Praise be to the God and Father of our Lord Jesus Christ." Seemingly the familiarity of that phrase influenced the later addition of the *exact* same phraseology here at 3:14. The earliest manuscripts, again, do not contain the phrase, which is limited to Western and Byzantine sources. Those who assert that the modern translations are trying to make God more "acceptable" to other religions by removing the limiting phrase "of our Lord Jesus Christ" have to explain the prevalence of that very same phrase in those versions ("Father of our Lord Jesus Christ" is found five times in the NIV New Testament, at Romans 15:6; 2 Corinthians 1:3; Ephesians 1:3; Colossians 1:3; and 1 Peter 1:3).

PHILIPPIANS 4:13*

KJV	NASB
I can do all things through **Christ** which strengtheneth me.	I can do all things through **Him** who strengthens me.

This variant is one of the many passages cited in evidence of the allegation that the Alexandrian (𝔓) text wishes to "remove" Christ. This particular variant "preaches" better than most, since the passage is one that is familiar with a large percentage of the Christian populace. It can be argued, of course, that Christ is the antecedent of the participle ἐνδυναμοῦντι, and hence the NASB is referring to Christ without having to repeat the name. It is no more confusing to figure out who the one strengthening Paul is in verse 13 than it is to figure out who the "Lord" of verse 10 is. The name of Christ is not found in ℵ* A B D* I 33 1739, a number of Latin versions, many other early translations, and a number of early Fathers. It is found primarily in the Byzantine manuscripts.

COLOSSIANS 1:14 AND "THROUGH HIS BLOOD"

Since the reading "through His blood" (διὰ τοῦ αἵματος αὐτοῦ) is in the minority of manuscripts, it is much easier simply to cite Mss. that *do* contain the phrase. Following the UBS 4th: 424 1912 2200 2464 *l*147 *l*590 *l*592 *l*593 *l*1159 along with some versions and a few patristic sources. There is no uncial support for the reading. This variant arose later in the transmission process, as the evidence demonstrates, and was surely the result of harmonization with Ephesians 1:7.

COLOSSIANS 2:18 — SEEN OR NOT SEEN?*

Here the variant revolves around the inclusion or exclusion of the single negative particle "μη." Metzger noted,

> The reading ἃ is strongly supported by 𝔓46 and good representatives of the Alexandrian and the Western types of text (ℵ* A B D* I 33 1730 it^d cop^{sa,bo} Speculum *al*). Apparently the negative (either οὐκ in F G or μή in ℵ^c C D^c K P Ψ 614 it^{g,61,86} vg syr^{p,h} goth arm *al*) was added by copyists who either misunderstood the sense of ἐμβατεύων or wished to enhance the polemical nuance that is carried on by the following εἰκῇ φυσιούμενος.[10]

---

[10] Metzger, *A Textual Commentary on the Greek New Testament*, p. 623.

TITUS 2:13 — GRANVILLE SHARP'S RULE AND THE KJV

The great scholars who labored upon the AV would have been the first to admit that their work was liable to correction and revision as the study of the biblical languages and the textual history of the Bible advanced. Surely they would have welcomed the study undertaken by Granville Sharp late in the 1790s. Sharp's work resulted in a rule of *koine* Greek that bears his name, a rule that was not fully understood by the KJV translators. Because of his work, we are able to better understand how plain is the testimony to the deity of Christ that is found in such places as Titus 2:13 and 2 Peter 1:1. The KJV translators, through no fault of their own, obscured these passages through less than perfect translation. Modern translations correct their error. And yet, KJV Only advocates continue to defend a rendering that is shared by such Arian translations as the Jehovah's Witnesses' *New World Translation,* and that *solely* because of their presupposition that "if it is in the KJV, it *must* be right."

Basically, Granville Sharp's rule states that when you have two nouns, which are not proper names (such as Cephas, or Paul, or Timothy), which are describing a person, and the two nouns are connected by the word "and," and the first noun has the article ("the") while the second does not, *both nouns are referring to the same person.* In our texts, this is demonstrated by the words "God" and "Savior" at Titus 2:13 and 2 Peter 1:1. "God" has the article, it is followed by the word for "and," and the word "Savior" does not have the article. Hence, both nouns are being applied to the same person, Jesus Christ.

In Titus 2:13, we first see that Paul is referring to the "epiphaneia" (ἐπιφάνεια) of the Lord, His "appearing." Every other instance of this word is reserved for Christ and Him alone.[11] It is immediately followed by verse 14, which says, "who gave Himself for us, that He might redeem us from every lawless deed and purify for Himself a people for His own possession, zealous for good deeds" (NASB). The obvious reference here is to Christ who "gave Himself for us" on the cross of Calvary. There is no hint here of a plural antecedent for the "who" of verse 14 either. It might also be mentioned that verse 14, while directly referring to Christ, is a paraphrase of some Old Testament passages that refer to Yahweh God (Psalm 130:8; Deuteronomy 7:6, etc.). One can hardly object to the identification of Christ as God when the apostle goes on to describe His works as the works of God!

The passage found at 2 Peter 1:1 is even more compelling. Some have simply bypassed grammatical rules and considerations, and have decided for an inferior translation on the basis of verse 2, which, they say, "clearly

---

[11] 2 Thess. 2:8; 1 Tim. 6:14; 2 Tim. 1:10, 4:1, 4:8; Tit. 2:13. W.F. Moulton, A.S. Geden, H. K. Moulton, *Concordance to the Greek Testament,* 5th ed. (Edinburgh: T & T Clark, 1980) p. 374.

distinguishes" between God and Christ.[12] Such translation on the basis of theological prejudices is hardly commendable. The little book of 2 Peter contains a total of five "Granville Sharp" constructions. They are 1:1; 1:11; 2:20; 3:2; and 3:18. No one would argue that the other four instances are exceptions to the rule. For example, in 2:20, it is obvious that both "Lord" and "Savior" are in reference to Christ. Such is the case in 3:2, as well as 3:18. No problem there, for the proper translation does not step on anyone's theological toes. Verse 11 in chapter 1 is even more striking. The construction here is *identical* to the construction found in 1:1, with only one word being different. Here are the passages, first in Greek, then as they are transliterated into English:

1:1: τοῦ θεοῦ ἡμῶν καὶ σωτῆρος Ἰησοῦ Χριστοῦ
1:11: τοῦ κυρίου ἡμῶν καὶ σωτῆρος Ἰησοῦ Χριστοῦ

1:1: *tou theou hemon kai soteros Iesou Christou*
1:11: *tou kuriou hemon kai soteros Iesou Christou*

Notice the exact one-to-one correspondence between these passages! The only difference is the substitution of "kuriou" (κυρίου) for "theou" (θεου). No one would question the translation of "our Lord and Savior, Jesus Christ" at 1:11; why question the translation of "our God and Savior, Jesus Christ" at 1:1? Consistency in translation demands that we not allow our personal prejudices to interfere with our rendering of God's Word.

Most attacks upon Granville Sharp's rule have been based upon less-than-full or accurate definitions of it. A review of the current literature shows that most modern grammars do not give full definitions when presenting Granville Sharp's work. Take, for example, the definition given by Curtis Vaughan and Virtus Gideon:

> If two nouns of the same case are connected by a "kai" and the article is used with both nouns, they refer to different persons or things. If only the first noun has the article, the second noun refers to the same person or thing referred to in the first.[13]

Kenneth Wuest, in his book, defines it this way:

> We have Granville Sharp's rule here, which says that when there are two nouns in the same case connected by a kai (and), the first

---

[12] Alford, *New Testament for English Readers*, p. 1671.
[13] Curtis Vaughan, and Virtus Gideon, *A Greek Grammar of the New Testament* (Nashville: Broadman Press, 1979), p. 83.

> noun having the article, the second noun not having the article, the second noun refers to the same thing the first noun does and is a further description of it.[14]

Note the absence of the second part of Vaughan and Gideon's definition, that of the two nouns both with articles. Dana and Mantey give probably the most accurate definition when they write:

> The following rule by Granville Sharp of a century back still proves to be true: "When the copulative kai connects two nouns of the same case, if the article ho or any of its cases precedes the first of the said nouns or participles, and is not repeated before the second noun or participle, the latter always relates to the same person that is expressed or described by the first noun or participle; i.e., it denotes a further description of the first-named person."[15]

However, much to my surprise, I have found that none of these definitions, even the one by Dana and Mantey, accurately reflects what Granville Sharp actually said or meant. It has been due to these less-than-accurate definitions that Sharp's rule has become the target of much criticism. One of the longest and best discussions that I have been able to find is found in A.T. Robertson's fine work (*The Minister and His Greek New Testament*, pp. 61-68), under the title, "The Greek Article and the Deity of Christ." It was here that I first found an accurate rendering of Granville Sharp's actual rule. Since that time I have been fortunate enough to track down an 1807 edition of Granville Sharp's work entitled, This work actually puts forth six rules, the other five being corollaries of the first.

Granville Sharp's rule, according to Granville Sharp, is:

> When the copulative καί connects two nouns of the same case [viz. nouns (either substantive or adjective, or participles) of personal description, respecting office, dignity, affinity, or connexion, and attributes, properties, or qualities, good or ill,] if the article ὁ, or any of its cases, precedes the first of the said nouns or participles, and is not repeated before the second noun or participle, the latter always relates to the same person that is expressed or described by the first noun or participle: i.e., it denotes a farther description of the first named person.[16]

---

[14] Wuest, *Wuest's Word Studies In the Greek New Testament*, 2:195.

[15] Dana and Mantey, *A Manual Grammar of the Greek New Testament*, p. 147.

[16] Granville Sharp, *Remarks on the Uses of the Definitive Article in the Greek Text of the New Testament: Containing Many New Proofs of the Divinity of Christ, From Passages Which are Wrongly Translated in the Common English Version* (Philadelphia: B.B. Hopkins and Co., 1807), p. 3.

The vital point that is available to the reader of Sharp's work is this: *Sharp's rule is valid only for singulars, not plurals; and it is not intended to be applied to proper names.* His rule only applies to persons, not things. As we can see, Granville Sharp's rule is much more limited in its scope than the more modern definitions reveal.

Does this more accurate and definite definition make a big difference? Indeed it does! There are seventy-nine occurrences of "Granville Sharp" constructions in the writings of Paul, using Vaughan and Gideon's definition. Hence, here we have constructions that mix singulars and plurals, descriptions of places and things, and constructions that reflect both nouns as having the article. A quick glance over the list reveals a maximum of fifteen exceptions, and a minimum of five. Even this ratio would be considered very good for a general rule of grammar. However, Sharp claimed that the rule *always* held true. Obviously, if the modern versions of his rule are accurate, Sharp was not. But when the constructions in the New Testament that truly follow Granville Sharp's rule are examined, a very unusual thing happens: *it is found to be entirely without exception!* As Robertson quotes from Sharp's work, "But, though Sharp's principle was attacked, he held to it and affirms (p. 115) that though he had examined several thousand examples of this type, "the apostle and high priest of our confession Jesus" (Heb. 3:1), he had never found an exception."[17] From my own research, I concur with Sharp.

Why, then, do the AV, the ASV, and a few other older versions incorrectly translate these passages? Robertson maintains that it is mainly due to the influence of George B. Winer and his grammatical work. For three generations his work was supreme, and many scholars did not feel inclined to "fly in his face" and insist on the correct translation of these passages. However, Winer himself, being an anti-trinitarian, admitted that it was not grammatical grounds that led him to reject the correct rendering of Titus 2:13, but theological ones. In the Winer-Moulton Grammar (as cited by Robertson), page 162, Winer said, "Considerations derived from Paul's system of doctrine lead me to believe that σωτῆρος is not a second predicate, co-ordinate with θεου, Christ being first called μέγας θεός, and then σωτήρ." However, Robertson put it well when he said, "Sharp stands vindicated after all the dust has settled. We must let these passages mean what they want to mean regardless of our theories about the theology of the writers."[18]

---

[17] Robertson, *The Minister and His Greek New Testament*, p. 62.

[18] Robertson, *The Minister and His Greek New Testament*, p. 66. Further scholarly corroboration of this interpretation of these passages can be found in A.T. Robertson's *Word Pictures in the Greek New Testament*, vol. 6, pp. 147-148; in Nicoll's *Expositor's Greek Testament*, vol. 5, p. 123; and in B.B. Warfield, *Biblical and Theological Studies*, pp. 68-71. Grundmann, in Kittel's *Theological Dictionary of the New Testament*, vol. 4,

JUDE 1, SANCTIFIED OR BELOVED?*

KJV	NASB
Jude, the servant of Jesus Christ, and brother of James, to them that are **sanctified** by God the Father, and preserved in Jesus Christ, *and* called:	Jude, a bond-servant of Jesus Christ, and brother of James, to those who are the called, **beloved** in God the Father, and kept for Jesus Christ:

This passage again demonstrates that there is no theological program being pursued by modern versions. The difference between "sanctified" and "beloved" in this instance is the difference between the terms ἡγιασμένοις (sanctified) and ἠγαπημένοις. The similarity of the terms is obvious, and the fact that either term "fits" in the context is obvious as well.

---

p. 540, says, "Hence we have to take Jesus Christ as the *megas theos*. This is demanded by the position of the article, by the term *epiphaneia* . . . , and by the stereotyped nature of the expression. . . . Hence the best rendering is: 'We wait for the blessed hope and manifestation of the glory of our great God and Saviour Jesus Christ.' "

Bibliography

Aland, Kurt, and Barbara Aland. *The Text of the New Testament.* Grand Rapids: Eerdmans, 1987.

Alford, Henry. *New Testament for English Readers.* Grand Rapids: Baker Book House, 1983.

Archer, Gleason. *The Encyclopedia of Bible Difficulties.* Grand Rapids: Zondervan, 1982.

Arndt, William F., and F. Wilbur Gingrich. *A Greek-English Lexicon of the New Testament and Other Early Christian Literature,* 2nd ed. Edited by F. Wilbur Gingrich and Frederick W. Danker. The University of Chicago Press: 1979.

Bainton, Roland. *Erasmus of Christendom.* New York: Charles Scribner's Sons, 1969.

Barker, Kenneth. *Accuracy Defined and Illustrated.* Colorado Springs: International Bible Society, 1995.

————. *The NIV: The Making of a Contemporary Translation.* New York: International Bible Society: 1991.

Brown, Francis, S.R. Driver, and Charles A. Briggs, eds. *A Hebrew and English Lexicon of the Old Testament.* Oxford: 1957.

Bruce, F.F. *The Books and the Parchments.* 3rd ed. Old Tappan, New Jersey: Revell, 1963.

Burgon, Dean John William. *The Revision Revised.* 1883.

Burton, Barry. *Let's Weigh the Evidence.* Chino, California: Chick Publications, 1983.

Comfort, Philip W. *Early Manuscripts & Modern Translations of the New Testament.* Wheaton: Tyndale House Publishers, Inc., 1990.

Dana, H.E., and Julius R. Mantey. *A Manual Grammar of the Greek New Testament.* New York: The Macmillan Company, 1955.

Davis, William Hersey. *Beginner's Grammar of the Greek New Testament.* New York: Harper and Row, 1923.

Faludy, George. *Erasmus.* New York: Stein & Day, 1970.

Fee, Gordon. "The Textual Criticism of the New Testament." In Frank E. Gaebelein, gen. ed., *The Expositor's Bible Commentary* Vol. 1, *Introductory Articles: General, Old Testament, New Testament.* Grand Rapids: Zondervan, 1979.

————. "Modern Textual Criticism and the Revival of the Textus Receptus." *Journal of the Evangelical Theological Society.* 21, (1978).

Fuller, David Otis. *Which Bible?* 5th edition. Grand Rapids: Grand Rapids International Publications, 1975.

Funk, Robert, and Ray Hoover. *The Five Gospels:* The Jesus Seminar. New York: Macmillan, 1993.

Gingrich, F. Wilbur. *Shorter Lexicon of the Greek New Testament,* Revised by Frederick W. Danker, 2nd ed. University of Chicago Press: Chicago, 1983.

Gipp, Samuel. *An Understandable History of the Bible.* Privately printed, 1987.
———. *The Answer Book.* Shelbyville, Tenn.: Bible & Literature Missionary
    Foundation, 1989.
Geisler, Norman, and William E. Nix. *A General Introduction to the Bible.* Chicago:
    Moody Press, 1986.
Grady, William. *Final Authority.* Schererville, Ind.: Grady Publications, 1993.
Green, Jay P. Sr. *The Gnostics, the New Versions, and the Deity of Christ.* Lafayette,
    Ind.: Sovereign Grace Publishers, 1994.
———. ed. *Unholy Hands on the Bible, An Introduction to Textual Criticism.*
    Lafayette, Ind.: Sovereign Grace Trust Fund, 1990.
Greenlee, J. Harold. *Introduction to New Testament Textual Criticism.* Grand Rapids:
    Eerdmans, 1964.
Hills, Edward F. *The King James Version Defended,* 4th ed. Des Moines, Ia.: The
    Christian Research Press, 1984.
Hodges, Zane, and Arthur Farstad. *The Greek New Testament According to the
    Majority Text.* 2nd ed. Nashville: Thomas Nelson, 1985.
Hoskier, H.C. *Concerning the Text of the Apocalypse.* London: Bernard Quaritch,
    Ltd., 1929.
James, Kevin. *The Corruption of the Word: The Failure of Modern New Testament
    Scholarship.* Williamsburg, N.M.: Micro-Load Press, 1990.
Josephus, Flavius. *The Antiquities of the Jews* in the *Works of Josephus.* Lynn,
    Mass.: Hendrickson Publishers, 1980.
Kittel, Gerhard, and Geoffrey Bromiley, eds. *Theological Dictionary of the New
    Testament.* Grand Rapids: Eerdmans, 1964. S.v. "ἕτερος" by Hermann Beyer.
———. *Theological Dictionary of the New Testament.* Grand Rapids: Eerdmans,
    1964. S.v. "μέγας" by W. Grundmann.
Kutilek, Doug. *An Answer to David Otis Fuller: Fuller's Deceptive Treatment of
    Spurgeon Regarding the King James Version.* Pilgrim Publications, n.d.
Letis, Theodore P. *The Revival of the Ecclesiastical Text and the Claims of the
    Anabaptists.* Ft. Wayne, Ind.: The Institute for Reformation Biblical Studies,
    1992.
Lewis, Jack. *The English Bible: From KJV to NIV.* 2nd edition. Grand Rapids: Baker
    Book House, 1991.
Louw, Johannes P., and Eugene Nida. *A Greek-English Lexicon of the New Testament
    Based on Semantic Domains.* New York: United Bible Societies, 1988.
Mangan, John Joseph. *The Life, Character, and Influence of Desiderius Erasmus of
    Rotterdam.* New York: The Macmillan Company, 1927.
Martin, Robert. *Accuracy of Translation and the New International Version.* Carlisle,
    Pa.: Banner of Truth Trust, 1989.
Metzger, Bruce Manning. *A Textual Commentary on the Greek New Testament.* New
    York: United Bible Societies, 1975.
———. *Manuscripts of the Greek Bible.* New York: Oxford University Press, 1981.
———. *The Early Versions of the New Testament.* New York: Oxford University
    Press, 1977.
———. *The Text of the New Testament: Its Transmission, Corruption, and
    Restoration.* 2nd edition. New York: Oxford University Press, 1968.

Moulton, W. F., A. S. Geden, and H.K. Moulton. *Concordance to the Greek Testament.* 5th ed. Edinburgh: T & T Clark, 1980.

Newman, Barclay and Nida, Eugene. *A Translator's Handbook on the Gospel of John.* New York: United Bible Societies, 1980.

Nicoll, W. Robertson. *The Expositor's Greek Testament.* Grand Rapids: Eerdmans, 1983.

Paine, Gustavus. *The Men Behind the King James Version.* Grand Rapids: Baker Book House, 1977.

Palmer, Edwin. *The Person and Ministry of the Holy Spirit.* Grand Rapids: Baker Book House: 1958, 1974.

Pickering, Wilbur N. " 'Queen Anne...' And All That: A Response." *Journal of the Evangelical Theological Society.* 21, (1978).

———. *The Identity of the New Testament Text.* Revised edition. Nashville: Thomas Nelson Publishers, 1980.

Pierpont, W.G., and M.A. Robinson. *The New Testament in the Original Greek According to the Byzantine/Majority Textform.* Atlanta: Original Word, 1991.

Pirkle, Estus. *The 1611 King James Bible.* Southaven, Miss.: The King's Press, 1994.

Ray, Jasper James. *God Wrote Only One Bible.* Eugene, Oreg.: Eye Opener Publishers, 1983.

Reinecker, Fritz, and Cleon Rogers. *Linguistic Key to the Greek New Testament.* Grand Rapids: Zondervan, 1982.

Riplinger, Gail. *New Age Bible Versions.* Munroe Falls, Ohio: A.V. Publications, 1993.

———. *The End Times and Victorious Living Newsletter.* January/February 1994.

———. *Which Bible Is God's Word?* Oklahoma City, Okla.: Hearthstone Publishing, 1994.

Robertson, A.T. *A Grammar of the Greek New Testament in the Light of Historical Research.* Nashville: Broadman Press, 1934.

———. *The Minister and His Greek New Testament.* Grand Rapids: Baker Book House, 1977.

———. *Word Pictures in the New Testament.* Grand Rapids: Baker Book House, 1930.

Ruckman, Peter. *About the "New" King James Bible.* Pensacola: Bible Baptist Bookstore, 1983.

———. *The Christian's Handbook of Manuscript Evidence.* Pensacola: Pensacola Bible Press: 1990.

———. *Custer's Last Stand.* Pensacola: Bible Baptist Bookstore, 1981.

———. *Hyper-Calvinism.* Pensacola: Bible Baptist Bookstore, 1984.

———. *Problem Texts.* Pensacola: Pensacola Bible Institute Press, 1980.

———. *The Bible "Babel."* Pensacola: Bible Baptist Bookstore, 1964.

———. *Why I Believe the King James Version Is the Word of God.* Pensacola: Bible Baptist Bookstore, 1988.

Ruess, Eduardus. *Bibliotheca Novi Testamenti Graeci.* Brunsvigae: Apud C. A. Schwetschke et Filium, 1872.

Rummel, Erika. *Erasmus' Annotations on the New Testament.* Toronto: University of Toronto Press, 1986.

Schaff, Philip, ed. *The Nicene and Post-Nicene Fathers*. Series I. Grand Rapids: Eerdmans, 1983.

Scott, Otto. *James I: The Fool as King*. Vallecito, Calif.: Ross House, 1976.

Scrivener, F.H.A. *A Plain Introduction to the Criticism of the New Testament*. London: George Bell & Sons, 1894.

————. *The Authorized Edition of the English Bible (1611)*. Cambridge, 1884.

Sharp, Granville. *Remarks on the Uses of the Definitive Article in the Greek Text of the New Testament: Containing Many New Proofs of the Divinity of Christ, From Passages Which are Wrongly Translated in the Common English Version*. Philadelphia: B. B. Hopkins and Co., 1807.

Silva, Moisés. *Biblical Words and Their Meaning: An Introduction to Lexical Semantics*. Grand Rapids: Academie Books, 1983.

Sturz, Harry. *The Byzantine Text-Type and New Testament Textual Criticism*. Nashville: Thomas Nelson, 1984.

Tischendorf, Aenotheus Fridericus Constantinus. *Novum Instrumentum Sinaiticum*. Lipsiae: F.A. Brockhaus, 1863.

Tregelles, Samuel Prideaux. *The Greek New Testament*. London: Samuel Bagster and Sons, 1879.

Trench, Richard C. *Synonyms of the New Testament*. Grand Rapids: Eerdmans, 1953.

Vaughan, Curtis, and Virtus Gideon. *A Greek Grammar of the New Testament*. Nashville: Broadman Press, 1979.

Von Soden, Hermann Freiherr. *Die Schriften Des Neuen Testaments*. Göttingen: Vandenhoeck und Ruprecht, 1913.

Waite, D.A. *Defending the King James Bible*. Collingswood, N.J.: The Bible for Today, 1992.

————. *Heresies of Westcott & Hort*. Collingswood, N.J.: The Bible for Today, 1979.

Wallace, Daniel. "The Majority-Text Theory: History, Methods and Critique." *Journal of the Evangelical Theological Society*. 37, (1994).

Ward, Norman. *Famine in the Land*. Grand Rapids: Which Bible? Society, n.d.

Warfield, Benjamin Breckenridge. *An Introduction to the Textual Criticism of the New Testament*. New York: Whittaker, 1890.

————. *Biblical and Theological Studies*. Philadelphia: Presbyterian and Reformed, 1968.

Watchtower Bible and Tract Soceity. *You Can Live Forever in Paradise on Earth*. Brooklyn, N.Y.: 1982.

Wessel, Walter. "Mark." In Frank E. Gaebelein, gen. ed., *The Expositor's Bible Commentary*, Vol. 8. Grand Rapids: Zondervan, 1984.

Westcott, Brooke Foss, and Fenton John Anthony Hort. *Introduction to The New Testament in the Original Greek*. Peabody, Mass.: Hendrickson Publishers, 1988.

Wuest, Kenneth. *Wuest's Word Studies in the Greek New Testament*. Grand Rapids: Eerdmans, 1973.

Indices

Greek Word Index

Biblical Reference Index

Subject Index

Person Index